India: Pre and Post-Independence, Indo-China War and Beyond

Reminiscences of an Indian Frontier Administrative Service Officer

India: Pre and Post-Independence, Indo-China War and Beyond

Reminiscences of an Indian Frontier Administrative Service Officer

Major Krishna Chandra Johorey, IAS (Retd), Padma Shri

as narrated to

Lt Gen Gautam Banerjee, PVSM, AVSM, YSM (Retd)

PENTAGON PRESS

India: Pre and Post-Independence, Indo-China War and Beyond
Reminiscences of an Indian Frontier Administrative Service Officer
By Major Krishna Chandra Johorey, IAS (Retd), Padma Shri

ISBN 978-93-86618-08-5

First Published in 2017

Published by
PENTAGON PRESS
206, Peacock Lane, Shahpur Jat
New Delhi-110049
Phones: 011-64706243, 26491568
Telefax: 011-26490600
email: rajan@pentagonpress.in
website: www.pentagonpress.in

Edited by Vibha Kumar

Printed at Aegean Offset Printers, Greater Noida, U.P.

DEDICATION

It has not been possible for me to access my own writings in the *National Herald.* My mentors at that time were the famous journalists – P D Tandon (later a minister in Uttar Pradesh cabinet) and Acharya J B Kriplani; Chelapati Rao and K Rama Rao being National Herald's editors, besides of course, the anonymous editor – Jawaharlal Nehru. Inspired by Prof. Banerjee, I also wrote for the in-house magazine of S M College, Chadausi, titled *Haley's Comet* in 1943. Later, in 1947 at the Indian Military Academy, I started a magazine titled *The Bugle*, under the guidance of Col Charles Wright, Capt Peter Gorb and my Under Officer Cadet S M Ghatak.

Similarly, I was also unable to access the reports of my tenures and tours in Bhutan and Tibet that I had submitted to the North East Frontier Administration, and to the Residency (later, the India House and now the Raj Bhavan) in Gangtok. Therefore, this book has found its shape from my oral recalling of events that I narrated to General Banerjee over a period of three years or so.

But for the authoring effort of Lt General Gautam Banerjee and support of my publisher Shri Rajan Arya, this narrative would not have seen the light of the day. I am grateful for their selfless interest in recording events and publishing this memoir.

In all humility, I dedicate this narrative to India's coming generation of administrators.

(Johorey K C)

Gurugram
Aug 2017
Shravan 2074

CONTENTS

FOREWORD

Major KC Johorey, currently aged 90 plus, is an old-time IAS Officer. Coming from a prominent family of United Provinces (later Uttar Pradesh), he studied at the Allahabad University before joining the Indian Military Academy in Dehra Dun as a Gentleman Cadet. Commissioned into the Corps of Engineers (The Bengal Sappers), he served in the Jammu & Kashmir Operations in 1948 – when he was at the forefront of the column that broke through the six months' seize laid by Pakistani raiders, and relieved the tenacious defenders of the Punch Garrison. Later, in 1952, he participated in a Bengal Sappers mountaineering expedition with the goal of scaling Mount Kamet, but had to call off the challenge at the verge of success. In 1953, he was selected to be transferred from the Army to Indian Frontier Administrative Service. This cadre was created at Pandit Nehru's initiative in the post-Independence time period, when the British era officers had migrated and administration of frontier districts was badly affected; this cadre was later merged with the Indian Administrative Service (IAS).

During the course of his long and eventful life, Mr Johorey has seen through many interesting aspects of India's independence: soldiering, frontier administration in NEFA, diplomatic assignments in Tibet and Afghanistan, and top civil service assignments in Goa and Delhi Administration. He was awarded with Padma Shri on recognition of his extraordinary service during the Chinese aggression in 1962, when he was the Deputy Commissioner at Bomdi-La (North-East Frontier Agency (NEFA), which is now the State of Arunachal Pradesh) – a rare distinction for a young civil servant.

The legend of Mr Johorey was known to most of us at the Bengal Sapper fraternity, not only because he was – and continues to be to this day – a die-hard Bengal Sapper, but also because one saw in him as the epitome of committed service to the nation and the society – an upright civil servant of impeccable honesty, even against formidable odds that they have to contend with, many times at their peril. And above all, the remarkable verve with which he took up the cudgels of his charge. It was his reputation that made Late Major General KC Soni, AVSM, nominating him as one of the key trustees of his estate at Roorkee – which he had bequeathed to the welfare of the Bengal Sapper veterans and war widows.

Impressed by this legend, the first opportunity I got to meet him was during my tenure as the Commandant of the Bengal Engineer Group, Roorkee, when I was also the ex-officio trustee of the Soni Foundation in Roorkee. Later, I met him during the Annual National Defence College Alumni Dinner in New Delhi in 2003, where I had a delightful and educative conversation with him. In 2008, I was appointed as the Colonel Commandant of the Bengal Sappers, and that gave me more opportunities to interact with him. Presently, the elder-younger relationship continues after I was appointed as a trustee at the Soni Foundation, and so I had the opportunity to administer that Foundation in close cooperation with him.

My long association with Mr Johorey convinced me to record the rather momentous and tumultuous events of the post-Independence India… the debacle of 1962, the Emergency of 1975 – the list is long – which he saw through his career, for the posterity to peruse. After my superannuation in 2011, I found that opportunity in spite of my think tank work; scripting of Mr Johorey's narrative began in 2015, albeit intermittently. That effort was somewhat helped by the rough notes made by Nehru Memorial Trust, wherein representatives of the institution recorded his oral history as part of research on Pandit Nehru. Finally, in February 2017, the manuscript was ready. In spite of his efforts to hide it in the true style of a gentleman, Mr Johorey was delighted – and so was I – to be blessed with an opportunity to throw light on this venerable Indian soldier-civil servant.

In this book, Mr Johorey shares his experiences with the undersigned, both being cognitively related by the hoary Bengal Sappers bond, for it to be scripted in the manner of a formal publication. It makes for a truly interesting reading, and opens up the visions of India's post-independence past for the readers to imbibe. Moreover, it offers an insight into the making of a good citizen, and a dedicated civil servant.

I am sanguine the readers would find the entire account eye-opening and inspiring. Those who take note of history would find many details which have remained obscured so far. To that extent, this book would find a place in the making of the Independent India.

My sincere thanks to Mr Rajan Arya of Pentagon Press for publishing, and Ms Vibha Kumar for editing this educational, awe-inspiring memoir.

Jai Hind.

Lieutenant General Gautam Banerjee, PVSM, AVSM, YSM (Retd)
Former Chief of Staff, The Central Command and former Commandant,
The Officers' Training Academy, Chennai; Distinguished Fellow,
The Vivekananda International Foundation, New Delhi.

ACKNOWLEDGEMENTS

This book is dedicated to my parents and teachers, who shaped my world-view and personality in the early, formative years of my life in Baudan. And I gratefully acknowledge the support of my wife Sudha Johorey (nee Lal), who gave up the comforts of the colonial mansion in Agra to follow me to the wilds of one of the most remote and isolated corners of India's anthropological paradise. I also acknowledge the inspiration and support from my Guru, Dr MS Swaminathan, and Ambassadors Arvind Gupta and Jayant Prasad. I specifically thank General Gautam Banerjee, who discovered and enlightened the spark in me at the fateful alumni Group Day Meeting at my 200 year-old regiment, Bengal Sappers. Acknowledgements are due to my children Geeta, Bella and Arun, and grandchildren Ambika and Ram – who have surpassed me and encouraged me to pen down my memories.

Lastly, my sincere thanks to my publisher Rajan Arya of Pentagon Press and my editor Vibha Kumar, who made it possible for this book to see the light of the day.

(Johorey K C)

Gurugram

Aug 2017

CHAPTER 1

FROM BADAUN TO ALLAHABAD

Badaun in 1930s

I was the first among the 10 children to be born in British India, in a sleepy old town called Badaun; it was a district headquarters. Badaun at that time was, and I am sure even now is, predominantly an agricultural district. At that time, there was no industry whatsoever – no electricity, no water supply, and the society was feudal in structure. The legal profession was at the top. There were a couple of doctors...but hardly any MBBS. Of course, there was a Civil Surgeon and a General Hospital. The only school was the Government High School. Population-wise, the city's demographic ratio was 52:48, that is, 52 per cent were Muslims and 48 per cent were Hindus and others. That composition influenced the character of this place.

There was perfect communal harmony in the Badaun district. There were some Shias and Sunnis. The only disturbance used to be when the *Alambardars* (Shias taking part in the procession) carrying *tazias* (name given to religious processions held mostly on 8th of Rabi' al-awwal by Twelver Shia Muslims in India and Pakistan to commemorate the death of Imam Hasan al-Askari, the eleventh of the Twelver Shi'a Imams) used to pass through certain streets to the local *Karbala* (battlefield) grounds. Of course, there were no overhead electricity wires at that time but the sensitivity of the other people, the Sunnis and the others, was taken care of. The District Magistrate's job was to maintain harmony and enforce law and order. In the city itself, there was no law and order problem. As I said, it was a sleepy old town with a few shops where one could get grocery and fabric. This was the Badaun where I was born, on the banks of the Ganges.

It was about half-an-hour drive from the river bank and less than 20 kilometres over a kutcha road.

Badaun was the headquarters of the district carrying the same name, which formed a part of the Rohilkhand Division. Rohilkhand was the name given by the British to an administrative division (*khand*) inhabited by the Rohilla Pathans. The division was made up of Badaun, Shahjahanpur and Bareilly districts, with the Divisional Commissioner posted in Bareilly. On the other side of the Ganges was Etah district, which stretched up to what is now called Narora, where an atomic power station has come up, and then on to Delhi.

In 1857, during what was called the 'mutiny', some British officers wanted to take refuge in Badaun. Then, in Badaun, the culture was firmly against permitting any bloodshed to occur. The story goes that the District Magistrate of Badaun saw some British officers who were given shelter by some of my relatives. He, along with some local families, took these officers across the river to safety among the friendly feudal elite – the local *Nawabs* (dukes). In return for that act of kindness, once the mutiny was over, two villages owned by our family were given *maafi* (literally meaning forgiveness; in this context, revenue exemption). Thus, these villages were called '*maafi ke gaon*' (forgiven villages). In recognition of the British sovereignty, we paid a *malguzari* (tax) of only seven rupees, as against other lands where the owners had to pay full revenue.

Coming back to Badaun, it had a high Muslim population and the Chairman of the Municipal Board was usually a Muslim – a 'Khan Bahadur' (an honourific title given to prominent subjects of the British Raj). There was no contest for the post – that was the convention. At one point, my uncle became the Vice-Chairman. When my father was the Chairman of the District Board, the Vice-Chairman was a Muslim.

School

There was a school in Badaun, which had perhaps been functioning from 1931, or even earlier. It was started by the British, and was called the Government High School. I distinctly recall that our house used to be full of people and their children, who usually came from rural areas to seek admission in the school.

I started my schooling in 1933. My first lessons in English were taught through the King's Primer (book) with a photograph of King George V on the cover. When I went to school, I had no knowledge of English. I started my learning through a Maulvi sahib – because in our community, the boys learnt Persian and Urdu, and the girls learnt Hindi and Sanskrit. Girls wore *dhoti* or *sari* and boys wore *kurta-pajama*. So, I was taken to the school by Quarbe Mohammad Ali, the

Maulvi sahib. The Headmaster asked for the date of birth or *janam patri* (new-born's astrological chart), which the Maulvi sahib did not have. The day, May 15, was the last day of the school and the rule was that one could not get admission till one was at least five years old. So, the Maulvi sahib said in Urdu, "Sahib, *ye to kal hi paida hua tha; paanch saal ho gaya iska*" (he was born yesterday, five years ago). So, May 14, 1927 was recorded as my date of birth. Later, when I was married, they got my *janam-patri* prepared. I did not make any change in my date of birth because I was already in the Indian Administrative Service (IAS) though. Many government servants of my generation, and I dare say even judges of the High Courts, did change theirs to get the benefits of longer service. I could have done so too, but did not have any inclination to.

The Headmaster was Narayan Das Banerjee. He was from the undivided Bengal, and was a member of the Provincial Education Service. He was an M.A. in mathematics, and taught us math and physics. Quarbe Mohammad Ali, the Maulvi sahib, taught us Urdu. He was a very fair complexioned Shia, always wore a Turkish cap and was a very good cricketer. He was of Arab descent, perhaps. The medium of instruction was Urdu; one may call it Hindustani. We were offered either Urdu or Hindi but in this school, most of us were offered Urdu. English was one subject. I was offered Urdu right up to Class X, and had science, mathematics, Urdu and English as the main subjects. I did not have Hindi. There was a Hindi teacher available, but very few were offered Hindi at that time. I studied up to Class X at Badaun, and then moved to Allahabad. First, I undertook the journey up to Bareilly – which took about four hours by the slow-moving, metre-gauge train. From Bareilly, I changed into a broad-gauge train to reach Lucknow overnight. After another overnight journey, I made it to Allahabad.

My father's name was Amir Chand Johorey; he was a lawyer. I do not know the origin of the surname 'Johorey'. It is said that it was more of a title than a caste name, because the 'Johris' of Rajasthan were traders while the 'Johoreys' of Johor Baru in Malaysia were rulers. The title's spelling is very much influenced by the Marathi language spoken in the adjacent state of Gwalior of the Scindhias, and that continues. My name, Krishna Chandra, was colloquially pronounced as 'Kishan Chand'. When the High School certificate was to be made, the Sanskritised spelling was used and my father's title, 'Johorey', was added. Actually, colloquial pronounciation of the first was the norm in those days. Caste names were not mentioned. Everybody we knew was called Lalaji, Maulvi Sahib, etc.

Home

Both, my paternal and maternal grandfathers, were in service of the Maratha State of Gwalior. Various princely states needed to employ officers, and so, my sister's father-in-law went all the way to Jind and Nabha to serve in the Khalsa state of Punjab, later rising to be the Revenue Minister of Jind. Likewise, one branch of the family shifted to Bhopal. Similarly, some of the Kashmiri Pundits came from Kashmir to Gwalior where Hukku, Mattu and Haksar were the senior officers. I visited these small princely states of Gwalior and Neemuch to see relatives on my sister's and mother's side.

We lived in a 24-room house – my grandmother occupying one room all by herself, which was unusual in a joint family. Ours was a big family and my mother had to feed not only 10 of us, but also the cousins, uncles and others in the joint family system. So, she was under great strain all her life, as taking care of 10 children to is no joke. We had a *goshala* (cow shed) and a stable. There was division of labour: *maali* (gardener) was employed for gardening; the kitchen was big, so we had a *maharaj* (chef) who came from the village to do the cooking. Then, there were two kinds of courtyards: in the inner wing, my mother would sit with her friends like the wives of the Nawabs, who would come in *tongas* (horse carts) to chat; in the outer wing, my father used to sit in his chamber to meet his clients in the morning. The evenings were an open house for friends, poets, politicians and others.

My sisters walked to the local Islamic School; later, on a *tonga* (a horse carriage). We boys walked to the school. There was no veil-rule for my sisters. Their Muslim classmates put their veils on, but they did not do so. When my mother went to the city, she used to put on the veil. In the city, we had two ancestral houses – in Kucha Panda (meaning the abode of Brahmins), and the other in Hussaini Gully – which were side by side. When mother had to go to perform religious rituals in our old family temple, she would put on the veil. But indoors, when Muslim women and Mullika – the District Magistrate's wife, who joined sometimes – would sit in the courtyard, there was no *purdah* (veil). *Purdah* was not used by women in the city either. In the rural areas, there was no *purdah*, no *chadri* – what is today called as burqa. My father's clients, many of whom were rich, did not wear burqas. But when their female servants came to the city, they wore burqas. Years later in 1963 in Kabul, Afghanistan, I discovered the reason. When I asked my house help as to why she came in *purdah*, she replied that she did so to hide her poverty.

Hindus and Muslims socialised quite often; like, on Diwali, the Maulvi sahib would bring a poem that he'd have written and I would read it out. Then we all would eat together. My family was strictly vegetarian. No meat was allowed inside our house; but then, my father had many guests coming in. He used to host an annual 'At Home'. The Commissioner came, so did the local Nawabs and all of my father's clients who could speak English. Other British officers, the District

Judge and the Superintendent of Police also came at times. Some members of the local mission of the Church of England and the family of Reverend Titus also attended the event. The mission is still there.

The Nawabs

There were a few prominent Nawabi families. One of them was Chaudhri Salauddin. He lived in the town because his wife was an MBBS or LMP doctor, posted at the *Zenana* (women's) hospital (that's how it was in the 1930s!). Chaudhri Salauddin was a well-known man – a landlord living in comfort because his wife was earning while he did what he liked. Maiku Mian was another aristocrat. There was Mir Mushtaq Ali of the Mir family of Sahaswan who were Shias from across the Ganges. Then, there was Khan Bahadur Wahid Baksh who was the Chairman of the Municipal Board while my uncle, Babu Ram Swarup, was the Vice-Chairman. 'Babu' was a very honourable word, not a derogatory word as it is now. The babus were all educated people. Wahid Baksh had a lovely beard, most gracious, absolutely silver – something like Vijaya Lakshmi Pandit's hair! He was very dignified as well.

I remember when he was going to *haj* (pilgrimage), we all went to the railway station which was very close by, at a walking distance. We were in the Civil Lines. On one side of the railway station was the Civil Lines, and on the other side was the British Colony where the District Magistrate, the Superintendent of Police and the District Judge lived. So, Wahid Baksh was seen off and we gave him a lot of gifts – including *patashe* and *pedas* (type of Indian sweetmeat) as *prasad* (religious offerings) for the haj – which he was required to bring back for distribution. The maker of the best *peda* was Mamman Khan Pahlwan. These *pedas* used to be offered in the temples too.

Religion, Caste

There was no untouchability in hour premises. Even the *khalifa's* (head sweeper's) wife – the *mehtarani* (sweepress) – who came to work in our house, was given the same treatment any human being deserves. Surprisingly, my mother had to put her *ghoongat* (veil) when the sweepress came in. She was allowed into our grandmother's room. If she sat on the floor, grandmother would ask her to sit on a chair. Considering there was severe untouchability issues in that era, this was a transformational leap for us personally.

The *khalifa* was a senior leader of the sweepers, and commanded a lot of respect. We could not call the *mehtarani* by her name; we called her *chachi* (aunt). To maintain hygiene and cleanliness, there was a door via which they would come in to clean the bathroom and toilets. The bathroom had cans filled with water. There was no electricity, and so, there was no system of water sanitation; maybe the District Magistrate's house had it. Pumps came only much later.

There were no communal disturbances between Hindus and Muslims. Among the Shias, there were murmurs during their festival – particularly during *Muharram* – that somebody might throw stones, and do similar things like that. There were temples and mosques side by the side. Trouble came later on, when the overhead electricity wires were put up. Then the Shias were told to reduce the height of the *tazias,* and that's when they protested. If the District Magistrate was clever, he would convince them; otherwise, he would ask them to change the route. Then on certain occasions, temple bells would be ringing or music played in front of the mosques, but there would be no conflicts. Sometimes, the British officers tried to make it a bone of contention, but they did not succeed because the Muslims would approach my father. He was a leading lawyer, so people listened to him. That is why after the elections in 1937 and before the 1942 movement, he was unanimously elected the Chairman of the District Board. I remember he gave a speech in which he assured all help to the minorities. In the villages, the landowners were mostly Hindus – *Thakurs, Rajputs, Kurmis* and few *Banias* too. The *Kashtkars* (share croppers) were both Hindu and Muslim, with many Thakurs among them. Some Brahmins had land. Brahmins who did not learn any Hindi, Sanskrit or the *Ramayana* used to work as cooks. Such was the division of labour at that time.

What is referred to as *manuvaad* (social order as laid down by Sage Manu) today, was non-existent. I remember that there were people who came to seek admission to the school hostel or to the hospital for treatment. They would come in bullock carts and ring up the Civil Surgeon for help. The government hospital beds were limited but the hospital was very neat and clean, unlike in Delhi. As the Health Secretary of Delhi, I had the misfortune of looking after the Irwin (now Jayaprakash Narayan) Hospital, which was in a terrible condition. Even in the government school, there was pin-drop silence when the Headmaster walked in.

Freedom Movement

In the 1930s, Jawaharlal Nehru and Subhas Chandra Bose were two distinguished leaders who came to Badaun. Naturally, the Indian National Congress was always in power in the municipality; but neither my uncle Babu Ram Swarup nor Khan Bahadur Wahid Baksh were Congressmen. They both had neutral inclinations. I do not think there was any Congressman in the

Municipal Board. The Congress party dominated in the Badaun area. The first elections were held in 1937. But before that, Subhas Chandra Bose came, and then, Jawaharlal Nehru too. Bose came when he was on his way to the Haripura Session of the Congress. He came for a few hours and went to the only hall – *Arya Samaj* Hall – where he spoke for an hour and a half. I remember very clearly as I was there. The Arya Samaj (a progressive sect of articulate Hindus) advocated independence. They allowed the girls to participate in social activities. Their school did not allow the parting of hair by the girls; unmarried girls just had loose hair, and wore *khadi* (hand-spun) garments. That was the dress code. My elder sister used to attend Arya Samaj activities wearing *khadi*. She supported the breaking of the Salt Law, when Mahatma Gandhi visited Badaun for an hour or so. At that time, my elder sister went there to participate in the symbolic Satyagraha, which upset my grandmother. Earlier, before I was born, Mahatma Gandhi stayed in our *kothi* (bungalow), which was the only decent place to stay at the time.

I was aware of all the political events taking place then. I went to see an aircraft for the first time when Jawaharlal Nehru came to Badaun before the elections in 1937. I was a young boy then. One of my uncles, Babu Raghubir Sahai, was an active Congressman. He was also a lawyer, but hardly a practicing one. He went there with his volunteers. All of them used to wear *khadi*. There was no aerodrome in Badaun. But there was a place called Barapatthar where 12-stone pillars demarcated an area where the troops of the British Indian Army used to camp while marching from Bareilly and Meerut towards Delhi, taking a shortcut across the Swat river and then cross the Ganges to reach Delhi for various ceremonies. That was the only open area, and so, the twin-engine aircraft landed there. In those days, there were no barriers; even if there may have been policemen, I do not remember any attempt at controlling the crowd. So, when people saw the aircraft coming in, they let loose and the pilot had to hurriedly apply the brakes to avoid an accident. With the sudden application of brakes, the aircraft did come to a halt, but the engine failed. Jawaharlal Nehru came out in his immaculate *dhoti*, *kurta* and what came to be known as Nehru jacket; no sherwani, but with a baton which he always carried. He then engaged in a sort of crowd control. He was annoyed by those followers who were rushing to touch his feet, almost on the point of beating them up. My uncle was there, trying to control the chaos when Nehru burst out in anger, "*Yeh log kyon aa rahey hain? Kya saab, apka intezam hai yahan*?" (Why are all these people coming here? You can't even control the crowd?). Uncle was very upset and angry that Jawaharlal Nehru shouted at him in the presence of all those people. Nehru must have stayed for a few hours, or maybe, overnight. He had come only to address an election meeting, and then went away to some other place. Of course, the aircraft could not take off, and was parked there for four days. It became a popular place of pilgrimage. The organisers must have arranged for a jeep or a car for Nehru to move on.

I was too young to attend the meeting. My elder sister attended it; my mother did not go. My grandmother, who was more of a royal, did not go because one of the old servants had come to meet her. This fellow was an orphan from the village, who went to join the Army at the Bareilly cantonment. There, he gave my father's name and our address in Badaun as his home address. Only when the policeman came for pre-recruitment inquiries, we found that this fellow had gone to join the Army. He used to come regularly on 60-days' leave, to see and look after my grandmother. He was a very nice person.

In the government formed in the United Provinces (UP) in 1937, Hafiz Mohammad Ibrahim – my father's friend – was the only Congress Minister with Govind Ballabh Pant as the Chief Minister. Subhas Chandra Bose had already been elected the President in February 1938 when he came to Badaun. It could be that the Congress Party was fighting in a by-election. This must have been when he was aspiring to be the Congress President again in January 1939. At that time, he was unhappy came and addressed a political meeting in Badaun for an hour and spoke exceptionally well. He did not come to our house. Mahatma Gandhi had spent a few hours in our house on his way to set up a *khadi* ashram in the neighbouring Chandausi tehsil (administrative centre) where there is a Khadi Production Centre, like the one at Rajpura in the Punjab, even now. In Badaun, people attended the Congress meetings in large numbers. The Salt Satyagraha was symbolic. Of course, the Congress swept the polls.

The Arya Samaj did not enter politics at all. It worked in the field of education, and was purely dedicated to educating the girls. Because Badaun was predominantly a Muslim town, they were worried about their influence over their girls. Later on, one of my sisters studied in the Islamia School for Muslim women. My father was the Chairman of the Managing Committee. In the Arya Samaj, Hindi and Sanskrit were taught. Then, there was the *mazaar* (grave) of Saint Sultan-ul-Arpeen, where Hindus also used to go for prayer and Prasad every Thursday. Even in 1947, there were no Hindu-Muslim riots in Badaun city. After Independence, a relative, Raghubir Sahai (a Congressman), was elected as Member of the Lok Sabha in 1952 and 1957 from Badaun.

There wasn't much political awareness among the people back then. Some people did participate in the freedom movement. Many people – including Ram Chander, Kishan Chander, my uncle Raghubir Sahai and Chaudhary Badan Singh – were arrested. I cannot remember any boycotting of the courts by the people. Some people gathered at the railway station to shout slogans of boycott and demand freedom. They did not have black flags, but cleverly carried black umbrellas to show their solidarity during protest against the British rule that were taking place in the country. They were told by the police to disperse. One of my uncles had a black umbrella but the moment the police beat him up, he threw it away. There was no damaging of the railway line. High school students, however, did not boycott the school; they were too young for that. The schools continued to function. But newspapers were being read. We used to get *The Hindustan Times* and *The Statesman.* Only four copies of The Statesman came to Badaun; besides ours, one was for the District Judge, one for the District Magistrate, and one for the Superintendent of Police. There was one local Urdu paper also. Saint Khwaja Nizamuddin Auliya was born in Badaun. His followers were called the 'Nizamis'. There was a Nizami press, and a Nizami was the editor of the newspaper. Later on, a small Hindi press was also started.

Allahabad and the 1942 Movement

I did my Intermediate from Allahabad. I was there for two years. In the last year, I had to leave college because of my association with the 1942 Movement.

I was in the Ewing Christian College, which was located on the banks of the Yamuna. It was an American institution and the Principal was an American named Dr C.H. Hazlett (1938-42). This college was started in 1902. Across the Yamuna was located the Yamuna Agricultural School (later the Allahabad Agricultural Institute, a deemed university). It was the first such school, probably started in 1910 by an American named Sam Higginbotham. The Ewing Christian College was the only co-educational college, and had only XI and XII standard, besides boarding facilities. There were just five girls, among whom one was a Bengali, one was from Lucknow and a third had come from Trinidad. Among the teachers were Dr B.B. Malvia who taught Physics, Professor Chattarjee who taught Chemistry, and Professor Mitra who taught Mathematics. Professor Biswas, a Bengali Christian, taught English. There were five hostels – Philadelphia, Princeton, Rhea, Turner and the one known as '1904'. I was in Philadelphia hostel. Princeton hostel was named after the Princeton University, which must have contributed to it. There was one master from Princeton. He used to stay in the hostel. I remember he taught me Rugby and Baseball, the American national game. One thing the Americans did was that they did not allow the police to enter the college. The Principal told A.D. Dixon, who was the Divisional Commissioner, that he would handle the problems within the college and that he should not interfere. When we students insisted that we fly the national flag, the Principal did not permit that. So, all of us boys went across to the *Kutcherry* (court premises) and hoisted the national flag.

Almost everybody from the college, except the girls, participated in the freedom movement. The worst kind of law-breaking according to the norms of those days that we did was to disrupt the Allahabad City railway station. Besides me, there was Ramu Menon who was half German, K.C. Raghavan, son of Ambassador N. Raghavan and Nadyam Bhaskar Menon, who later on joined the Royal Indian Air Force. Ramu Menon and K.C. Raghavan had come from Malaysia. Being separated from their parents who had joined the Indian National Army of Subhash Chandra Bose, their money orders had stopped coming. The three of us went and 'raided' the Allahabad City railway station, throwing away furniture and papers, and sloganeering. We did not hurt anyone. We had no weapons. When the police came running to chase us, we escaped and reached the Turner hostel. Once, I went with my box camera to Pratapgarh railway station and took a photograph of Khan Abdul Ghaffar Khan. He was travelling by the Punjab Mail train to attend the All India Congress Committee (AICC) meeting at Bombay (now Mumbai) in August 1942. We used to go to Anand Bhawan whenever Jawaharlal Nehru went there. But during the time when he and his colleagues were all in jail, the Swaraj Bhawan became our meeting point. Acharya J.B. Kripalani was there sometimes. His nephew, a young handsome man, and Kripalani himself used to give me books to read. Narayan Dutt Tewari was also in Ewing Christian College as a day scholar. Mubarak Mazdoor, too, was there...so was Acharya Narendra Deva's son, Ashok Verma.

I was not a member of the Congress Party but took active part in their public meetings and rallies. I attended all meetings and activities of the Congress Party, helped in making flags and banners, and joined in shouting slogans and causing disruption. There was no All India Students' Union. I was a member of the Allahabad University Union and was elected unopposed to its Judicial Council. Then there was the Socialist Circle in which Indira Gandhi used to participate. She was not married then, and was known as Jawaharlal Nehru's daughter. She was a very quiet person. We had a photograph of her sitting in the middle while on my right was Mahendra Singh, a topper of the class whose notes on history I used to borrow. He was also a leftist at that time. Later on, he joined the Indian Police Service. There was Acharya Narendra Deva's son Ashok Verma, and Ramu Menon and K.C. Raghavan who had come from Malaysia – and having been given introduction from there to Vijaya Lakshmi Pandit, formed part of the 'Circle'. Once, we set fire to Feroze Gandhi's cinema hall. We did not know it was his. There was this Gazdar's Ice Cream Parlour owned by Feroze Gandhi's *mausi* (maternal aunt). We used to go there for ice cream and watch English films in his cinema hall. In 1944, that was the only cinema hall where English films were shown. We used to go cycling from the Yamuna Bank up to Civil

Lines to see English movies, and maybe buy books sometimes. It so happened that at the end of a film, we did not stand up to the display of the British flag on the screen with 'God Save the King' playing in the background. We were abused, and that provoked us. So, when we were on the point of being arrested, K.C. Raghavan (who was Ramu Menon's first cousin) said to him, "Before you reveal our identity, I will lift you up and throw you down from the third floor, and you would be dead". Ramu Menon was very angry, and was gearing up for a fight. I stopped him, saying, "Do not do this. Let us quickly change our clothes and disappear". So, we changed our clothes and ran away from there.

The four of us were very close because we were in the same hostel. We used to get some money from home, but it always fell short. When money orders of the four of us failed to reach us, Vijaya Lakshmi Pandit used to help us out. She knew us as we were regular visitors to the Swaraj Bhawan and Anand Bhawan. C.S. Venkatachar, who was the first Indian ICS Commissioner, also quietly helped us out with money to survive. I could not help my group much because I was skint myself. Although as and when my money order came, I did share it. We lived frugal; we had only two ties which the four of us would share. We also used to share clothes – wear each other's coats, chappals and other things.

There were few Communists amongst us too. Ramu Menon had definite Communist leanings. As soon as the Russians joined the Allies in the Second World War, Ramu Menon and the Communists said that they would support the War effort. They declared that it was a 'People's War'. Out of the four of us, Ramu Menon took the Communist line. That was where my differences came with Ramu Menon. We were very good friends but after Allahabad, we dispersed. Later on, he had become the First Secretary of the Communist Party of Great Britain before his demise in London. The only other Communist whom I knew was Mubarak Mazdoor. I was a Socialist myself. Ashok Verma and Hemvati Nandan Bahuguna, too, were in the Socialist camp. But the Socialists never opposed the Congress movement. We were opposed to the War. We used to listen to the broadcast of Subhas Chandra Bose quietly. There was open sympathy with the anti-British, pro-German factions, and people used to enjoy the British losses. Even in Badaun, as my sisters used to tell me, it was the same feeling. It was no concern of ours as to how might a victorious Japan behave.

Allahabad University was a residential university with many hostels; there was also a Government College. Dr C.H. Hazlett, the Principal of our college, forbade us from destroying any college property. He also made sure that we were not arrested within the campus. He allowed us the freedom of speech and movement. The college authorities were sympathetic, otherwise they could have given us away. The Principal told Commissioner Dixon very clearly that he could arrest us outside the college and do what he liked, but not to interrupt our academic trajectory.

To avoid arrest, we left Allahabad...and all four of us dispersed to various places. For one year, I had to be sent to Shyam Sunder Memorial (S.M.) College in Chandausi. This was because my father was told by British officials that I was found indulging in political agitation. They did not touch me because my father was a title holder. I was asked not go to Allahabad; if I did, I would be arrested. So I was sent to Chandausi, which was a village but had a very good college – the S.M. College. For one year, I studied there because I was virtually expelled from Allahabad, and passed my Intermediate Science from this college. I resumed my studies in Allahabad in 1944, and took active part in all political meetings. In 1937 elections, the Congress had won very few seats because of creation of separate electorates, and that led to communal disharmony. M.A. Farooqui was in the students' movement. He was one of the few from the Indian National Congress who won the election.

We did not go to the University that year. Afterwards, when we came back after one year, K.C. Raghavan and Bhaskar Menon went to Triplicane in Madras and joined the Madras University. Bhaskar Menon joined the Air Force, and became a very distinguished pilot. I do not know what happened to Mubarak Mazdoor; he probably continued in Allahabad. He was an out-and-out Communist; he even took the name '*Mazdoor*' (labourer). Moonis Raza was also a Leftist. Of all the Urdu-speaking people who were there, none of them voted for the Muslim League. When C. Rajagopalachari came to give a talk, we went to listen to him. Some of us also went to listen to Muhammad Ali Jinnah's speech when he came to Allahabad.

The 'Quit India' Movement

On the call of 'Quit India', all Congress leaders were arrested. Indian Communists were definitely opposing the call and propagating as to how good the Soviet Union and its Communist Party was. They had definite links; there was no doubt about it. Even in Badaun, one of my cousins used to show me pictures of the oil town of Baku, and a collection of beautiful Russian pictures and books. So Communist cells were there. One branch of Leftist students were sympathetic even then; even if they did not participate in the Quit India Movement. Ramu Menon said that the Second World War was a People's War and, therefore, we should not disrupt the railway lines. We just wanted to participate in the Movement, not hurt anybody but just cause disruption. He even went to the extent of threatening us, saying that he would give us up to the police. He must have been really convinced against the Movement. In our college, we did not indulge in any vandalism. First, there was no violence from the British side. However, there was one example of Padmaja Singh, a young boy, who was shot dead as he climbed up a pole wanting to hoist the National flag. Maybe there were people beaten up severely too.

As I said earlier, I had to leave Allahabad for Chandausi, where I studied at the S.M. College. At that time, Army convoys used to come and pass through Chandausi. They camped in our football ground for the night. S.M. College was a government college, named after Shyam Manohar – a local *zamindar* (owner of many plots of land), who must have given the initial donations. For one year, I stayed in the Hailey Hostel, which was named after William Malcolm Hailey, the Governor of Punjab. That was only a boys' hostel. There was no hostel for girls there. I was the editor of Halley's Comet, a publication started by us. In S.M. College, my tutor in English was Professor Banerjee, a very nice person, while Professor Mewa Ram was the Mathematics teacher. All the teachers were very devoted. They were all focussed more on academics rather than politics. Professor Rajnath was very fair-skinned; maybe he came from the North-West Frontier Province or Punjab; he was absolutely brilliant in English. A follower of Swami Rama Tirtha, he gave me a set of 12 books titled In Woods of God-Realisation, authored by the Swami himself, which I read intently. The Rama Tirtha movement was very strong in Punjab then. S.M. College produced two members of the ICS: Bhagwan Sahay and Vishnu Sahay. Chandausi was also the home of Kunwar Sir Jagdish Prasad, one of the members of the Executive Council of the Viceroy. Another Councillor was from Allahabad. Here, I concentrated on my studies. I had to pass the examination and get back to Allahabad. I did that in July 1944.

Allahabad University, 1944-47

Back to Allahabad, I went straight to the university. Allahabad University was a residential university, and were four hostels. It was, therefore, very difficult to get admission in Allahabad University hostels. It would be a delegacy if one belonged to Allahabad, but for the outsiders, the hostels were open to students from various parts of India (mostly for students from the science stream). I was admitted to the Holland Hall but when I opted for Bachelors in Political Science, Modern History, English Literature and the Faculty of Law for a Bachelor's degree, the delegacy put me in the P.C.B. Hall, a hostel named after Sir P.C. Banerji, the Vice-Chancellor in 1917-19.

In 1944 when I was in Allahabad, we used to cycle from the college to go to Anand Bhawan. Anand Bhawan was open to all, and people would come and go the whole day. Reginald W. Sorensen and Woodrow Wyatt, both Members of the United Kingdom (UK) Parliament, came there. I met Stafford Cripps in Anand Bhawan. I also remember meeting Feroze Gandhi and Indira Gandhi there. I first met Feroze Gandhi at the Gazdar Ice Cream Parlour which was owned by his aunt. 'Gazdar' is a Parsi name, and so is 'Feroze'. He was very handsome and used to wear *khadi* clothes. He joined us in processions and meetings of the Congress Party. Ashok Verma, Acharya Narendra Deva's son, Upadhyay, son of Professor Ishwari Prasad, the Head of the History Department, also used to join. Amarnath Jha, the Vice-Chancellor of Allahabad University in 1938-47, kept away. His father, Sir Ganganath Jha, was a pucca Oxonian, a Knight and the Vice-Chancellor of Allahabad University during 1923-32. He did not approve of the students going out for pro-Congress processions. We also had a 'Friday Club' in Allahabad.

At the University, I had English Literature, History and Political Science as my subjects. Professor Tara Chand taught us Medieval History. Ishwari Prasad, who also wrote a number of books, taught us Modern India. I think the most eminent and learned was Professor Moolchand, the Head of the Political Science department. An erudite scholar, he was an expert on Greek polity. Political Science consisted of two parts: Political Theory and the Constitution. Political Theory was taught by five or six different Professors. Thomas Hobbes, John Locke and Jean-Jacques Rousseau were taught by A.B. Lall. Lall's interpretation of Hobbe's thesis was that man is a hedonistic calculus. By nature, he is hedonistic and later on, the State takes over the controls. Then, he taught us the theory of Communism, Nihilism and Political Science. Constitution, which included the Indian Constitution of 1935, British Federalism and so on, was taught by different professors. All were extremely knowledgeable in the subjects they taught, and very fluent in English as well. They used to speak extempore, and there was total silence in the class. We had great respect for those teachers. Romantic poems of P.B. Shelly and John Keats were taught by Harivansh Rai Bachchan, who taught English Literature at the Allahabad University from 1941-52. There were tutorials also. Once or twice a week, about eight of us sat down like friends, as in Oxford and Cambridge, with the appointed tutor who taught us. Professor Kelly Malhotra's wife, an English lady having come from Oxford, also taught us English. She was very friendly with the Nehru family. Amarnath Jha took about 10 lectures on William Shakespeare. Bachchan used to write in Hindi, but the surprising part was that he never taught us Hindi Literature. I remember Bachchan because of his *kavi sammelans* and *mushairas* (poetry sessions). My language was Urdu, and so, I used to attend wherever these took place – in the Hindu Hostel, the Muslim Boarding House or wherever. I do remember going and listening to him, but in the class room he never talked in Hindi.

The medium of instruction was English throughout. In Ewing Christian College, the medium of instruction was English as well. Even if that was not the case in the Government High School, by the time we passed out, we had picked up enough knowledge of English to understand the lectures. Nobody talked in Hindi in a class of English Literature, or even in the Political Science class. Among our teachers were Professor Shafaat Ahmad Khan and Professor V.N. Gadgil, the economist. Besides these eminent men, the university also had the distinction of having Mahamahopadhyay Sir Ganganath Jha and Sir K.S. Krishnan, the Physicist in the faculty. Teachers never talked of politics in the classroom. They also did not attend public meetings; most of them were busy in their academic pursuits. In private life, of course, they were close to the Anand Bhawan. Professor S.C. Deb was a very simple person and used wear *bandh-gala* (buttoned up) coat that was in vogue those days. He taught English. Professor R.D. Ranade taught Philosophy. He used to wear silk *dhoti-kurta* and his trademark Marathi turban. Cigar-smoking Amarnath Jha used to visit the Banaras Hindu University to deliver lectures on English Literature; Sarvepalli Radhakrishnan, who would later become the President of India, was a teacher in that University. I remember Ashok Pratap Singh, son of the Raja of Bhadri, K.C. Raghavan and myself cycling all the way to listen to Dr Radhakrishan. We attended a few lectures and came back by rail.

I was impressed most by Amarnath Jha, who was a *pucca* sahib. Bachchan's expositions were more in the nationalist mould, the subject being raised to spiritual and philosophical heights. In his writings – *Madhushala* and *Madhubala in particular* – there was an element of poetic justice. Saghar Nizami and Shakeel Ahmad Badauni were poets; there was a Leftist touch in their Urdu poetry. Nizami wrote the poem *Bhikharan Aayee, Bhikharan Gayee* (Arrived as a Destitute, Exited as a Destitute). He was from Meerut. He used to come and stay with us in Badaun. I met him years later when he was honoured with the *Padma Shri* award. At that time, Shakeel Badauni was not famous. Whenever there was a *mushaira*, his seat would be towards the end.

Mushaira and classical music congregations were very common in those days. Every year, there would be a classical music conference when people came from Bengal also. I remember Pandit Narayan Rao Vyas and Ustad Fayyaz Khan came and stayed in our house; because there were no hotels, the participants used to be put up in various homes. Once there was a Chatterjee father-daughter duo – the father playing the violin while the daughter danced. Dance those days invited whistles rather than appreciation. But this dance was something very different and gripping. Classical music was heard with rapt attention – no shouting and perfect silence. Many of the singers were Muslims. My father was a great patron of music. We had teachers to teach us tabla and harmonium. My two sisters also learnt music. Apart from cooking, music was one of the qualifications for the girls to be married to the right family.

Allahabad was the hub of freedom movement. I used to go to the Anand Bhavan, usually with K.C. Raghavan, not very often though. We were short of money, so we would go and Vijaya Lakshmi Pandit would give us some money. We would also meet the girls – Chandralekha, Nayantara and Rita – who had been left out from arrest on account of the movement. We took them out for ice cream or some snacks and long debates. Then, there would to be large gatherings whenever any of the British Members of Parliament came for a visit. Jawaharlal Nehru never disallowed anyone – anybody could walk into his balcony; more the crowd, the happier he would be. There was no security. He would come out and talk when there was a big crowd of admirers. He would welcome them to the balcony. Once, I saw him going on a bicycle. If I had my camera at that time, I would have clicked a photo! I never had a chance to talk to Jawaharlal Nehru, though I did hear him when I had climbed up to the balcony where he was talking to Reginald W. Sorensen and his wife. He was saying: "Look at these crowds! They all want to be with me. They are all very poor people. I have not called them. They have come because I have come out of jail".

Nehru had his own views. Whenever he was in Allahabad, people would come to get a glimpse of him from morning till evening, until the gates were locked. Once Vijaya Lakshmi Pandit and Rafi Ahmed Kidwai came to our hometown when my father bought some shares of the Associated Journals Limited – the company which owned the nationalist newspaper, the National Herald, and that attracted me to that paper. In Allahabad. Acharya J.B. Kripalani gave (me) some pamphlets for me to write book reviews. I remember getting paid some 10 or 15 rupees on two occasions. In 1947, when I was selected for the Army and joined the Indian Military Academy in Dehra Dun, two cheques arrived. The envelope had 'Associated Journals Limited', not the 'National Herald' written over it, but someone had put a stamp of 'Quit India' on the envelope with the help of an improvised stamp made from peeled potato and ink. That was one method of improvising a kind of stamp. It reached the Academy, which had an all-British staff – from top to bottom. That was in January 1947. By that time, it was decided that India would be independent. No cognizance of the 'stamp' was taken.

CHAPTER 2

FROM ALLAHABAD TO THE ARMY

University to Military Academy

During the period 1942-43, after having been shunted out of Allahabad, I remained virtually in hiding to avoid arrest. I had to go somewhere instead of sitting at home. I joined S.M. College in Chandausi, and finally passed the Intermediate Science examination with Physics, Chemistry and Mathematics. Today, one calls them engineering subjects; if one takes Botany, Zoology and Chemistry, he is said to be opting for medicine. I certainly wanted to go for engineering. That was the purpose for which I had taken Physics, Chemistry and Mathematics. But once I returned to Allahabad and the university, I could not get admission in science stream. That was the period between 1944 and 1946.

In those days, I stayed in the P.C. Banerji hostel, where my seniors included people like Shankar Dayal Sharma, who became the President of India later on. He had been in the universities of Lucknow and Allahabad where he had done his Law. Devendra Narayan Sinha, the veteran freedom fighter, was there, and there were other very brilliant minds. All of them were preparing to join the civil services. Allahabad was known for being pro-government. There were two streams: one comprised of people who wanted to join politics, and the others were those who wanted to join the civil services. Those who were in politics were in the forefront. I never wanted to join politics because in politics one had to make a lot of compromises. So, I took BA and thought I would go into the legal profession – following my father's footsteps. One brother was already an engineer from Thompson College, Roorkee – a very coveted institution. There was the constraint of finances also.

There was no Indian Civil Service; the 'Federal Public Service Commission' had more or less stopped recruiting during the War years. Recruitment to the Indian Civil Service was stopped, and entry to even the Provincial Civil Service was closed. Having passed BA, I was expected to start earning. The family was made up of professionals. There were lawyers and judges in my immediate family while relatives on the mother's side served as ministers in the princely States. They were from what was called the aristocratic and intellectual elite or the educated upper crust of the Indian society – actually the upper middle class who had the educational background, awareness and certain urge to go higher in life. I had already been trying to earn some money by writing in the National Herald while interacting with J.B. Kripalani and P.D. Tandon. Now, I wanted to earn regularly because at that time, only one of my brothers was earning and my father was getting old. We were 10 of us. Financially, we were hard up. I had to make a choice about my career.

I was in the Arts stream, and therefore, not qualified for engineering or medical stream. Having done BA, I had taken a dual course of Law and MA in Political Science from Allahabad University. I was in touch with top faculty, and was interacting with the best minds in the country. The Vice-Chancellor was Amarnath Jha; Dr. Tara Chand and Ishwari Prasad were famous historians, and in Physics, there was Professor K.S. Krishnan. I wanted to remain in the university till I got a job.

It was very clear that India would be Independent, that it was only a matter of time. Negotiations were going on, to which I was a witness as a student and as a visitor to Anand Bhawan. At this stage, having a nationalist background and having joined the Quit India Movement, I decided to respond to a call to join what was still the British Indian Army, but was to be the Army of an independent India soon. I knew very well that was the only government service available. It was a very honourable profession but there were risks involved, and nobody in the family had ever joined the Army.

The Selection Process

There was a three-tier competitive examination for the Army. First, there was a very short preliminary examination. These preliminaries were held at different centres to select suitable candidates. In the first selection, many were weeded out. Next was the state level or area level interviews held in Lucknow. Finally, one had to appear before a Selection Board. In the Selection Board, the procedure was that about 30 boys were invited to stay at the Selection Centre for three days. Every candidate wore the same dress of shorts and shirts – not military uniform – and given a number; no names were taken. Throughout those three days, the candidates were put through various tests. There were Group Testing Officers and psychiatrists who put the candidates through discussions on various topics. The Group Testing Officers were all British. There were three written objective tests which were meant to evaluate the candidate's reflexes. They would flash a picture and then ask the candidates to write down their impressions in the form of a story. Those were the kind of tests that were conducted. All this was serious business because whether in the Indian Army or in the civil services, officers had to be leaders of men. Slated for higher administrative or management positions whether in civil, military or business organisations, they had to lead their teams of men and women and take the right decisions. At the end of the three days, the results were announced.

Without consulting anybody, I had responded to the call; and having been called up, went to Lucknow to appear in the preliminary interview. It was called the Area level or the State level interview. There, one British Brigadier and one or two more officers asked questions for an hour to test my educational qualifications and find out if I could converse in English. Much weightage was given to the family background. They must have also checked up from the intelligence agency, but they did not ask any questions about my involvement with freedom fighters. They must have known that my father was a British title holder. Physically, I looked all right. There was a four-page proforma, like the Union Public Service Commission (UPSC) of today, to be filled. I must have been cleared at the weeding out stage, and so a letter from the Army Headquarters arrived asking me to appear for a formal interview. I undertook the journey to Lucknow again for a second interview with the British Brigadier and a few more officials – I do not remember them – and it took about three hours. After that, I went back to Allahabad. Some days later, I was called to the 'Services Selection Board' in Bareilly. That was the third tier examination at the national level, to be conducted at the 'Services Selection Board' which was somewhat similar to the UPSC. I went to Bareilly and stayed for three days in the Services Selection Centre to undergo group tests, interviews, psychological tests, academic, objective tests and the like.

In Bareilly, there was also the physical fitness test. The candidates had to go through an obstacle course within a specified period of time. The timings were noted and out of eleven obstacles, if one could clear eight within a certain time, he was cleared. It was very objective. There was no scope for any recommendation or *sifarish* (sponsorship). We did not know anybody, and nobody knew our names; only the numbers were displayed on our chest. The Group Testing Officers were watching us all the time while situations were painted to which we had to respond.

Our power of reasoning, rationalisation and debating skills were tested as well. There were no political questions at all. If any of us wanted to argue a case, he had to explain his justification; or if a picture was shown, one had to respond with his reflex interpretation. Finally, after one was selected, he had to proceed to the military hospital for medical examination. Once all these tests were cleared, one got the letter of selection.

On the final day, I remember there were two Indians on that Board. One was Colonel Hira Lal Atal, a Kashmiri Pandit, probably closely related to Jawaharlal Nehru whom he called by the first name. After retirement, Atal was posted as the Chief Commissioner of Tripura. The other Indian was Akbar Khan, a huge Pathan or Punjabi, who later became a Lieutenant Colonel in the Pakistan Army. The Chairman, Hira Lal Atal said, "Gentlemen, only four or five of you will be selected to serve in the Indian Army. However, those of you who are not selected may know that there is no such thing as rejected. Perhaps when you get back, you will have something better coming". Atal was a King's Commissioned Officer, one of the Sandhurst products, carrying that stamp, and had perfect British accent. He was very fair. We therefore mistook him for a British. In those days the Army Officers did not wear names tabs on their uniform. He said, "My name is Hira Lal Atal. I am an Indian. I am not British. Do not write 'Quit India' in your answer sheets, because I will not quit India".

Final Selection

After I was selected and there was a time lag and I got seven days to join. So, I came straight home and told my father that I had got selected and I have to report to the Indian Military Academy at Dehra Dun by a certain date. My father immediately asked, "Is this your decision?" Earlier whenever he asked me, I used to say that I wanted to be a journalist to which he once said, "All right, you be a journalist, do what you like. Do not ask me for money. You have done your BA so be on your own. If you think that you can become M. Chalapathi Rau in one day, you are sadly mistaken. He had to struggle for long". So, when I said I have decided to join the Army, he said, "Fine, all right, you join". Though it was a risky life, he did not stop me.

Mother was a bit worried and my sisters were all up in arms because soldiers of the Army were considered to be sacrificial lambs. They protested, "What is this? There is enough to eat, why do you want to go to the Army?" It of course had much value in the marriage market where it was at number two, the ICS being at the top. To add to my dilemma, the marriage of my elder brother, who had qualified as a lawyer, was fixed for the very next day. So, I attended the wedding in Bulandshaher and from there proceeded straightway to catch a train to go to Dehra Dun and join the training on time. I joined the Indian Military Academy in Dehradun in January 1947. I had to leave my MA in Political Science and the Law course at the Allahabad University.

It was not only because of my love for adventure that I joined the Army. The other reason was that it was the only opening available for good employment. Secondly, when I read Jawaharlal Nehru, I was impressed with what he conveyed through his book, 'An Autobiography'. The exact words I do not remember, but the underlying spirit behind it was something like this: "For me, not the comfort of the shores, because the storm within me is much more strong, and therefore, I want to be on the waves". When I joined the freedom struggle, I would have been shot by the police for damaging railway property which was a criminal offence. Similarly, in the Army, one's career could end if one was not fit enough, or one might be court-martialled if one was a bad boy, or if one went into any action, one could die. That was the challenge.

It was out of my love for adventure and the opportunity that came my way, I would say both, that I joined the Indian Army. My urge was to be on my feet, depend no more on money orders and do something honourable, challenging.

The Indian Military Academy (IMA), Dehradun

Prior to the setting up of the IMA in 1930, officers for the British Indian Army were trained at the Royal Military Academy, Sandhurst, U.K. These officers were known as 'King's Commissioned Indian Officers' (KCIO). The commission was bestowed by the King-Emperor and the words were: "*To ——————, our worthy and most beloved, I commission you to serve the British Army and King George V and successor kings of the Realm*". So, one was a King's Commissioned Officer and owed loyalty to the Empire.

When I joined the IMA in 1947, ours was the last batch to be trained by the British and the first to be commissioned after Independence. By that time, the Partition was complete. An Indian Commission (IC) number was allotted to each of us who completed the training and passed out from the Academy. After the Indian Constitution was adopted in 1950 and the commission was granted by the President of India, we had to take another oath. Just as a Vice-Chancellor signs in the degree certificates, the President, Dr Rajendra Prasad had signed our commissioning parchment, our roll.

During the training, we were referred to as 'Gentleman Cadets' (GC). That was the traditional designation. We were not officers, we were like students in a university. Every Gentleman Cadet was allotted a GC Number which was our identity during training, reflected on our books, clothes, and all other articles of use, as much as in documentation related to training matters. We wore cadets' uniforms, but we were not subject to the Army Act, nor was there any provision to cover the risks of training as it is today. We were gentlemen trainees and therefore governed more by traditions and practices rather than formally legislated acts.

About 80 per cent of the training was devoted to academic subjects, leaving just 20 per cent to military education. Actually, the IMA was like a public school, one could call it an exclusive public school where everybody lived in the campus and the training was very rigorous. We were not allowed to step out of the Academy for the first six months, and no visitors were allowed inside. Unlike a university where one finds a free atmosphere, the rules in the Academy were like as it is in a public school. Discipline and order was the corner stone of our existence. Within the campus, we were self-sufficient in everything. We could even see a film once a week. The staff was entirely British, from top to bottom, including the Physical Training (PT) Instructor. Military subjects were very simple: basic tactics, drill and physical training. We first learnt to handle the rifle, which was a soldier's weapon. We also learnt to use the light machine gun, known then as the 'Bren Gun' and the pistol which was carried by the commanders of crew-served weapons or detachment of troops. Thus we were taught the use of only four weapons: the rifle, light machine gun, sten-gun and pistol. Every GC carried a rifle that was permanently allotted to him. Although we were trainee officers, we had to completely submit to our trainers who were Sergeants. There were two Captains who were in charge of all of us.

The academic staff taught us Geography, History, Constitution, Geo-politics and various other subjects, the wide coverage being necessitated because we were being trained to be military officers. An officer is a leader of men, and a gentleman who is instilled with a sense of honour and dignity. For example, even while cycling or marching on the road, we were expected to behave in most dignified manner and strictly observe the Academy's code of conduct. During the training period of two years one could be thrown out if one were inefficient, or injured, or medically unfit, or unable to go through the strenuous life, or for lack of discipline - whatever be the reason. Weakness of character was one of main reasons for expulsion from training because it was thought that while physique and education could improve, character deficiencies, like the telling of lies, could not be fully eradicated.

I recall two incidents. We used to go on bicycle, once a week to the town, to have some ice cream or to buy some items. We had to come back by a certain time; I think, the latest was 9 p.m. in the winter. Once in our group one cadet did not have the lights on in his bicycle while another cadet just stood by the roadside to ease himself. Just then one of the Military Police Non-Commissioned

Officer, a British Sergeant, appeared and asked, "What is your number, Sir?". The cadet gave a wrong number and a wrong name. The Sergeant, of course, was not fooled. The other cadet did not have his bicycle lights on, and so, his offence was not so serious. They were both charged. It was just like a court. We were lined up in front of the Commandant. The Sergeant was asked to identify the defaulters. The cadet who gave the wrong name and number was Pereira, I remember. He confessed and said: Sorry. But for having lied about his name and number, Pereira was out of the Academy the very next day. The other cadet admitted: "Sir, something was wrong with my lights, I am sorry". He was let off after being awarded some punishment in the form of imposition of certain restrictions for three days. So when one committed an offence, one was expected to own up.

I remember the training in the Academy because the Commandant was a very senior military officer, distinguished by the Crown award of 'Order of the British Empire' (OBE) and a 'pukka Sahib'. Right from the Physical Training Instructor to the Commandant, who was like a Principal or a Headmaster, the British Government had sent their best trainers to the IMA. They were all British. The teachers were the very best, graduates from the Oxford and the Cambridge Universities who accepted junior positions to just came to serve in India. Another reason could be that they may not have found good offers in other fields; but when in the military academy, they gave their best. One of the Sergeants (Havildar) instructors, Peter Gorb, was an Oxonian, a topper at that, who came to teach us English. A.E. Foot, the first Headmaster who served the Doon School from 1935 to 1948, was one such Englishman. The Forest Research Institute (FRI) – which is the pride of India and even today remains one of the world's best in that field – and the Royal Indian Military College, now known as the Rashtriya Indian Military College (RIMC) which remains a matchlessly top school, had the benefits of being served by such committed Englishmen. The IMA was established when the British Indian Government, acceding to the demands of the Indian leaders, found it difficult to send larger batches of Indian officer cadets to England for training.

If one was to be awarded a punishment, he was called to report to the 'Orderly Room' at quarter to one p.m. and 'marched up' to the Commandant. Whereas if one had been a good cadet and scored good marks in academics, he was called to report at quarter to four p.m. and given a cup of tea. I had scored very good marks in Physics and Mathematics. One day my tutor, Captain Parry of the Royal Engineers, asked me, "What wrong have you done?" said, "I do not remember". Then he said, "You have been called and I will have to march you to the Commandant". So, I was called at quarter to one p.m. to be 'marched up'. After being 'marched-in' to the presence of the Commandant, one's name was announced and he was expected to reply with "Yes, Sir" and a salute. Then he would be questioned and dismissed with whatever punishment that he deserved. So was I 'marched-in'. The Commandant was sitting there. The Sergeant called out, "Gentleman Cadet, K.C. Johorey, 447!" "Present, Sir", I replied loud and clear. The Commandant showed me a letter with my name on it and asked, "Is this yours? Is this letter addressed to you?" I said, "Yes, Sir". He then asked me to open it. When I did so, there were two cheques, one of ten rupees and another of fifteen rupees. Before I could say anything, the Commandant asked, "Are you a member of the Congress Party?" I said, "No, Sir, I am not a member of the Congress Party". He then asked, "What is this money for then?" I said, "I used to write occasionally. Once I had no money coming from home, the Money Orders had stopped. So I wrote book reviews. One of my photographs was published in the National Herald newspaper. The photograph was of Khan Abdul Ghaffar Khan, sitting and drinking water at Pratapgarh railway station. He was very thirsty and had got down to drink water; it was very hot in the first week of August. I had a box camera and clicked the photograph which was published". "Are you sure?" asked the Commandant. "Yes", I replied. The next question was, "Did you have any sympathy with the movement?" I said, "Yes Sir. I will be telling a lie if I said no. All boys at that time had sympathy". He again asked, "Have you still have such sympathies now?" "Yes, we are certainly looking forward to Independence", I replied, "But I have been selected for the Army, so I am now a government servant". He said, "All right, take it", and gave me the cheques. He could have dismissed me from the Academy.

Partition of the Indian Army

In the Academy, there were some Indian officers from the Princely States, like Kanwar Zorawar Singh from the House of Jaipur. The Gentleman Cadets did not exhibit any disagreement among themselves when they discussed the issues relating to the coming independence except the Gaikwad of Baroda. He said, "I do not know whether we will accept integration with the Union of India". Though in 1947 the process of integration had not commenced, there were questions raised as to what would be the position of the Sisodia Rajputs or the Marathas. At that time, besides the Indian Army's regular regiments, there were regiments of the Princely States which were drafted during war to fight under the Indian Army, and commanded by British officers. There were hardly any Indian officer commanding a Brigade. There were few Indian Lieutenant Colonels, but mostly the Indians were Captains and Majors. After 1947, when Indian instructors were posted for the first time, Captain I.S. Gill, who was a World War II veteran from the Royal Engineers, was one of them. These instructors were thorough professionals and fiercely loyal to the Independent India.

Nothing changed at the IMA on the 15th of August 1947. We were continuing our training except that the British flag over the Academy was replaced and the Academy's flag was hoisted on its place; it was not the Indian flag, but the Academy's flag. The Academy colours had the emblem of 'Heaven's Light, Our Guide', and the 'Star of India' over a background of steel grey and red. No one, none of us, were showed any concern, it was business as usual. Then some riots started and we were given live rounds to protect the Forest Research Institute and the adjoining areas. We were trusted to keep good order. We were told that never before the cadets had been issued with live rounds to maintain order, without having being enrolled and covered under the Army Act. At that time we did not concern ourselves with what might have been our constitutional status, and we carried out patrolling. Nothing violent happened in that area. The Headmaster of the Doon School was made a Magistrate (First Class) and given the judicial powers. The British officers remained within the campus. There were no riots in Dehradun city but in Jwalapur and some other places trains had to be escorted by the Indian Army regulars. Violence and killings started only beyond, in Delhi. Even between Saharanpur and Delhi, we did not have any report of violence.

When the Partition came, I would say that the British played a very dirty game. On 13 October 1947, all of a sudden, during the dinner, we were asked by Major A.J. Wilson, the Academy Adjutant, to stay put. After the dinner was over, Major Wilson came and said, "Now, gentlemen, those who wish to opt for Pakistan please sign this paper. We leave in about two hours, at 5 early in the morning". This announcement came as a shock to us. Among the cadets who opted for Pakistan were Shafqatullah Khan and Hidayatullah Khan Hoti, the Prince of Chitral, who was an old Doon School boy. There were some Muslims from Allahabad, like one Nur Ullah Kazmi, who also opted for Pakistan. Our senior Gentleman Cadet, Prince Vijit, the Gaikwad of Baroda, advised other Gentleman Cadets from the Princely States to stay back. None of the Sikhs and Hindus opted for Pakistan. An Anglo-Indian Gentleman Cadet, Roman Miranda, opted for Pakistan as he was from Karachi. Two other Anglo-Indians, Edward Alfred Cater and Leslie M. Tobin, also opted for Pakistan. The other Anglo-Indians stayed back. Among the European cadets was Ronald Amery and four or five others who chose to stay back in India. The cadets from Lucknow and Bangalore also stayed. There were Punjabi Hindus from Peshawar – from the Kapoor family related to the film star Raj Kapoor, and the Khannas – who could have opted for the Pakistan; but they did not.

Next morning we escorted our classmates when they were taken to the Saharanpur airfield. We were armed so that nobody attacked them. They were put into an aircraft and sent to Kakul where the Pakistan Military Academy (PMA) was established. All the Punjabi Muslim and even the Frontier boys who were not in favour of Partition, went to Kakul in Pakistan. Later we learnt that within six months some differences had cropped up between the Frontier and the Punjabi cadets who went to Pakistan. Sixty Gentleman Cadets in all went to Pakistan. Ironically, these cadets soon found themselves fighting against the Indian Army in Kashmir. So in 1948, within a week or 10 days after I was commissioned, I found myself in Naushera and then in Poonch where I took part in the Battle of Poonch. Our batch representative, General Pramod Anand, remains in touch with the survivors of our batch to this day.

Half of our teachers were transferred to the Pakistan Military Academy which they had set up at Kakul. Major A.J. Wilson, the Academy Adjutant, opted for Pakistan while Captain Canning, the Battalion Adjutant and the son of the Lord Canning, stayed on in India. Captain Parry, the Engineer, also stayed on, as many others did. Among our Indian instructors, Atiqur Rehman, who was from Muradabad and had married the daughter of my Professor, Sir Shafaat Ahmed Khan, opted for Pakistan as did Tikka Khan, the future Chief of Pakistan Army, and two or three more. The British had removed or stole some of the weapons and memorabilia from the Academy Museum. As to how these had been taken away, I do not know, nor do I know if they took any documents or research papers also. There was no damage to the Forest Research Institute, and nobody was harmed in the Rashtriya Indian Military College or the Doon School. The Partition was announced in August 1947, and by 14 October, the Indian Military Academy was partitioned. The Academy's role was absolutely impartial, purely humanitarian and non-political.

The Indian Military Academy Post-Independence

During 1947-48, many Indian leaders visited the Academy. They were Vijaya Lakshmi Pandit, Vallabhbhai Patel, H.M. Patel and Sarojini Naidu, Governor of the United Provinces. The Defence Secretary, Lord Louis Mountbatten and Lady Edwina, Field Marshal Sir Claude Auchinleck and General Sir Roy Bucher also visited the Academy. For Lord Mountbatten and the British Indian Army Chiefs the Academy had reserved a place of pride. Sardar Patel and Vijaya Lakshmi Pandit had discussion with the officers. We had a glimpse of them. We admired them greatly. There was no direct interaction with them; such things were not done.

The training curricula carried on. The tradition of strict discipline continued. As it happened in an ashram in the old days, parents did not go and disturb them to find what their children were doing. Similarly, no parents were permitted to visit except when they were invited once a year. A Gentleman Cadet could visit his home only during a term-vacation; I was not allowed to go when my sister was getting married, even when the Chief Justice rang up the Commandant.

Brigadier A.B. Barltrop, the Commandant who stayed back and served the Indian Army, spoke on the motto of the Academy. The motto was: "The safety, honour and welfare of one's country come first, always, and every time. The honour, welfare and comfort of the men one commanded come next. One's own ease, comfort and safety come last, always and every time". This is the motto imbibed at the Academy. This was what Captain P.K. Sehgal of the Indian National Army had said when he was being tried by a court-martial at the Red Fort in Delhi. He said, "I was trained and educated in the Academy in Dehradun where this was the motto and, therefore, I joined the Indian National Army". That statement helped his case. The Academy remained totally non-political and stayed neutral in policy matters. In my batch, there were 185 Gentleman Cadets who passed out to be commissioned into the Indian Army on 11 September, 1948. Once a year, an eminent personality was invited to be the chief guest at the Passing Out Parade and take the salute. The Prime Minister did not come but for the first time an Indian leader, Sardar Baldev Singh, the first Defence Minister of India, took the salute and addressed the Passing Out Parade.

CHAPTER 3

YEARS IN THE ARMY

First Posting

What was called a 'Police Action' against Nizam's rule in Hyderabad began on 13 September. After the Passing Out Parade, the Defence Minister talked to us and the next day we read in the newspapers that Army had started action to defeat the pro-Pakistan rebels in Hyderabad. But I was not sent to Hyderabad. I was sent to Kashmir. The course itself was cut short by two or three weeks because of the three factors. One, there were not enough officers in the Indian Army; and two, Pakistan had invaded Kashmir; and three, the Hyderabad operation was underway. So, departing from the practice of holding the Passing Out Parade for every course on a fixed Saturday of the sixth and the twelfth month, we were told that the date of commissioning had been advanced. This was obviously done with the approval of the Government of India.

After commissioning, I reported to the Engineer Centre at Roorkee. I was assigned to the Corps of Royal Indian Engineers. On academics at the IMA, I had the highest marks in Physics, Chemistry and Mathematics. Captain Parry of the Royal Engineers selected me for the Corps of Engineers. We had to give our choice as to the arms we wished to join. The Army had many wings, Infantry, Artillery, Engineers, Cavalry, meaning the armoured corps, and Signals. These are the fighting arms. Then, there are services like the Medical, Supply and various others. The Academic Board assigned the wing to which one had to join. There were certain principles laid down for the assignment - like in the IAS one was assigned a State cadre but fifty per cent officers had to be from outside the home state. I opted for the Artillery as my first choice and Engineers as the second. So, I was assigned to the Bengal Engineer Group of the Corps of Engineers, and I reported to the Bengal Engineer Group and Centre, Roorkee. It is a 200 years old training centre where newly commissioned young officers are attached for a month or two to be introduced to the regimental values and traditions. But we were posted to the field in Kashmir just after four days. We were not told about the exact location but I was assigned to 69 Field Company which was fighting in Kashmir. I was asked to report for duty at Pathankot. I left Roorkee on the same date at mid-night.

In the context of the Indo-Pakistan War in Kashmir 1947-48, the term 'tribal raid' was a misnomer. It was not a raid. It was a deliberate and cleverly executed attack planned by the British officers, even if we did not know that at that time. I do not know why this term was used by the Government of India or the Ministry of Defence. Newly commissioned Pakistani cadets must have been assigned to the newly created Pakistan Army regiments as junior officers, as Second Lieutenants. They however, could not have anything to do with the higher planning; none less than a Brigadier or a Major General could do so. At that time, there were hardly any Brigadiers in the undivided Indian Army. In our own Army, the senior most officer was K.M. Cariappa, who was a Brigadier. No doubt therefore, the attack on Kashmir was planned by the British officers of the Pakistan Army but the final decision had been taken by the Government of Pakistan. Then final planning was done at the level of the Pakistan Army's General Headquarters and below down to the brigade headquarters.

The British officers who stayed back were unquestionably loyal to India. There was no question of divided loyalty among these officers. The most prominent among them was Major General Sir Harold Williams, who later retired from the post of Engineer-in-Chief. He continued to live his life in India. He was a great soldier and was admired even by Pandit Nehru. But those who went to Pakistan, their point of view was – and this has been confirmed – that their loyalty was to the British Crown, and therefore, they were not bound to listen to Lord Mountbatten who was not their Governor-General. Strangely thus, there were two sets of British officers who were fighting each other at least at the planning stage! The British officers in Pakistan did not fight or participate in the raid; they just sent junior Pakistani officers forward. They were only planning and advising them.

I am convinced that Lord Mountbatten wanted to be the Governor-General of India and Pakistan, both. That was why he had been retained at New Delhi. There was to be one combined Commander-in-Chief. However, Mohammad Ali Jinnah did not allow that to happen. He went one day prior to the scheduled Independence Day and assumed the mantle of Pakistan's first Governor-General. So, the loyalty of the Pakistan Army was to the Government of Pakistan. Similarly, the loyalty of the Indian Army was to the Government of India. Yet, the British officers in Pakistan continued to seek guidance from the British High Commissioner in India, Sir Terence Allen Shone, who is reported to have asked them, "Why are you asking me? I am the Ambassador of Britain in New Delhi". I believe, in one of his dispatches, he informed this matter to His Majesty's Government. All this came to notice later on, but the sum total was that the tribal raiders were provoked in the name of religion to be used in that War alongside the Frontier Constabulary and other irregulars. The Pakistan Government must have paid them, but the planning, of course, was done by the British officers. In some places, they had engineered riots, like the one in Gilgit in which Brigadier Ghansara Singh, the Governor and one of the top officials of the State of Kashmir, was killed. Some of the rioters were local soldiers. Communal tension had been aroused and only a spark was sufficient to start such riots of most barbaric kind.

In the early British Indian Army, there was no communal tradition. Later on, Pakistan may have raised regiments on religious lines when religion justified nationhood and separation took place. When Pakistan attacked Kashmir, I think, they formed up all kinds of irregulars and referred to them as 'raiders' for public consumption. That was why the Government of India could not decide as to how to respond to the attack. The usual response to an attack is to respond by counter-attacking across the international borders. But in this case, besides Kashmir's political status, the façade of 'tribal raid' kept the Government of India uncertain as to whether to send troops to Kashmir or wait. Later, once the dilemma was settled by Kashmir's accession to India, the decision was taken to do so. These are all a part of history now.

A Company Officer in War

I was posted to 69 Field Company of the Bengal Sappers. The unit was assigned the task of opening the line of communication with Poonch. Poonch was surrounded from all sides by the enemy. The task assigned to us was to break through the enemy's cordon and build a road from Rajouri to Poonch that would be jeep-friendly. Poonch was a very beautiful district. There was the beautiful palace of the Raja of Poonch situated at one end of the town. The population there was mixed. Situated between the Dogras on the Jammu side and the Kashmiri-speaking people in the Kashmir Valley, neither was Poonch a part of the Kashmir Valley nor were the 'Poonchis' a Kashmiri-speaking people. They were the people of the hills with their own language, tradition and religion. This fact was not very widely known outside the Jammu and Kashmir. Some Poonchis had relations in Mirpur.

Poonch was surrounded. The garrison at Poonch was on half-rations because no supplies could reach there, not even an aircraft could land. Then the troops had to be put on quarter rations. They could fight without food for two or three days more but they could not fight if they had no ammunition. So, the local Commander gave us a deadline. That was the reason why we were sent to try to save Poonch. We were told to break through and take the supplies somehow or the other. We started building the road amidst sporadic firing. Brigadier Mangat Rai, the Chief Engineer, came personally to see us take off on the way to Poonch. Finally, we were able to join up with Poonch garrison on time. Completely exhausted by now, I was able to report the road link-up to the Brigade Commander who had set up his headquarters in the Poonch Raja's Palace. The Garrision Commander, Lieutenant-Colonel Pritam Singh, wanted to capture Mirpur, Bagh and Kotli – the latter, though higher, could have been easily occupied. Due to international politics however, the Indian Army was told to ceasefire when we were in an advantageous position and so the advance to Mirpur was given up. If Mirpur had been taken, the Kashmir Valley would have been saved all that trouble that it is we are put to today. With all the sacrifices and hardships we suffered, it was a very successful operation. We operated in Poonch for a month or so and then, in 1949, I was detailed for the Number 1 Young Officers' Degree Engineering Course at the College of Military Engineering, Kirkee, Poona (now Pune).

College of Military Engineering

I joined the College of Military Engineering at Poona to qualify as a military engineer. Earlier, engineer officers had to go to Chatham in the United Kingdom for training, like the Indian Civil Service (ICS) officers who used to go to Cambridge for training and grooming after the selection. The Government of India could not afford to send the engineer officers to Cambridge or Chatham. So it decided to upgrade the School of Military Engineering, Roorkee, and so the College of Military Engineering was set up at Kirkee in Poona. We were the first batch of Indian Army engineers to be trained in India. The British Commandant of the School of Military Engineering, Roorkee, Colonel R.E. Holloway, was promoted as Brigadier and posted as the Commandant of the College of Military Engineering. Among the Indian instructors in the faculty, I remember Professor Bose and Professor Biswas. Half of the staff of the College was Indian and the other half was British.

At the College of Military Engineering we were fully preoccupied with studies. We were not in fighting and had been taken off executive responsibilities because there was a need to fill up the shortage of military engineers. Had I been assigned to the infantry, then I would not have been sent for engineering degree; we all had already qualifies in infantry training. It took three years of training to qualify as an engineer. It is very important to understand here the role of the Engineers. The Corps of Engineers is a specialised arm of the Army. The Engineers are responsible for planning and execution of civil engineering works for military purposes. In war, they have a major role in combat. They are one of the first elements to move to battle for the purposes of breaching the enemy's defences, field fortifications and obstacles like, ditches, mine fields, rivers or canals road blocks and so on. In defence against enemy's attack, the Engineers create obstacles to stop or divert the enemy's forces and cause attrition to his men and material and so block him from approaching own defensive position. Finally, the Engineers also have the role of occupying defensive positions and fight in infantry role. Military engineering is a challenging mandate which involves construction of defences under enemy's fire and preparation of crossings over mine fields and rivers for the rest of the army to pass. We were motivated by the Engineer's gallant performance at Ghazni in Afghanistan during the Anglo-Afghan War in the 1830's. In that campaign, our unit went from Roorkee all the way to Ghazni where they stormed that Ghazni Fort. For that act of supreme bravery and ingenuity, the Bengal Sappers had been decorated with the 'Battle Honours Ghazni'.

In peacetime, the Engineers, apart from training and preparing for war, engage in construction works like accommodation, provision of essential services, bridges, roads etc. in the cantonments. In our time, construction of civil engineering assets like buildings and roads was quite simple. The main focus of specialised training was in breaching mine fields which the enemy laid to defend itself – a very risky job; one could be torn apart, even a tank could be blown up. So that was the role of the Engineers and that was what I was training on.

After the Course, my new posting was to 100 Field Company (Sirmoor) which was deployed on the Pakistan border in the area opposite the Ichhogil Canal in the Punjab. The nearest railway station was Butari. It was a 'concentration area' where our battle formation was to be concentrated in wait for the government's order to launch attack cross the Ichhogil Canal. The attacking formation's crossing across the Canal was the responsibility of the Engineers. We had to be the first to breach the enemy's defences and launch an assault bridge over the Canal for the attacking troops to carryout assault. Subsequently, our role was to help the Army to move, manoeuvre to fight and survive in the hostile environment.

Having injured myself in sports, I was evacuated to Military Hospital and after recovery, was placed in temporary low medical category and posted to the Bengal Engineer Group & Centre at Roorkee.

Mountaineering

I was very fond of mountaineering. During my army days, there were two major events in my life. One was the first Indian expedition to Mount Kamet in 1952. I was a member of that team. The only 'non-Indian' member – actually he was more devoted to India than any other British officers – was Major General Sir Harold Williams, the last British Engineer-in-Chief, who lived his life as a true Bengal Sapper in India and lies buried in the Roorkee Cemetery. I was selected and invited to join the expedition to Mount Kamet. This was the starting point in my love for the mountains which had actually started during my training at Dehra Dun. There were six volunteers in this expedition. Major-General Sir Williams, the famous mountaineer Major N.D. (Nandu) Jayal, Lieutenant P.P.S. Bhagat, Major M.A. Valladares, Lieutenant Manohar Lal and myself – out of the six, only Manohar Lal and I am still living. This was the first time that the Indians took to mountaineering as full members of the climbing team. Before this, mountaineering was exclusive preserve of foreigners while the Indians were taken on hire only as guides and to carry loads. We had seven 'Sherpas' (expert porters). I was a climbing member of the team in 1952. All of us had taken earned leave and were not on official duty, which was the practice those days.

In 1952, this was also a test case because the British were preparing to climb the Mount Everest in 1953. So, General Harold Williams advised the Government that we should also join as the members of that team since we had no experience of mountaineering. Only Nandu Jayal, who was from the Garhwal Hills, had done some trekking as a student of the Doon School. General Williams, true to his British habits, must have done some trekking, but none others had been to any such venture. But we were motivated by our love for the mountains and the thrill of climbing the Himalayas.

In that expedition, I was in one of the three leading teams. Gurdayal Singh, a master from the Doon School was also there. Gurdayal, Nandu and myself formed a team. In mountaineering, teaming up is in terms of 'ropes' who attempt to climb together and reach the summit. When one 'rope' returns, then the next team goes up. All three of our 'rope' were very fit and therefore, our team was selected for the final assault. General Williams remained at the Camp V; at the age of 55 or so, it was a record for any person to have spent two nights in that oxygen depleted altitude. In those days, we had no oxygen, no wireless sets, no doctor and no contact with the Base Camp. It was a pure adventure sport.

After 14 days, we reached the height of 23,000 feet where we established the last Camp V. Then, one early morning we started off. As we were about to reach the summit which was less than a hundred yards away, suddenly heavy mist blanked out every sight. We had to stop there because Gurdayal complained of cold feet. Nandu Jayal, being more experienced, suggested that we carry on. He asked me. I said that I was fit; I was the youngest. The senior most in age among the three was Gurdayal Singh. He said, "Look, mountaineering is a sport. What is the use of reaching the mountain-top, if when one comes back only to have his legs amputated, or die of exhaustion?" There was a philosophical discussion. It was not a race or a competition to reach the top first. The top was just one spot in the climb where one wanted to be for himself. There was no clapping, no audience; it was not a theatre. One could call it a *tapasya*, a religious submission, the feel of exhilaration at that height being the reward. We therefore decided to return because we could not leave Gurdyal Singh.

But we had a casualty when on the way back, P.P.S. Bhagat died. At the Camp V, as he was sliding down, he hit an ice axe and was injured. We had no doctor. By the time we reached Bampa, the nearest habitation, he just collapsed. Few hours later, he died in his sleep. He was cremated at Bampa village and then we walked for two days to take his ashes to the holy shrine of Badrinath. Although he was a Freemason – Freemasons did not subscribe to religion – General Williams also had a dip and *darshan*. He was a remarkable man.

Yes, the Army gave us the facilities. But technically, I was on leave. If I died in the mountains or became disabled, there would be no compensation or benefits, as it happened when P.P.S. Bhagat died. Nowadays, the police, students and everybody else is taking up mountaineering. But in those days, it was a pure sport and one paid for it. We took leave. I was on leave for two months and I paid for the equipment, travel and food. But support was given by the Army by way of transport facilities, camping gear etc. because these were very expensive. Even the climbing boots cost 90 rupees in those days and were neither manufactured nor available in India. So, they had to be imported. Because of the Army's support, the Government of India allowed the import of such equipment. But for the Sherpas, we had to bear the expenditure. My share of payments was about 2,000 rupees. Looking for the success of our venture, we paid happily.

Then, we came back to our training Centre at Roorkee where I had been posted after training at the College of Military Engineering. I was the Officer Commanding (OC) of a training company and trained recruits of my battalion in marching, bridging and devising military engineering solutions.

In 1953, when the Everest Expedition was formed by Sir John Hunt, we were waiting for an invitation. Out of the three, if one was to be selected, then Nandu Jayal would go; he was very fit. If two were to go, then it would be Jayal and myself. Gurdayal had not been very fit by that time. Expeditions those days had to be launched from at India as its base. Apparently on General William's advice, the Government of India decided that no foreign expeditions would be allowed without Indian participation. But the invitation never came. At that time, we did not know that they had deliberately kept the information from General Williams even if he was a British. The Government of India waited in vain. The reason was that the British did not want to share the glory with India. They selected Tenzing Norgay who was of Nepali origin and chose to hoist only the Nepalese flag. There was no Indian participation. We Indians were still happy because Tenzing was our man. However, the British flag and the British members stole the show. There was intense nationalism in that.

The Government of India then decided that every foreign expedition must have two Indians as climbers, as full members. As a full member, one had to pay for everything. And it was so that I was asked to join the French team which was preparing to climb the Nun Kun Peak in 1953. I was appearing in a promotion examination at Lucknow while on tour from Roorkee. They telephoned me in the afternoon and asked if I could take leave and join the Indo-French expedition. It was for the first time that India and France collaborated. When the French were given permission, they immediately decided to invite two Indians as co-members. I was granted leave by the Army to join the expedition. The other climber was Flight Lieutenant Nalini Dhar Jayal from the Indian Air Force, who joined later on. This was another Nalini Dhar Jayal, not the famous mountaineer Nandu Jayal's cousin, who was also from the Doon School.

The Indo-French expedition to Nun Kun in 1953 was another great experience. For two months, we were lived with the French, sharing their tent and food. Having established the final camp, we were to proceed for the assault the next day when I realised that my leave had finished. Because of the changing weather conditions one could not be sure of going ahead and returning at a fixed time. One cannot plan everything in the mountains; mountains have to be respected. So, I took leave of my fellow mountaineers. I could not overstay. The French very reluctantly bid me goodbye because they had banked on my reaching the top. Only the French were left to complete the expedition because Jayal was not fit at that time. Nalini Jayal stayed at the Base Camp while I came back to join my unit.

CHAPTER 4

FROM SOLDIER TO CIVIL SERVANT

The Call of the Army

As I reflect, the first thing that comes to my mind is that I did not want to join the British Indian Army, which it still was in 1947 when I joined up at the IMA in Dehradun. The British were still in control and the Army was known as the 'British Indian Army' or the 'Indian Army'. The Indian Army had acquitted itself with great credit throughout the British regime, particularly during the First and the Second World Wars. No matter what the political situation was, the Indian soldiers acquitted themselves with honour wherever they went. Even during the Second World War, while the negotiations for grant of independence were going on against many political confrontations, it was certain that India would become Independent soon. Indian leaders were trying to bargain, "All right, we join the war efforts, but what happens to us afterwards; would it be a Dominion Status or within the Commonwealth or full Independence, which was the goal of the Indian National Congress", they would question. However, when it came to the question of leading the independent India's Army, it was clear that of Indian officers serving in the British Indian Army, while serving under their British superiors, very few had held senior command positions. K.S. Thimayya was one of those who commanded a battalion and a brigade in the Second World War. In the First World War, no Indian had served as officer in the Indian Army – neither was any in the Indian Civil Service. Maybe, a few doctors or Viceroy's Commissioned officers were there. There were Indian soldiers, but mostly the Indian Army was led by British Officers.

The Indian soldier fought for honour. It was a volunteer army, not a drafted one. They were honourable men who joined to keep to their soldierly tradition.

For example, there was not a single case of any looting or molestation by the victorious Indian soldiers in Bangladesh; officers made sure of that. While serving in the British Indian Army, the Indians had a very good reputation. Recently, there was a British Broadcasting Corporation (BBC) serial which showed how the Indian soldiers and officers fought in the battles of Sangro and Cassino and won great respect from the locals for their gentlemanly conduct; some photographs, including that of a Sikh soldier who must be about 80 now, were also shown. Many of them were welcomed in the Italian homes as their liberators. Afterward, when the war was over, some of the Indian soldiers married European women and brought them home, very honourably, as their wives. One of my first teachers was Kunwar Zorawar Singh from the princely state of Jaipur. His wife was a very beautiful, Greeco-Italian lady named was Afroditi. Of course, she did not were a veil (*ghoongat*) but she covered her head and put a *bindi* on her forehead in the traditional Indian style. Colonel Dr J.N. Ghosh, decorated with the Military Cross for service in Europe during the war, returned home with Enice, an Italian lady as his wife. Dr Ghosh and his wife were very valuable members of our team which visited the remote districts and villages of the North-East Frontier to set up dispensaries.

Similarly, there were others who won laurels, like Captain I.S. Gill, one of the first Indian officers, who was half British. During the Second World War, he was serving with the Royal Engineers when he was parachuted twice to operate behind the enemy lines in Italy as well as in the Yugoslavia, and he did a fine job. He was one of the team which rescued Josip Broz Tito, the rebel leader of the Yugoslavs fighting against the Nazis. That was the calibre of the Indian Army officers. Later on he married and after retiring in the rank of Lieutenant General, settled down in Madras (now Chennai). Earlier, his father had been elected the Mayor of Madras. A Punjabi who spoke Tamil fluently, he died recently. Viewed from all these angles, I was in no doubt, apart from my own hesitation to be a part of the British system, which joining the army was an opportunity to fulfil my aspirations. By 1947 there was no doubt in my mind that we were not going to have to serve under a foreign master. Even if the British Officers in the Academy acted as our masters, tutors and superiors, during the training we were not 'commissioned' as officers, nor did we have to take any oath. We were just 'Gentleman Cadets' and were not subjected to the Indian Army Act. The word 'gentleman' implied that an officer had to be a gentleman, displaying all the attributes of a gentleman, to be an army officer.

So, I did not find any contradiction in my joining the Quit India Movement and then joining the Army. At that time, I was clear in my mind; as every educated Indian was. When the two cheques against my honourarium for writing few articles in the paper 'National Herald' was received while I was under training at the IMA, Dehradun, and I was marched up to the Commandant on a charge sheet, I had explained my position that we all wanted Independence, but I was not a regular member of the Congress Party. I said, "I took some photographs of Khan Abdul Ghaffar Khan at the Pratapgarh railway station and these were the cheques in payment, sent to my hostel in the Allahabad University who had re-directed these to the IMA. I therefore wish to accept the money". The Commandant allowed me to accept it, and wrote a very general letter to give his opinion. If he was narrow-minded, he could have written that I was an ex-Congressman and that I should be expelled. But not a single cadet was expelled from the IMA on political grounds. There were people like Prince Vijit, the Gaikwad of Baroda, who was openly very pro-British, but some of the Princes were downright hostile; all of us did express our political views quite frankly at that time. But our Commandant, Brigadier A.B. Barltrop was a very distinguished, fine man, highly decorated with the Order of British Empire and the Military Cross. He had fought in the two World Wars and was well educated. In his report he stated that the future officers of the Indian Army, who were going to serve the Government of India, wanted the British to quit. Later on, he reported this to the Government of United Kingdom (UK).

In fact, there were three such reports to that government. One was from one of a British Political Agent who tried to convince Apa B. Pant, a prince of Aundh State and its Prime Minister in Maharashtra, to arrest Achyut Patwardhan and Aruna Asaf Ali when they came into his State. It was a very small state, one can call it a postage stamp state. So the Political Agent who had intelligence reports coming in, asked the Raja Balasaheb Pant, father of Apa B Pant: "Will you please arrest them?" The Raja said: "Look, they have not harmed any single British subject". He further said: "My people have not killed a single British subject because it is against our principles, it is against our dharma. They have not violated any local law. If they have cut the railway lines, that would be an offence committed in the British area. But if they take refuge in my State, I cannot arrest them, they are refugees. I cannot hand them over, unless they violate any of my laws. If they resort to violence in my area or if they kill somebody or do anything against our law, our procedure, the Criminal Penal Code (Cr.PC) will be enforced. You may arrest them when they go to Poona". So, that was a report the Political Agent at he sent directly to the British Secretary of State. As a punishment, he was recalled immediately. Apa Panthad studied at the Cambridge, and later joined the Indian Foreign Service.

By that time an interim government, with Jawaharlal Nehru as Vice-Chairman of the Viceroy's Executive Council, had been formed. As I remember, Vijaya Lakshmi Pandit and Vallabhabhai Patel visited the Academy and addressed us.

Lord Mountbatten also visited and addressed the cadets. All these developments vindicated my choice of joining the Indian Army.

The Call to Frontier Service

By the time I came back from the Kun Lun mountaineering expedition and joined my unit, there was a circular from the Government of India asking for volunteers who wished to opt for transfer to the 'Indian Frontier Service'. Apparently, Prime Minister Jawaharlal Nehru had been to Assam after widespread damages to life and property had been caused by floods following an earthquake (described as *bhoomikampa* in local parlance) on 15 August 1950. There were thousands of casualties in the frontier villages on the Assam-Tibet border in what was then called the North-East Frontier Agency, NEFA in short (the word 'Agency' implying the administration). When Nehru went there, he found that out of the six district officers, that is, the Deputy Commissioners, four were foreigners. These officers were not willing to continue to serve in India and were keen to leave for Britain. After the partition, some members of ICS had gone to East Pakistan, some went to Delhi, and some British Officers had taken retirement and gone. Only one or two remained in Shillong. Some had joined the tea gardens. Later, after I joined the Frontier Service in NEFA, I remember very well Geoffrey Allen and Peter James amongst them who were my predecessors. Then there was John Halliday and David William Mackenzie. Three or four such officers had joined the tea gardens in Assam and maintained their relationships with the tribals.

When asked by Prime Minister Jawaharlal Nehru about the shortage of such key state-executives, Gopinath Bardoloi, the Chief Minister of Assam, told him that he did not have enough officers after the partition, and the few he had, were manning the State Secretariat. So, it was decided by the Central Government to invite applications immediately from officers from the Army, Navy, Air Force and other All India Central Class-I Services – IAS, ICS etc. with a minimum of five years' service, for deputation as administrative officers to the Frontier Districts. In the circular, it was indicated that Head of the Department would not withhold the applications; he could do so in those days. Even now, no officer in the civil or defence services are permitted to respond to any such call directly.

NEFA was technically a part of Assam, but was directly administered by the Governor of Assam who was the agent of the President and who worked through executives known as the 'Political Officers'. The system was somewhat similar to that adopted by the British to control the Princely States and Frontier Agencies. Here, Political Officers were posted, who were like ambassadors representing the British Crown, reported directly to the Crown and to the Viceroy, and not to the Governor-General. Political Officers were selected as an elite corps from the Indian

Civil Services (ICS), the Army and the police; there was no direct recruitment to the 'Indian Political Service'. Political Officers were mature and adventurous people, committed representatives of the British Empire who opted to serve at places like Peshawar, the Razmak Agency and Kabul, and deeply devoted to the local tribes over whom they ruled. They were what one may call the 'blue-blooded empire builders'. The post of Governor in Frontier Areas were more or less reserved for the officers of this cadre. That was the era of 'The Great Game' that was being played between the British and the Russian Empires in the Frontier Areas, Kabul, Kashgar and Lhasa, all across from the East to the West of the Himalayan Ranges where the British Indian Empire's interests extended.

Starting with about seven of them, there were only three or four Indians who remained in the Political Service at the time of the partition. One was Ishkander Mirza who went to Pakistan and later rose to be the President before Ayub Khan imposed military rule. Another was J.N. Dhamija who chose to stay back in India, though the Dhamijas came from the North-West Frontier Province (NWFP) which was now a part of Pakistan. Mirza Rashid Ali Baig (Tara Ali Baig's husband), was also in the Indian Political Service. This service was later abolished and merged when the 'Indian Foreign Service' (IFS) while the 'Indian Administrative Service' (IAS) were formed. The ICS was stopped and it took about a year to select and train a new IAS cadre. Some members of the ICS were merged into the IAS and they retained their seniority. The ICS had also been divided when some of its members opted for Pakistan, but not straightaway in 1947. There were two streams in the ICS; those who were academically inclined, were in line for the post of High Court Judge and Chief Justice; if one had the aptitude for administration, then one could rise to be a Chief Secretary. Some of them, including High Court Judges, stayed back for a year and more. Justice William Broome of the Allahabad High Court stayed back in India. He married an Indian and did not go back to England. Similarly, as I remember, T.J.C. Acton, the Commissioner of Rohilkhand Division, Bareilly, and some others who later became great writers, went to Pakistan.

Nehru, the Prime Minister, was his own External Affairs Minister. He loved the tribes. He loved the mountains. So, the Ministry of External Affairs (MEA) became the nodal agency for administering the NEFA. The decision to find officers from other services to man the post of Frontier Officers in remote districts was responded by over two thousand applications. So, a high powered five-member Selection Board and some Advisors was formed. The first batch of 14 was selected thus sometime in the middle of 1953.

I saw the circular calling for deputation to the Frontier Service after I came back from the Indo-French Expedition to Mount Nun Kun. The notice circulated clearly stated that the conditions of living were very hard and those who wished to volunteer, could forward their particulars. The Defence Ministry had made it clear that the unit commanders should not withhold any application. So, I gave my particulars to the Adjutant and he forwarded the application to the Ministry of Defence, from where it was sent to the MEA. That was how it started.

After a month, I got a call for interview before the Special Selection Board of the Union Public Service Commission (UPSC) consisting of the Foreign Secretary, Defence Secretary and member-advisors of the UPSC. Afterwards, in December 1953, I was informed that I had been selected and that could take leave of my unit to report to the South Block in New Delhi for training and deputation to the Ministry of External Affairs. There was to be what was called a 'probationary period', like it is in the IAS and other all India services. If not found suitable during the probationary period, one could be sent back to the parent cadres. So, I arrived at Delhi and reported to the Ministry of Defence. They gave me the training programme. The unique feature of this curricula was that the training was not to be held in the Metcalfe House, New Delhi, where the IAS probationers were trained before the Academy at Mussoorie was established. In those days, the training was for six months when one learnt horse-riding and studied a bit of the Constitution of India and a few economic issues. The Prime Minister had decided that there was no need for a full course of six months at the Metcalfe House. What training after all would need to be imparted to officers with five years of service in the ICS, IAS, IPS, Army, Navy and Air Force, he opined, after they had been through the processes of selection in their own services and gained requisite experience for five years. The selected candidates therefore had their training reduced to a few week's orientation. In those days, 'capsule courses' were not known.

The orientation was for two weeks when the heads of various Departments came to give talks. The course was inaugurated by the Prime Minister himself. Normally, the inaugural speech is for 30 minutes or so and then, there is 'tea' before the speaker would say, "Congratulations, carry on and thank you", and leave. But in this instance, like a headmaster, Jawaharlal Nehru asked, "How many are present here?" The Foreign Secretary who was sitting to his right, said that it was 14. At the same time, the Joint-Secretary who was in charge of the training said, 13. Both of them spoke at the same time. So, Nehru said, "Make up your mind, is it 14 or 13? How many are present here?" He was like a headmaster taking a roll-call of the students. Then the Joint-Secretary said that out of 14, 13 were present because one officer could not arrive. That was Major Renalte Khathing (Bob), a unique person. A Tankhul Naga, he was far away in the Manipur Hills and though he had got the message, could not come either because of the distance, or probably the Maharaja of Manipur did not relieve him. After Independence, he has been appointed as the Administrator of Manipur. There were only two graduates in Manipur at that time, Maharaj Kumar Priya Vardhan Singh himself who was a graduate from the Allahabad University, and Major Bob Khathing. Bob Khathing was a very brave soldier. He had been in the 'Chindits Operation'* with Major General Orde Charles Wingate. He lived through that operation to become a Member of the British Empire (MBE) and also won the gallantry award of 'Military Cross' for his exploits. Although Bob Khathing was a Minister for the Hills in Manipur, he opted for the Frontier Service and was selected. He could not come.

One of the selected was Rajkumar Bharat Singh, the Prince of Bharatpur who was the Commandant of the President's Bodyguard. He arrived at 10 O'clock after attending to his duties. He was still in his uniform. Nehru asked all of us to stand up one by one and give our names. Then he asked, "Bharat Singh, why does one want to join, what is that urge which brings young men to the unknown frontiers, giving up the comforts of regular service?" We were after all regular officers, not emergency cadres who are relieved after five years, and that commission meant a service liability for the rest of one's lives in the air, land and sea. In the circular, it was stated very clearly that the conditions of living were very hard and the officers were expected to live among the tribal people and administer them without the amenities. It was not that one would get a bungalow to live or a Personal Assistant to assist.

Nehru spoke for 45 minutes. He said, "Someday, there will be the live frontiers. You are going there. You know, geographically, they have been isolated. They are our kith and kin and you have to administer them with great care, because the tribal people are not only simple but they are attached to their freedom. If a tribal says that this was his area, that must be so. There, even the fishing and the hunting rights are all defined by their customs. They have their own social system, their own system of administering justice, ready and rough sometimes, sometimes very cruel, but so it must be. Under these conditions you must administer well. The typewriters can go later on, but the pen and paper, and the flag should go first". That was the theme of his talk. He mentioned that someday there would be live frontiers. Indeed after long internal wars, China became united under the banner of Communism in 1949, and with the old imperial glory impressed into their mind, they had started moving into Tibet from 1950.

* The Chindit Operation was the largest of the Allied Special Forces operations executed between February 1943 and March 1944 in the war against Japan. The 'Chindits', as the commandoes were referred to, operated deep behind enemy lines in North Burma. Tragically, Wingate, their leader was killed on 24 March 1944, a few weeks after the launch of the operation.

No doubt, Jawaharlal Nehru was very clear in his mind. Today people criticize that it was his 'Forward Policy' which upset the Chinese. There are various other theories. Some say that it was the Dalai Lama's asylum. Others opine that we should have left the North-East Frontiers outside the Indian Union and that our taking possession of NEFA was a provocation. I do not think so. Every Indian has a right to the fruits of freedom. There is no question of a Naga or an Adi or a Padam or a Mishmi or a Ladakhi being denied schooling and left to remain deprived of freedom. Till 1953, there was just one school at Pasighat in what is now Arunachal Pradesh. That was all. That kind of neglect had to be corrected.

Jawaharlal Nehru kept on talking till Indersen Chopra, the Chief of Protocol, came and whispered into his ears. Indersen Chopra was a Sandhurst trained, highly anglicised member of the erstwhile Foreign and Political Department. He used to call himself Anderson Chopra. He whispered that the Nepalese Ambassador in Delhi had been electrocuted.* Jawaharlal Nehru was at that time speaking at a very high level of discourse like the influences working in the Frontiers and the role of the Chinese. Thus interrupted he said, "Oh! I am sorry. Gentlemen. A very fine young man, the Nepalese Ambassador, a very good friend of mine, he died", before carrying on with his talk and keeping his decided schedule. He started at 10 am and the tea had to be delayed to 11:30 am. He spoke for one and a half hour and spoke very clearly. After two weeks, there was another training programme at the Raj Bhavan in Shillong where we were accommodated. There, some remarkable people like Dr Verrier Elwin came to talk to us.

To the North-East Frontier

In January 1954, the Government reorganised the entire North-East Frontier area. The whole of the North-East Frontier Agency was about 35,000 to 40,000 square kilometres, and constitutionally a part of Assam. The British had given this area names such as, Abor Hills District, Mishmi Hills District and Balipara Frontier Tract. The British Deputy Commissioner of the Border District was also the ex-officio Political Officer, with plenipotentiary powers over and above what a District Magistrate or Collector had, combining in himself all the administrative functions. The area, South of the McMahon Line, was now reorganised into six administrative divisions. Apart from Tawang, starting from the West, first came the Kameng Frontier Division and then the Subansiri Frontier Division, each named after the Subansiri, Kameng and Siang rivers which flowed through them. Then came the Lohit Frontier Division which was inhabited by

* Bijaya Shamshere Jung Bahadur Rana, the Ambassador, died of electrocution on 29 December 1953 while taking a bath.

the Mishmis, Idus and Chulikata tribes and named after the Lohit River. Finally there was the Tuensang and the Tirap Frontier Divisions on the Burma (now Myanmar) border. The NEFA was bordering the Tibet Region of China and Burma on North and East respectively; the borderline ran somewhat like an arch is one looked at the map. Much later, the NEFA area was restructured under a new state of Arunachal Pradesh; I happened to be posted there at that time.

I was posted to the Siang Frontier Division. Siang is one of the five rivers which flow from the Northern watersheds on the Indo-Tibet Border to the South into River Bramhaputra. I was posted as an Assistant Political Officer to the Siang Frontier Division with my headquarters at Along. It was like a district headquarters of today. When I say headquarters, there were just two huts. One was for Rashid Yusuf Ali, the Political Officer, who was selected in the first batch and was my boss. One could call him the District Magistrate and Collector. I was number two to him. I was one of the two Assistant Political Officers who were selected in our batch and posted to this Division which later was restructured into three districts with new names. There was a reason behind finding fresh names. In British days, the region was known by divisive names such as the Abor Hills District, Balipara Frontier Tracts, Mishmi Hills District and Naga Hills District. This was the policy of 'divide-and-rule', and the dividing lines had kept the tribes from being on the best of terms amongst themselves. The tribes in the Kameng Frontier Division were mostly Buddhist while many practiced pre-Buddhist animism and rituals, while in other Frontier Divisions people practised Buddhism, animism, Christianity and Hinduism of varying forms. But no matter how much one tried to draw dividing lines, cultural boundaries always transcended the political boundaries, and as always overflowed linguistically as well as culturally, just as it is in the case of McMahon and Durand Lines. On both sides of the dividing lines, the people were almost the same and there was free flow of trade and ideas.

People talk of 'fluid' and 'live' frontiers. At the inaugural lecture to us probationers, Jawaharlal Nehru had talked of the live frontiers, by which he meant that these frontiers had been live at one time; there were routes going across and live trade and social intercourse flourished. The significance of the agreement with China, which was finally signed in 1954, may have prompted Nehru's that statement. I, however, did not understand its full import till I was posted to Tibet, because our main role and training was aimed at running the routine civil administration. Jawaharlal Nehru had also said, "The staff must go along with the flag, and the typewriters can follow later on".

True to that advise, physically and literally, we landed at the Jorhat airfield at Rowriah where we had to wait for some days before moving on. Firstly, we could not go to Along because there were no roads. The Brahmaputra River had eroded the banks and damaged all the approaches. There was no bridge on the Brahmaputra at that time and one could not even go by ferry boat to Pasighat. Therefore, we had to be taken by air. Along had a very small, hastily levelled air strip and restricted by rather complex weather conditions. So, we had to wait. Having joined and initially trained at Delhi, we went to Shillong to be briefed by the Governor, the Chief Minister and various heads of departments. We learnt the law, the local traits of various tribes, and what we could of their languages in two weeks' time. After that course we went to Tezpur, where we daily went to the airfield, wait for the clouds to disappear and come back unrewarded. This routine continued for another two weeks or so. One fine morning, the dashing pilot of the Indian Air Force said, "Let us board and take off quickly to land at Along". So, we went, Captain Utonkomoni Chakilometresa, Rashid Yusuf Ali and myself, each with a small bag of some essential clothes.

Captain Utonkomoni Chakilometresa was a very colourful person. I did not know that he was a tribal from Chittagong Hills on the East Pakistan- Burma border, and knew Burmese and Bengali well. He generally wrote U Chakilometresa as his name. 'Utonkomoni' could be a word of Sanskrit roots like many of the Thai names which are so derived. 'U' is also an honourific and the Burmese equivalent to 'Shri'. Chakilometresas are a recognised tribe these days.

Pasighat-Along

So, U Chakilometresa, Yusuf Ali and myself, three of us landed at Along. This was the administrative hub. It had pucca buildings, a pucca treasury building, a dak bungalow (state rest house), and a government farm. It was the air-head for supply of commodities. We had put some steel sheets with the help of the Indian Army, and prepared a ground where aircraft could land once a week with food, medicines, papers and *dak* (official correspondence) from the secretariat at Shillong. However, there was no electricity in Along. Later, a doctor also joined and started working from there. So, that was how the administration was got established at Along. My predecessor had his headquarters at Dibrugarh first, then at Pasighat before moving to Along, which was four to five days journey away. We were received by the very colourfully attired people, all in their red garments and feathered embellishments. They had two houses for us, one for the *burra sahib* (big boss), that is, Yusuf Ali, and behind that, another. The houses were actually huts made of bamboo, palm leaves and cane. Even the tables and the bed were made of bamboo. There were no mattresses, no electricity and no furniture. The houses were very clean and airy. That was all. We had taken some food or rations. Food had to be airdropped on the small airfield which was also used a dropping zone.

The people were very healthy and strong. They were very strong because they lived on simple food. The modern diseases had not crept in. There was no Sexually Transmitted Diseases. They hardly had any skin diseases and they had shining bodies. After they came in contact with people from the plains, change had to take place. The British introduced alcoholic drinks like rum, but at the time, we never found a drunken fellow, although drinking was open. The tribal society was simple and cases of law and order were of that nature.

We started our work. People kept on visiting us. We kept on meeting the people to know their problems, aspirations and expectations. Then, after 15 days at Along, we started travelling. Some of the villages were newly habited and no administration had reached there. The villagers had never seen a coin. They had no medicines or any other facility of that sort. There were small forces of the Assam Rifles deployed in those areas to keep vigilance, if cursory due to the rudimentary conditions, over the border areas as well as for the security of the villages. Some of the Assam Rifles personnel were Gorkhali-speaking people. It was a police force which also provided 30 to 40 personnel to the district headquarters to guard the treasury.

We continued travelling and meeting people. They came with their personal problems and legal cases, including land – someone had violated the tribal code which had the sanctity of law or violated the governing rules, these were simple cases. Then there was the matter of distribution of salt. A public distribution system was introduced because otherwise the people had to go to Tibet or come down to the plains of Assam to get some salt and barter goods with the local produce. They could not go to the plains after the earthquake of 15 August 1950 and so they were trapped within their own places. So, we did the distribution of salt and also carried out legal and judicial work, controlled the law-and-order situation and attended to the social problems. Sometimes simple cases of divorce came. There were hardly any cases of murder. At least in the first three years, I did not have to handle any murder case. There were no lawyers there. There was the *Kebang* – the court was called *Kebang* and I used to preside.

State administration was introduced very gradually, we were not forcing on them the Indian Penal Code or the Criminal Procedure Code or the Evidences Act. There were few written judgments available for reference; some of these were written by Peter James. I found some of them were very simple, like, "In view of the complaint of the village, I find that this particular trophy should be kept in the community centre of so and so village". But all these solutions were arrived at with the consent of the people. Many times they would come and claim that a particular step was taken in their favour by the judgment of the earlier Political Officer. I respected that. The disputes and differences were simple, direct and open. The system could even be called as democratic because everybody had a say in the open court. Day after day, the complainant would repeat the same thing. There is one tribal word, *'idakkam' which* in English means 'however' or 'nevertheless'. In many of the old notes, one would find the use of expression, "under the circumstances, however...." and then, a repetition of what his predecessor had already stated. The Adi-Gallong clan were experts in the art of repetition. They would repeat the same arguments which were given by his 'learned brother' or supporter. The defender would either accept his guilt or repeat his part of the story again and again. Then the spokesman of the litigant would repeat the same argument, and so would the hearing proceed.

Law and order was not a major problem before we landed there. In the entire NEFA, the 'Achingmori incident' in 1953 was the only serious case to take place. The Base Superintendent, Pradeep Barua, was murdered along with Major Ripudaman Singh of the Assam Rifles and 13 others on a misunderstanding that they had come to liberate the slaves. These officials were engaged in opening up the heretofore un-administered areas by extending the state's presence. This scheme was called as the 'New Opening.' After 15 August 1947, the government had announced that there would be no slaves hereafter. Slavery was very common among the tribals in those days. After winning over a fight, a tribal chief would take some young men, women and children from the defeated village to his own and keep them as slaves. Whoever was powerful brought slaves. The British hardly interfered with them. We also wanted to respect the local traditions, but we could not allow criminal acts like murder to go without any trial and punishment. At the Independence, all the peoples had been declared as free and slavery was made illegal because we did not believe in slavery, just as we did not believe in untouchability. But this was misunderstood because a tribal chief had decided to keep his own slaves. That suspicion led to the murder.

But the tribal society was stabilising. They were still at a stage which could be better described as conforming to the Hobbesian theory of 'noble savages'. That meant that the tribal was courageous, truthful, and honest but he was also a savage in exercising brute force and hedonistic calculus. Many of their practices in dealing with murder, property, sex or kidnappings had to be tempered with civilised mores. It was a system that had to be tampered with modern justice. Of course, we could not judge them by our own standards of morality. They had their own norms and if they violated those norms, there was violent retribution by tradition. But at the same time, we had very clear instruction that although we would give them the fruits of development, we would not allow any heinous crimes to be committed. For instance, even if in Shariat it states that an offender's hands be cut off, one cannot follow that no matter what the orthodox clergy opines. In the modern world, that kind of solution is totally unacceptable and if any polity allowed that, it would not remain worth its status. There were no lawyers. So we used our judgment in the best interest of justice and in accordance with the wishes of the local people. We associated the local people who would express opinions openly. A court case could go on, but it never took 12 years as it takes now. It might take four to seven days, because the number of cases were few. In the briefings given to us, it was stated that we would respect all the local traditions, and the very first thing to do was to learn about the tribal traditions. But very little literature was available on that subject. The British seldom went to these areas and there were very few accounts; neither were there the district gazetteers which a District Magistrate was supposed to go through to acquaint himself with his area of responsibility.

There were small chiefs and many tribes. They were all forest-dwellers who did 'Jhum' cultivation. Hardly any rice was grown and food was scarce. There were few natural medicines, and no doctors, education or schools. As I found, the British kept from interfering with the tribal lifestyle not because the British Raj wished to let them preserve their culture, but because they did not have any deliberate intent of keeping the tribes as museum pieces. Theirs was a deliberate policy to keep the unruly tribes away from the tea gardens, and not to allow inter-tribe hostility to spill over to Assam. So long as they did not loot the tea gardens, the British were happy. One British official, Peter James, was very popular with the tribes. He neither visited them frequently, nor did he set up schools and hospitals. All he did was to go to them during the Christmas time with a 20 to 30 pony-loads of silver coins and cases of rum, and lot of salt and basic things like food, rice, salt, condiments, etc. He would just go and have a good time. Peter James was very popular because he danced with them, lived with them, and gave them gifts. The intent as well as the policy was purely economy-driven. Similarly, there was a British Mission in Tibet where the Head of the Mission did not interfere with the Tibetans or the Dalai Lama.

Siang Frontier Division now has three districts; but in those days, Pasighat sub-division was nearest to River Brahmaputra which flows into Assam, as well as closest to the tea gardens. The Minyong tribe lived there. Across the Minyongs were the Padams and the Pasis. This area was also the abode of the Adis. 'Adi' is a word in Sanskrit which means of 'real origin'. The Adis were very fair, tall, with fringe hair and quite volatile in nature. They were so very conscious of their appearance and status that they would not allow a Minyong to come in to their area; the head of the district at Pasighat, who was a Minyong, would not go to Along. There was tremendous rivalry between the tribes, and even between two villages. The senior-most tribal leader was Boken Ette of the Ette tribe. Ette tribesmen were very handsome and looked somewhat like the Kashmiris. They used to wear skirts up to knee-length and a red coat. The red coat was given by my predecessor to identify the village headman, whom some of them used to call 'Raja', meaning King. They had their own *kheti* (farmland) and their domestic animals, and enjoyed a very high status among their people. Whatever the headman said, people listened to him.

Tours and Camping

When we went on tour, we had to hire local porters to carry our camp-equipment and seven days' food with us. These porters were mostly women because in the societal division of labour, men would go to the forest for hunting, making trails, house-building, cutting of trees, fighting, etc., while the women – being physically weaker – undertook less taxing jobs. But the population was much smaller in those days, and so, they were reluctant to leave their chores to come work as porters. When I went from one village to another, the local porters would come to carry the loads and at the end of my journey, they would go back to their villages. Our tour journey started very early, at 5:00 in the morning and whichever location we arrived at midday, we stopped, put up a camp and met the people. So, the first six months were spent mostly in touring. We were out for 15 to 20 days in a month, after which we came back to the headquarters to see the mail brought up by the local postman. There was no post office except at Pasighat, which was a six-day journey from the district headquarters at Along. Disbursement of due payments, and such administrative chores were attended to during these days. This was the simple, direct administration.

Languages were many, and communication was a problem. We had to adapt and learn; and within three months, I could speak their language fluently. We had the *dwi-bhashis* or the interpreters who knew Assamese and Hindi because in the plains of Assam, they had started to speak a little bit of Hindi. I knew no Assamese and no Adi, but within three months, I could speak Adi and conduct cases. We also had to pass a language examination. The practice carries on; today for example, if an IAS officer is posted to Tamil Nadu, as my son was posted to Pudukkottai, he had to pass an examination in Tamil language as well. If one knows the local language, half the battle is won. So, gradually we communicated through broken Assamese and broken Hindi.

Sometimes, when we camped in the village, in the mornings we went around to see the village *khet* and what primitive arrangements there were. The court cases started in the evening (when they came back from the *khet*) and it would go on for two-three hours. After that, there was dancing and music and other events. The local music was simple. By about midday, one was tired enough to drop dead. The same routine would be followed day after day. Most disputes related to the land-use. If there was any land dispute between the two parties, we went to the *khet* and I gave a judgment straightway. One man would indicate a stone as a boundary mark while the other fellow would indicate another. On fishing rights, one party would claim a limit which they would not allow to be crossed. The issues also related to rights on hunting, fishing and forest produce. There was no forest department and no police department. I had no policemen to rely on. Men of the Assam Rifles were there, but they were there to assist in marching and setting up the camp at the end of the day's march and guarding it. We never used the Assam Rifles for law and order for three years that I was in Siang Frontier Division.

For the first six months of my civil service, up to 15 August 1954, I remained posted at Along, that is, the divisional headquarters. Then I was posted to Pasighat, which was an independent Sub-Division. It was a more settled place where there was a school up to Class IV or V, which we got upgraded later on. Along was my area of training at the district level, and now I was to be in-charge of the Pasighat Sub-Division.

CHAPTER 5

SERVICE IN PASIGHAT SUB-DIVISION

Life at Pasighat

I arrived at Pasighat on August 16, 1954, to be precise. Dr. Verrier Elwin's assessment was that if there was any trouble after the flag hoisting on Independence Day, it would begin from Pasighat – which was the most sensitive area. I did not travel via Dibrugarh or the plains of Assam. I moved along the upper reaches of Along to reach Pasighat, and took over as the Sub-Divisional Officer with independent charge. In that post, I communicated directly with the headquarters at Shillong and with the Advisor to the Governor in Delhi. My reports were sent directly to the Political Officer, Yusuf Ali, at the beginning and later his successor, P.N. Kaul.

When the first British forces went from Pasighat to Along, one garrison was totally massacred in a house which is still there. So, the British met with a lot of resistance. One British officer was murdered because he laughed at a tribal funeral. This person went out of curiosity and mocked at their rituals. They were offended if a camera was taken. They were very suspicious of outsiders; that was their mechanism of defence. Not only were the tribals suspicious of outsiders, but even among the villages across the Valley, they used to send chilly-messages. A "chilly" message meant: "I would fight with you if you come to my area. Do not come till I invite you". They were suspicious of each other in these unexplored regions.

But after Independence in 1947, a few tribals used to come to the plains of Assam and when we went in 1954, there was no resistance. The first batch of officers who were posted to the NEFA were warned to be very cautious and careful in dealing with the tribals. The only example of resistance was in the Achingmori incident, one year ago in 1953. Achingmori was a remote village in what is now called the Subansiri District. It was the abode of the Nishis who were colloqually called 'Daflas'. They were well-built and tall tribals with unkept long hair, who wore just a loin cloth; they looked like they were out of those typical pictures of the primordial cavemen. Administration was practiced by sending columns with salt and a flag to remote areas with one civil officer, a few men of the Assam Rifles and with some people from the already explored neighbouring villages. So, one column went there with salt to explore the area and to extend the administration. Pradeep Barua, the Base Superintendent and Major Ripudaman Singh of the Assam Rifles went there with a column. When Pradeep Barua and his team went to Achingmori, somehow there was some misunderstanding. Barua had joined the service in 1953, one year before I did. He was of the rank of Tehsildar. Major Ripudaman Singh, commander of the Assam Rifles detachment, was very popular among the tribes; he used to amuse locals by taking off his turban and showing his long hair. The people there were slave-owners. They got the impression that the team had come to liberate their slaves. So they decided on a pre-emptive attack to kill them. Duipui was the tribal who had murdered the entire team. The attack took place as soon as Barua arrived at the camp. They had just put the loads down and the camp – a few shelters and bathrooms – was being set-up with the help of the local people. Men of the Assam Rifles had put aside their weapons, and everybody had started cutting and clearing the jungle. Barua was issuing salt to the villagers who kept coming in groups. That was when the attack took place. Within minutes, the Dafla tribals came from the bushes and massacred the whole column. Barua, Ripudaman Singh and all others were killed except one person who escaped and brought the story back, after several days.

When the news reached Delhi, they began to think that there must be something seriously wrong with our policies. The murder was enquired into and statement of the villagers was recorded, followed by a trial. The Daflas had confessed that they murdered the column of officials because the officials had come to abolish the custom of slavery. Actually, that was a misunderstood message. Some of the village headmen in red coats, who had accompanied the officials to an inter-tribal rally, told them that slavery was soon to be abolished. The Adi-Gallong people and the Daflas were always fighting each other. The Daflas thought that the Administration was pro-Adi. So, they murdered the entire column. Later, I went to that area with my colleagues and we talked with, pacified and mingled with them. Personally, the column leader Ripudaman Singh was very popular. I have the feeling that our two officers and the whole column was murdered because they chose to be with the wrong kind of people.

Pasighat Sub-Division was a very challenging assignment, particularly because there were a large number of accounts and financial transactions. Distribution of salt was an important responsibility. There was no salt available in that areas in those days, and the disease of goitre was quite prevalent. So the government had sanctioned free distribution of salt in remote areas. Salt used to be dropped. Salt used to come from Dibrugarh – dropped by aircrafts and then further moved by porters. It was a very popular political present from the government to the locals. Actually, salt distribution was something like a predecessor of the public distribution and supply system. In any case, we needed salt, wheat, rice and *dals* for ourselves, on payment, of course. Rations were supplied similarly to the Assam Rifles and the government schools. Some rice also had to be acquired because the local produce was quite diffused, and there was no system of buying and selling. There were no bazaars. It was a very primitive barter or exchange system; these days one cannot imagine those things. There was hardly any currency or money in circulation.

Work at Pasighat

There was no bridge on River Brahmaputra and boats were used to cross it. There was no easy way of reaching my place. Due to heavy floods in the wake of an earthquake in August 1950, the banks of River Dihang – a tributary of the Brahmaputra – were eroded. The dak-bungalow, offices and roads disappeared. We had to travel by air from Dibrugarh and Jorhat airfields by a Dakota of the Indian Air Force, and land at a hastily-improvised airfield at Along – the new district headquarters of the Siang Frontier Division. Once in a week, an IAF aircraft used to drop essential supplies. There were no roads either at that time, not even from Pasighat to the plains. By 1954, a few airfields were made in certain selected areas and some 'dropping Zones' were cleared – these were small patches of more or less level ground which had been cleared of the jungle and marked by a flag where an aircraft could drop supplies. The entire Agency's needs were dependent on air maintenance. It was very unsatisfactory and expensive arrangement, but that was the only solution. Such was the infrastructure.

Take the case of the opening of a new school. Even if a District Magistrate or a Minister wanted a new school, there were certain procedures which would take a long time. Even if a school was sanctioned, the corrugated galvanised iron sheets had to be got by airdrop. The food for the teachers and others had to be airdropped. If sent by land route, girl-porters from one village would go down to carry the loads up to the next village, from where another set of girls would be sent; one village did not allow girls from another village to come. Most of the girls were doing the work of cultivation of land and they probably would not like to work as porters. Whenever I travelled, I needed a minimum of 15 to 20 porters to carry my food and other essential things. I could carry only few things. Villag rs would not cooperate by giving more porters.

We started making what we used to call 'porter tracks'. I could say that I was my own engineer. At that time, there was no engineer in the whole district. There was one person of Overseer rank, like a Junior Engineer today; that was all...and maybe, one Assistant Engineer at Pasighat. So, with our own resources, with the help of the local people, we started making tracks which the porters with loads could negotiate. Every time we went to a village, we had to walk, cut through the jungle and sometimes, even build bridges of cane and bamboo. That was the infrastructure to be built. It was really a part of coming into contact with the local people, a sort of exploratory move.

Before 1947, there was nothing there. Pasighat had the first school to start in that area that was spread over 35,000 square kilometres. Soon, we set-up a small school and appointed teachers. We went around the villages and found out what their requirements were...it was a sort of planning by response and consent. We would go to the village square to meet the elders, sit down and exchange gifts. The village headman would come with some eggs held in very intricately woven bamboo baskets, very colourfully done. They would offer the gift in a ceremonial gesture as it was the practice in the old days of the Rajas. He would also bring chicken. His wife would come and bring a jar of *chhang* (local brew or rice beer) as a token of friendship, to say that we were welcome. We would then enquire from the village headman, "Alright... *bataiye* sahib, what do you want us to do for you?" Then the headman would say, in broken Assamese, "Morey to pundit lagey", that is, I want one 'Pundit', meaning a teacher; the school was without a teacher. We would return with our notes, write to the government in Shillong, to the Secretariat, to send a teacher immediately. So, within about six months, we got a sanction to recruit six teachers. The first preference was education.

As stated, there were very few footpaths or inter-village paths. Gradually, we converted these into jeep tracks over a period of two to three years. New roads were sanctioned from time to time. We followed the Public Works Department (PWD) procedure and the PWD was the disburser, the disbursing officer had to have a gazetted officer in the government. There were no contractors, so there was no question of inviting a tender here. A contract would be signed for the provision of labour and payment would be made directly to the porters or the labourer. It was an open administration. If 100 rupees was sanctioned, everybody would work for 100 rupees. The labourers had to be from the work place and they would work only up to that point which fell in their area. The British did not encourage labour coming from outside, except a few of the Nepalese load carriers from a labour agency. The village people demanded that they should provide them labour; they were very conscious of their rights. At the end of the day, after all the porters had been paid in cash, many of the girls would proceed to the nearest silversmith and exchange that cash with a garland or a necklace made out of coins. Whenever I would next go to that village, the girls would very proudly wear the necklaces. So a goodwill was created.

We had to be very cautious in dealing with people at that time because of the Achingmori killings. There was no hostility, however. We never talked of politics, only about development. It was true that the local tribes had not experienced any state administration. They had only seen the benign British officers very remotely when they visited a few key locations. For example, Peter James never visited Along. His headquarters was Dibrugarh and then he moved it to Pasighat, where the floods washed away his house, the dak-bungalow and the entire set-up. Then, his official house was also burnt down probably because he lit a cigarette when drunk; it was not the local people's mischief – that was established. The government did not punish him for that, and immediately sanctioned a grant with which another house was constructed. I had put up the National Flag on it and lived in that house.

To sum up, administration was simple and direct, with minimal staff and least interference. Secondly, it was very open and transparent. Every expenditure, including those on roads and airfields, were well accounted for. We used to allot work openly to the village community as a whole in the presence of the tribal leaders. I would then say, "Alright, if you finish work up to that point, tomorrow I will come again and I will give you the money straightway". Payment was disbursed in the presence of all the workers. Accounts had to be maintained meticulously, and thumb impressions were taken.

The locals' attitude is well-illustrated by one episode. There was a pucca dak-bungalow made by the British where I was to disburse the salary of the *chowkidar* (caretaker-guard). There, it was his wife who appeared to record the presence of her husband. I accepted the customary gift of a chicken and seven eggs, and asked her to call the man. She said that he could not come because he had gone hunting, but if I wanted to meet him, he would certainly come. I had observed that the fellow turned up only once in a while. She then demanded that since the man was present, she had come to receive his salary. But I was a bit puzzled because if I disbursed the wags to the wrong person, I could not forgive myself, nor would the Accountant General accept it. So I said that the money was there and I wanted to give it to him, that she should send him to receive it. The *chowkidar*'s wife took it as an offence. She said, "We are not working for the government for the sake of money. We do it for the prestige because my husband has been given a red coat. He would come the next time". So, I had to take a decision. I did not take this money back and did not disappoint her. I gave her the money after taking her thumb impression and writing down her name. I did write a report stating that the amount had been disbursed to the *chowkidar*'s wife and not to him, and that the audit should accept this. That was the system there. If I had not given the money to the lady, she would have been very annoyed and the whole village would be up in arms against us. They had agreed to maintain the dak-bungalow, and that meant that they had accepted the Administration and protected it in their village.

Tribal Administration

For seven years, from 1947 to 1954, there was hardly any progress. Given the 'hands off' policy regarding the tribes, this was inevitable. Progress came because of the Chinese movements and I credit Prime Minister Jawaharlal Nehru for that. He could have continued the policy of keeping off and desisting from expanding the state administration to forward areas. But that would have been catastrophic; the administrative vacuum had to be filled by people either from across the frontier (i.e. Tibet) or from our side. India could not have left a political vacuum there. That indeed had been the purpose of delineating the McMahon Line. Today, some sections of the intelligentsia, columnists and analysts criticise that.

Dr Subrahmaniam, a friend of mine, feels that it was because of the 'Forward Policy' that the Chinese attacked India. But what was the Forward Policy but a natural process of inclusive growth and bringing progress to the peoples living on the national margin? The case was similar to the Andaman and Nicobar Islands. The Andamanese are the people of India, local tribes and descendants of people who were exiled there; many among them were criminals. But the people from Europe who went to the USA were not all pilgrims either. Therefore, even if the Islands had once been a penal settlement, it was not possible, not advisable in fact, to let the same state continue forever. So, the reach of the state had to be extended and administrative machinery established to cover the areas which had so far been left out of state administration. Similarly, as the Indian settlements moved into the North-East Frontier Agency (NEFA), it had to be seen that state, too, moved up to take control.

The Political Officers were on top of the administrative hierarchy. Then there was my own second Magistrate, Dying Ering, who was the first Matriculate from that area. He was a prominent person, and therefore, the Governor of Assam asked me to look after him and his wife. Then there were the Assistant Political

Officers, the Base Superintendents, Deputy Collectors or Tehsildars, Naib-Tehsildars and *Gaonburahs* (village headsmen) in red coats. The other village leaders were given various kinds of responsibilities but were not paid anything. The tribal people had a lot of respect for the village leaders in red coats, whether in Nagaland or in other places. In Nagaland, the village leaders also used red blankets because it was very cold.

In the old days, every District Magistrate had a manual to guide him through his functions. But we did not have even that. We took guidance from the book titled A Philosophy for NEFA by Verrier Elwin. Then there was the prominent villager headmen called Gaonbura, who was given a red coat and also an interpreter known as dwi-bhashi – both helped in running the administration. We had gone with very simple objectives, and all our time was devoted to public service. But we made sure to implement our laws in a gradual, non-intrusive fashion. There was nothing else to be done from morning till evening but to serve the population's needs. I had to deal with streams of visitors all day. There was no question of one minute being wasted.

We were told to associate the people with governance at a grass-root level. Whenever I went to a village, I had a meeting of the Panchayat. It was called *Kebang*. The *Adi Kebang* was a very powerful institution. It had judicial and executive functions, and it ensured maintenance of law and order. If someone was to be arrested, the Kebang – like a court – sent a man to do so; just as what 'Bobby' did in London. The deputed man would go to the offender's house, knock on the door and proclaim: "In the name of the Queen, I call you to come to the *thana* (police station)". That person would readily obey the summons. That system was still going on. We did not have to issue any written summons. If an offence was committed, like somebody was mischievous or there was a case of theft, and when such a message was received, the offender would be called by the *Kebang*. I sat as a Magistrate in the middle of the *Kebang*, surrounded by both the parties, and held open count in the village. Anybody could attend the proceedings – men, women and children. That was the basic system for speedy administration of justice through the *Kebang*.

We consulted the *Kebang*, the local village council, which was like *panchayats* in other areas on most issues. In Pasighat, the Gaonburas, in red gown, would attend the *Kebang*, which used to go on for hours together. They would all sit underneath a tree and undertake judicial functions. If there was a dispute on land or water or fishing, both the parties would plead their cases in the *Kebang*. Both, the judicial and the executive functions were conducted there. If I wanted to arrest an offender, a Gaonbura or village leader in a red coat would go and bring him – there was no need for use of any force. He would say: "*Migom* sahib *bula raha hai aapko"* (*Migom* sahib calls you). They called me '*Migom*' which meant, an elderly person, a senior for whom they have great respect. Even now, when the Chief Minister of Arunachal Pradesh meets me, he addresses me as Migom, even though I would call him 'Sir'. It was in the *Kebang* that they said they would like to have more development...and for that, money was needed. We used to transmit the feelings of the people to the Governor, and to the Central government in Delhi.

I would like to recount one incident in our block. We were supposed to give a report on the number of pits dug. One put the bio-refuge, all the kitchen waste and everything in a pit, and it turned into manure after some time. So the *gram sevak* (village worker) went and told the villagers: "We would make a pit and mark that location". When I went to the village in the evening, I found the women crying. I asked: "What is the matter? Why are you weeping?" They said: "Sahib, your officer told us to dig the earth. This is Mother Earth. Digging is only associated with death. We bury our dead. Secondly, you are putting *kodali* or *phaora* (shovel) on the breast of our Mother Earth. We are the product of the Earth. So, it is a very bad omen, and God help if somebody dies". I considered that should someone die today or tomorrow then, we would be blamed for it. So I reported this incident immediately. I wrote: "I don't think we should have that target of 20 pits per village for even one village in the whole district. I would not recommend that. Please do not insist". My superiors agreed. The performance appraisal was now on the number of water points one had cleared, the miles of roads one had constructed, the number of schools started and so on. These were the indicators of development.

Even today, the World Bank relies on statistics. But one cannot rely on these figures. For example, if consumption of cloth is take as an indicator, the figure will be very high in Ladakh where one is loaded with it to protect from extreme cold, whereas in South India, even High Court Judges attend court in chappals, fine dhoti and a black turban; Dr S. Radhakrishnan (later the Second President of India) used to wear chappals and dhoti to the Banaras Hindu University to teach! So, the consumption of cloth in Madras was much less than in Ladakh. That could, therefore, be no indication of development. Besides digging manure pits, there were many other relevant factors like longevity, education, etc. to evaluate development. Fortunately, the government understood my point of view. On the other hand, we had the highest people's participation ratio in road-building. Although the output was not very high...qualitatively, the roads were made good enough for one jeep to go when the above-mentioned two members of the State Re-organisation Commission visited.

People of this region were among the worst sufferers from floods. Floods did so much damage that even a whole hill could be washed away. Many of the villagers lost their cultivation, animals and possessions. In Pasighat, the court and the treasury buildings were washed away by the flood waters of River Dihang on the upper reaches of the Brahmaputra. So, those buildings had to be rebuilt. The affected people were supplied with some clothes, salt, food and medicine by the Administration. Some relief was given from the Governor's Relief Fund. But for housing nothing was given. The villagers themselves got together and rebuilt their houses. There was no compensation given, not even against deaths. Assam was also very heavily rocked by earthquakes. But there was no National Relief Fund in those days.

Relations between the Administration and the tribal chiefs was very cordial. Tribal chiefs were associated with all aspects of the administration, for judicial as well as executive work, and planning. We used to meet them, and do the planning. The planning was not done in the 'Yojana Bhawan' (central planning office), as it is done these days. We were the first to start some planning from the bottom up. P.N. Luthra, who was our first Development Commissioner (1957-60), sent us clear directives asking us first to ascertain the needs of the people. So, when we went to a village, we found out what exactly they wanted. Everybody would want a school. Somebody would want a bridge or a road. So, we would reach a consensus and then we would prepare a plan. Thus, district level plans were made and then it was compiled at the headquarters of NEFA Secretariat in Shillong. Now, of course, the Secretariat has been shifted to Itanagar, the capital of the state of Arunachal Pradesh. From 1954 to 1972, it took roughly 20 years to evolve this statehood into Arunachal Pradesh. First, there was an Agency Council to administer the region but there were many misgivings regarding its efficacy. New Delhi was very reluctant to grant statehood, but Indira Gandhi finally concurred: "What power can we give them but to associate them so that at least they may speak their mind? she asked before going ahead.

Once I led a local delegation to the Republic Day, when Dr. Rajendra Prasad was the President. From the North-Eastern area, there were some tribal people from Tripura and some Adis; an interpreter had also come from Tripura. I was detailed to take them to Delhi. The President had invited the tribal chiefs to the Rashtrapati Bhawan after the Republic Day. When we reached there, I introduced everyone to him. The interpreter started speaking in Bengali. So, Dr. Rajendra Prasad said to me, very softly: "I can speak to them directly. I do not need an interpreter". He then talked to them in Bengali. The chiefs from Tripura were quite impressed with the President's knowledge of Bengali.

Tribals had competing claims among themselves. The *Minyong* and the *Padams* on one side, and the *Gallongs* on the other side. A feeling of rivalry existed between them. If there was any inter-village dispute, then the feeling of tribal loyalty rose very high. One had to be very careful in dealing with such situations. That is why Gallong is a separate district today. It is called Gallong district or by its administrative area – as West Siang, North Siang and Pasighat district. Other parts are still known as Minyong or Padam district. The best course to deal with tribal rivalry was to let them talk. They would talk for days together...over simple matters like keeping a trophy in a village. A large trophy which might have been bought by ancestors from Tibet and which they valued very much – an old utensil for example – was much valued as dowry, and that might be the object of contention. Similarly, there were many shades of inter-village rivalries – sometimes over outsiders marrying tribals, but the problems could mostly be sorted out.

Economy and Development

The British left the tribals alone. It may have been because of their respect for the tribals but basically, they were very practical administrators. My predecessor, Peter James, was a very practical administrator. A very tall, fine person and a bachelor, James used to travel with mule loads during Christmas as winter was the best time because there was no rain. Whenever he travelled, he travelled with about a dozen of supporters and mules. Even mules could not go to some areas. The British practice was to go to a village, camp there for two to three days, and then move on to the next village after constructing a dak-bungalow or carrying out some bit of development and judicial work among the people. The Inner Line Regulations gave him all the powers. The judicial system was based on and administered in accordance with the deep rooted tribal customs. There was no police. He, however, did not distribute seeds of food crops which the villagers wanted for terrace cultivation. This work was left to the initiative of the successor to the ICS, that is, the IAS Political Officer who was also the ex-officio District Magistrate or Judge and Collector of the Treasury.

There was urge among the tribal people; when they saw an aircraft flying, they also wanted to travel in that aircraft. Knowledge of language was very important in understanding their customs and as we were advised to learn the local language, we understood the aspirations of the tribal people. The first seeds were sown at a meeting of the students where they asked for more jobs, especially as more matriculate students came out. To be a matriculate was a big achievement in those days. What would they do after that? There were no jobs. Jobs meant training, and they were not trained. So, we sent some students to the nearest college of Agriculture. They hardly came to Delhi at that time.

In response to that urge, the Government of Assam had not done enough for the development of NEFA. Assamese was the lingua francaof at least of two states – Arunachal Pradesh and Nagaland, but not of Manipur. Manipur had a very distinct Manipuri language. Tripura had Bengali language. The Chief Ministers of Mizoram, Arunachal Pradesh and Meghalaya spoke English and Hindi. They also spoke Assamese among themselves. But the tribal areas were neglected. In fact, when the development work started, the leaders of Assam said that NEFA meant 'No Entry For Assamese'. They started critisising the Political Officers because they felt that their grip over NEFA and the prominence of Assamese language was being targeted.

The tribal economy was based on what is called the 'Jhum' cultivation. Jhum is shifting cultivation. The tribes got together, a family or a group of families or even an entire village, and they cut and slash the jungle. After the trees and shrubs had been cut and cleared, the women would take over to prepare the terrace fields and plant seeds. In tribal societies, planting work was allotted to women because fertility of the soil and its produce were expected to be higher when undertaken by the hands of the women. Men were allotted to harder work like cutting trees.

Everybody knew that Jhum was very damaging to the environment because the slopes caused the top soil to wash away, leading to severe land erosion and climatic changes. As population grew, a system of 'Jhum cycle' or a period of gap between successive Jhum cultivations was introduced. Originally, seven years was the minimum period of gap. If a village needed some land for cultivation, they selected a patch in consultation with the local oracle and the *pujari* (priest), and then took the decision unanimously. Then they would clear the selected hill for cultivation in the following year. The terraces would then be prepared, and seeds planted for edible crops. It was not a money economy; there was only the practice of barter limited to exchanges with friends and neighbours. That was the basic economy.

Then, we got a graduate in agriculture and established the first agriculture farm of over 100 acres in Pasighat, where modern methods of agriculture were introduced. In this farm, we taught the villagers about better methods of terracing, which was otherwise a long and expensive process. For example, we taught them to place the cut trees in lateral fashion rather than longitudinally so that the run-off and sliding soil could be trapped and stabilised within a terrace. That was the beginning stage. It took one or two seasons to show results.

The tribals were a very hardy people because their food habits were simple. Their food had no spices and ghee. Milk was hardly known and there were very few chickens. Occasional sacrifice of a 'Mithun' – a cross breed of yak and buffalo – for distribution of meat to the community was an occasion for festivities when nothing else mattered. There was no dairying in Pasighat. So a dairy was started.

A piggery was also established; we got some high breed pigs, and introduced them in the village economy.

There was a whole village outside Pasighat where lepers with families were allowed to settle. It was a village with a school and families living in it, and known as the Hanson's Disease Hospital. We did not use the word leprosy because of the stigma attached to it. We referred to the village as Dr Hanson's village for Hanson's disease. In 1956, we had only one doctor, Dr Bhattacharya, a very dedicated man who was very well-respected. Nowadays, there are special risk allowances for such jobs. At that time, there was no risk-allowance. Government officials did not need arms, and had no fear going to remote areas to improve health services and agricultural farming. They listened to the people and tried their best to attend to their administrative needs. It was an eye-opener for me to learn from a devoted volunteer like Dr Bhattacharya, the Medical Officer in charge of the H.D. Hospital, that the children of leprosy patients were born normal and did not inherit the disease. However, he cautioned that direct contact with the skin and sores should be avoided. When we introduced the so-called 'Forward Policy' in spreading the administration, sulphone treatment was started for the lepers. The doctor could not go to each and every village. So, the patients came willingly to live in the village with their wives and children. We used to draw up a separate programme for the dignitaries to visit the leprosy hospital.

I remember, we initiated many development works and increased economic activities in blocks of villages. The 'Community Development Project' consisted of schemes like opening road communications – making footpaths, mule tracks and jeep tracks – to bring literacy, elementary education, health care, animal husbandry, cattle-breeding and improved agricultural practices within the reach of the people living in frontier areas. We could do all this because our tenures were long – unlike these days, where a District Magistrate is shifted every one or two years depending on the whims of the Chief Minister. After being posted to Pasighat on 16th August 1954, I stayed in that district for three full years. In most of my stations, I stayed for three years, which gave me reasonable time to plan and work. I found that one can spend a lifetime in a place like Siang or Bomdi-La trying to do something worthwhile for the people and the area. These were very hard stations, and that had to be accepted.

The Community Development Project was started in 1952 at Pasighat and by the time I reached there, ta 'block' had already been established. That was the first year when the block became functional and community development work started. That was also the first and the only community development block in Arunachal Pradesh where we had *gram sevaks* (village volunteers) and social and education organisers working on agriculture, veterinary services and running a school. Multi-pronged activities were taken up under the Community Development Project, which was a part of the First Five-Year Plan and administered by backing from the Central government. There was hardly any income from revenue collection, just four rupees per house, per year. When the British tried to introduce that collection, it caused a lot of heart burn to the tribals, with them demanding to know the reason because they considered themselves as a free people. Finally, a token amount of four rupees was symbolically collected. After independence, that arrangement was continued but the policy was against enforcing it strictly; unlike the colonial days in British India where if one did not pay one's *malguzari* (taxes), one's land was taken away by the Collector. We carefully followed the clear instructions from the Administration on the policy of revenue collection; if somebody deposited four rupees, it was well and good.

The basic economy was based on livestock husbandry, mainly *mithuns,* pigs and cows. The cows were few, and were mostly owned by the Nepalese. Pasighat was the most cosmopolitan place. There was a second-generation of Sikh family of carpenters named Ganga Singh and Gyan Singh. There were migrants working in saw mills located across the Brahmaputra River. These people must have come about a hundred years back and spoke fluent *Adi* language. Then, there was a Nepalese settlement of Banskata village whose headman was Bhim Bahadur. The *sarpanch* was known in Nepalese as *Gam.* There was also a *Sardar Gam,* which meant a very respectable person. Then there was a small trading community represented by Chirkutram Sewanarain. So, these were the only non-Adi residents.

Many people say that the plains-people have come to these areas and exploited the tribals. I do not agree with that view. Chirkutram Sewanarain came here with a can of kerosene oil on his head, walked for days and delivered kerosene oil because of which tribal homes were lit for the first time. That was before electricity supply was introduced. He also brought salt. Even the Tibetans used to buy salt from us. So, these few people from the plains were of great help to the local people. It had become fashionable those days for the activists to say that the Marwari came from the plains as exploiting traders. It was true that in an area where there was no education, a few maybe monopolising, profiteering or even cheating kinds trickled in. Generally, however, the outside traders were very well-respected. In fact, they were sometimes even called to settle the petty disputes. Important non-tribal leaders in Pasighat were Ganga Singh, Gyan Singh, Bhim Bahadur and Chirkutram Sewanarain. A few traders from Bihar were also there along with their labour gangs. Chirkutram was from Rajasthan. He hardly had any education, but he could write in his own language and maintain his own ledger and accounts.

Most transactions were through barter system. Paper currency, though valid, was not popular; coins were used instead. In most parts, accounting was done by bamboo sticks. Business practices among the Adi-Gallongs, Miniyongs and Padams were well established by customs and conventions within the clans and the tribes. Fiscal practices, too, were simple. In our block, it was very successful because we did not have contractual system for execution of works. The PWD announced that one kilometre of a road would cost so much, and released some money. Then villagers were called up, given the implements and tools and asked to execute the work. The marking was done by junior engineer officers. Initially, - I also led columns to mark alignments where no footpath existed. We did ot have a big paraphernalia, like Executive Engineer, etc. The number of people b ing less, the Administration was intensive. If anything went wrong, it was reported straightaway. Unlike Delhi, it did not take a whole day to meet any state f nctioning of consequence like the Deputy Commissioner; here, the small population and simplicity of the system was of much help to the people.

Another feature was the single line of administration. That means the entire administrative apparatus worked as one team and not in compartments. There was one hierarchy in the Administration. Nowadays, sometimes, each department wants to have its own Executive Engineer, who would then take orders from a Chief Engineer located in the state capital. At the district level, we had what was called the District Secretariat. Villagers came here for many purposes, like to get some rice from the Supply Department or to collect items released from the police *malkhana* (custody) or to obtain a gun-licence; these were the things which a simple villager or a citizen wanted.

There was a local leader called Orin Myong. He was a *Minyong* who had been to school and so could speak Assamese and Hindi, but not much English. He was made in-charge of the first cooperative that we started. In giving a name to the cooperative we were told to patronise Adi, the local language. The cooperative was, therefore, named as *Kebang Koret* (*Kebang* meaning *Panchayat* and *Koret* meaning a trading organisation). That was the nearest description of a cooperative. It was not run by the government but by a *Panchayat*. It was a success. We started off in a small hut and stored few things which the people could buy from there, instead of having to go to the bazaar. That was a very small beginning for the Kebang Koret, which expanded later on. Later, it had its own mill too – the Kebang Koret Mill.

Money allocated for development programmes was not very high because the policy was not to pump beyond the capacity to absorb. The local people were not trained and for every project sanctioned, workers had to be found from outside and selected very carefully. For example, in road-building, the labourers would have to be brought from outside because if the villagers were to undertake that project, they would not be able to do the cultivation. Labour was always in short supply. That was the reason why we started with footpaths only before graduating to jeep and other bigger tracks. By and large, considering 35,000 square kilometers of spread, the Plan Funds were very limited. With such miniscule amount of money, one could not achieve fast progress. In 1947, there was no bridge on the Brahmaputra River, no railway station, no electricity, no school. But within 10 years' time, as political evolution came, the pace of development increased, as did the population. I think, in those days, the entire population was of about three lakh. In the overall context, as compared to the population and the area, the funds were very little, and scope for utilisation being limited, these were released only for very simple schemes which we could implement within our own tenure.

Visit of Central Leaders

There was the first visit of Dr H.N. Kunzru and K.M. Panikkar, members of the States Reorganisation Commission (SRC), which was followed by a visit of Home Minister Govind Ballabh Pant. Kunzru was quite a respected leader and the President of the Servants of India Society. I had met him earlier in Allahabad, and also had the pleasure of meeting him much later at the Indian Council of World Affairs in Sapru House (New Delhi), where he lived.

Two factors hastened the reorganisation of the state. One was the attack on the touring official column and the killing of two officers and others. It was a serious incident, and the Cabinet must have considered the factor of local frictions and misunderstandings. Another reason was the earthquake and floods in Assam, in which thousands of people were killed, property destroyed and life brought to a standstill. The point is that there was need for better administration.

The SRC came to Pasighat in 1955, just before I went to Tibet. I got a message that the SRC was visiting in two or three hours' time. Visit of the SRC, appointed by Government of India, to a remote Sub-Division across the Brahmaputra, and between Brahmaputra and McMahon Line, was a major event. We were told that the villagers could ask them any question that they wanted to. They gave us a very short notice, and arrived from Along to Pasighat by a special aircraft. The communications being what they were at that time, I could not complain that I got a short notice. The proposal for the reorganisation of states dates back to Dr B. Pattabhi Sitaramayya's views on the Linguistic States. It was a natural evolution of post-independence administrative progress to cover remote tribal areas right upto the McMahon Line. Pasighat was a full-fledged, independent Sub-Division, and also the most developed area where the people were more awakened and demanding – it was a potential trouble spot. It had suffered the most at the time of the earthquake, and was closer to the plains of Assam. So, Pasighat had all the elements of good or bad connotations of a civilized and volatile society.

I invited all the village elders. Hundreds of people came and lined up, but for the meeting with the members of the SRC, only about a dozen people come. I could not bring together more people in that short time. K.L. Mehta was very angry with me because when anybody came from Delhi, they were shown respect by garlanding, music, dance etc. Traditionally, the guests were taken to the guest house, and there was a programme of dancing and singing for two hours. I did not do that as the SRC was visiting on a very short notice, and one needed time to walk up to the villages which had no telephones or wireless sets. Even then, the villagers would have gone to cultivate their land. There were about 15 to 20 non-officials at the airport. In the meeting, the local elders told the SRC members that they wanted their own rule and did not want to be administered from Shillong where the NEFA Secretariat was located. Truly, Shillong was very distant as one had to cross and re-cross the Brahmaputra to go there. One had to come down to Assam and then go up to Shillong in Meghalaya, and it took several days to reach there.

I accompanied the SRC members to meet some tribal leaders at the High School for Boys in Pasighat. The leaders gave some kind of a memorandum to them. I had told them to ask whatever they wanted to ask the members, who were there only for an hour or two at the most. The tribal people had their own views and, therefore, they brought a representation which was carried to Delhi by the SRC members K.M. Panikker and Hriday Nath Kunzru. My local leader, who was in the car, proudly stated that they wanted more development, more health-care, education and communication by roads, and naturally, more representation of the voice of the people in governing their own areas. A representation was given but there was no demand for creating a separate state. There was a demand to create an assembly and for more senior officials to be posted in the administration. People of the NEFA were demanding more roads and schools. There was an urge for development among them. There was also an urge for representation because they found that neither the members of the Legislative Assembly nor the Chief Minister of Assam ever visited them. They wanted Jawaharlal Nehru to come more often; they had seen him only once.

People aspired for better administration. Although the NEFA was administered by the Governor of Assam as the Agent of the President, the system was a past relic. In the region between the McMahon Line and the plains of Assam, the Brahmaputra Valley as it was popularly called, the 'Inner Line Regulations' were very strict. These regulations were required when the frontier area was isolated and geographically cut off, but it also stifled development. The members of SRC had also brought in their aircraft the members of the Press. I showed them the some development works. Dr H.N. Kunzru wanted to visit the development projects and see what was happening. I also took them into the leprosy village and the Hanson's Disease Hospital. People who suffered from anson's disease were more or less outcastes in the society in the rest of India, as i was considered to be a disease which struck because of past bad karma and sins. We had been told to reorganise medical treatment at priority, and so the Leprosy-cum-Civil Hospital was started. At that time, Hanson's Disease was not very widespread. There were about 15 families discovered in my Sub-Division. So, a kind of village was made where they lived normal lives and were given Sulfa drug therapy. As I said earlier, one Dr. Bhattacharya volunteered to be there. I always invited the visitors to a village of leprosy patients. Dr. Kunzru and K.M. Panikkar were a little hesitant to enter the village. Kutik Myong, the local leader, came along. I was driving and Dr. Kunzru sat next to me. Panikkar, who was the younger, sat at the back of the open jeep. When we reached, he asked: "Where are we going?" I said: "We are going to the village which has patients of Hanson's disease, leprosy". He said: "Oh!" I assured him: "Do not worry, Sir, one will be well-taken care of. Before we enter, we have to wash our hands; and when we come out, we have to wash our hands again. I go there every day with my wife, and I talk to the children, and I have no problems". When we arrived, the villagers sang the National Anthem. We went to each hut. They showed the weaving of cloth which was for sale; leprosy was not a contagious disease.

People always demanded more and more representation in the government. But the civil administration realised that if the tribal areas are opened to political parties, each would assert its partisan agenda and then development would not take place. There would be fights and communal disturbances in the villages. There would be no end to manipulation and petty politics. With each hill having a different dialect, there would be 45 Divisions in NEFA then. So how would they ever unite? That was one reason why we named the area as 'Kameng'; and thus, avoided identifying it as Buddhist or non-Buddhist, or Adi or Minyong or Padam district.

The SRC was to elicit the views of the local people as to how to reorganise the state. The NEFA, which was constitutionally a part of Assam, was in the first stage of evolution. From the stage of Agency, it was to evolve into a full-fledged state. So, the members of the Commission went around checking up the languages, ethnicities, religion etc. Much later, Arunachal Pradesh and various other states were formed and finally, when Indira Gandhi visited as the Prime Minister, she created the seven states. I also spoke to her when I expressed my, as also the local leader's view, that people wanted more say and participation in the government. There was just one Member of Parliament for the whole of NEFA – Chowkhamoon Gohain.* He was a Buddhist from the Assam side of the Indo-Burma border. Later, J.N. Hazarika became the MP when Jawaharlal Nehru co-opted him as a Parliamentary Secretary (1952-62). But there were no political parties, not even a formal Congress party. Even then, the tribal people had hoisted the National Flag at the time of Independence. Earlier, whenever there was a Congress session in Guwahati, some people went to attend it.

Dr Verrier Elwin was another visitor who stayed in Shillong, and was first called as the 'Assistant Anthropological Advisor' and then as 'Advisor on Tribal Affairs'. He did not like the title. He gave us a series of six lectures and so did Dr B.S. Guha, the Director of the Anthropological Survey of India. These two gentlemen briefed us about the right approach to the tribal people. "Do not approach as the superior human being, respect their dignity, and respect their traditions. There was a case when a British officer laughed at a tribal-funeral or had taken photographs. That led to a fight and he was killed. It was a recorded fact. Therefore, one had to be very cautious while approaching the tribal people," they told us.

When G.B. Pant, the Home Minister, visited, I drove him myself. Pant was a very huge person and a man from the hills. So, those people said that Pant was their own man, a *pahari* (hill-man). Except Mahatma Gandhi, nobody else was much known in that area. Chinese coins with Sun Yat-sen's image had been found in the area and these were brought by the border traders. We used our coins with Gandhiji's image. The locals thought that Mahatma Gandhi was a Naga, and so, he became well-known in that area. The girls used to sing a song: *Gandhi Raja.* Jawaharlal Nehru was also known because he had been there. Govind Ballabh Pant's head used to shake, and so he could hardly sit in the jeep. I had only one jeep and I drove him. Behind me was the tribal chief.

We got the instructions that Pant was a strict vegetarian. But the programme was that he would be received with ceremonial honours. So, seven *mithuns* had to be sacrificed, and he was to pass through that site so that he was purified by the village priest. He asked me: "Do I have to eat?" I said: "No, Sir, one does not ave to eat; one just has to pass through the spot, and that is all. They are sacrifi ing seven animals in your honour because you are a Cabinet Minister and nu ber two in the Government of India". He asked: "What will happen then?" I repl ed: "This whole village will eat the meat for three days and there will be a party. They will eat and enjoy. All this is in your honour". We passed through the spot

*A nominated member of the first and second Lok Sabha representing the tribal areas of Assam.

and stopped for a minute. They made him wear a garland and then, the priest came and said to me: "Sahib, we may have to pray extra for him". I asked: "Why, what has happened?" He said: "He is shaking. We have never seen a man like him before and we only pray that he goes alive from here. If he dies here, we will have to sacrifice another seven *mithuns*...which we cannot afford". I said: "He is not going to die. He fought the British and liberated you, and so he is here". That was the humorous side of it. They thought that he was some Superman. They were very much impressed by his personality though.

Pant saw the developmental activities in Pasighat. He spoke to the people in Hindi, which I translated into their language. He assured them that their customs, language, religion, faith and everything would be respected and nothing would be imposed on them. They felt reassured. The British propaganda was that the Hindus would come and stop meat-eating and drinking among the tribals, and would take away their women. This propaganda was a deliberate and sustained last ditch effort by the British who wanted to make that area a Crown Colony. Whether it was out of love for the tribal people, one does not know. So, that was the story of Pasighat.

When Mahatma Gandhi visited the Guwahati Session, he said that the women of Assam wove poetry into their looms. That was in reference to one of the customs in which a girl, before her marriage, had to weave a *mekhla (*a long skirt but not a saree). Different districts have different names for it; in Mizoram and Manipur it is called *phanek*; in Pasighat area of Adis it is called *gaale.* Each village has its own colour scheme, just as in Rajasthan one has very colourful Jodhpur turbans and Jaipur turbans. Some of them are displayed in the museum of Dr Elwin, a well-known anthropologist. I had a very good collection, but I gave it away. In every village, when one went there, a small, hand-woven gift was offered. Mill-cloth had not penetrated till that time...it was all local hand weaving. We used to make yarn available to them at a reasonable, concessional rate. The bundles of coarse yarn were dropped by air to keep the local economy going.

Religion and Custom

In Pasighat, people were *Adis* or nature worshipers. The Adi's supreme deity was *Donyi-Polo*. They were what one may call *Suryavanshi* and *Chandravanshi*, decendents of the Sun and the Moon. They also believed in a figure, a formless thing, something like Shiva and Shakti. They had their sacrifices and their own priests.

Christian missionaries had tried to enter the region, but they had been resisted. Outside, for example in Assam, they were present. But in Pasighat, there were no

Christians at that time. Missionaries used to take away some boys to the Mission, and there was a big debate on it. There was no demand for a Church or any other religious practice. We, from the government, were very scrupulous. We did not endorse temples or mosques, and completely left the tribals to be on their own. But whenever there was a festival, the Dussehra, for example, they would join and enjoy. Rama and Sita, bows and arrows attracted them immensely. But even now, they perform sacrifices during their own *puja* (worship). There was an attempt by external elements to proselytise them by sending some literature to the people. I remember having received a postcard threatening me, and stating that the Communist Party would kill me for introducing Hindi in school! I sent it to the higher authorities. There were mischievous elements who were just trying to entice the tribal boys away to the plains of Assam and convert them in the name of schooling. But when a school was already functioning in Pasighat, there was no reason for the people to fall in that trap.

The moment one crossed over the Brahmaputra River, there was a Christian Mission, a beautiful tea garden, air-conditioned clubs and schools of the tea garden owners. The church activities were in Assam, across the Inner Line limits. The policy of NEFA Administration in keeping the tribals segregated was criticised later on. But it was necessary at that time for their own protection because when the floodgates open and suddenly the tribals are exposed from a primitive simplicity to the contemporary complexities, there would be more damage than good. For example, when some mill-woven cloth was distributed, there being no washing facility, many diseases started. If one had silk clothing, it had to be washed, but the local woven clothes were all right. It was so hot and humid going to the forest, that girls would remove their blouses and just have a *sarong* on. That was a simple practice. The moment they entered the village, they would put on their blouses. When they come to a village or a bazaar to sell their oranges in those conical baskets, then they would put on a blouse. Otherwise, there was no inhibition. It was a very simple existence. Having seen all this, the Commission finally decided to recommend continuation of the existing system of administration, that is, through the Governor of Assam (and his Advisor) who was the Agent of the President of India. One could call it a direct rule from New Delhi.

Tribal marriage custom was that before a child was born, two families would meet and one head of the family would say to the other: "I will give you seven cows and this girl is mine". If agreed, then that girl's marriage was settled. It was a dowry in the reverse, what they called as 'bride-price'. Inter-tribal marriage was very rare, but it happened at times. Some of the cleavage was created by the missionaries. They translated the Bible into the local languages. Slowly and gradually, they sowed the seeds of separation. The British Deputy Commissioner and the British missionaries worked very hard, and did a lot of social work there. There is also clear historical evidence that they wanted to make that area a Crown Colony. The claim that Mahatma Gandhi and Subhas Chandra Bose made promises to Z.A. Phizo was all bogus; it was all planted. Who met Mahatma Gandhi? Even I could not meet Mahatma Gandhi. I was active in the movement. I do not know whether Phizo met Mahatma Gandhi at all. So, Phizo's was truly a separatist movement.

All the six political officers and six assistant political officers in six Frontier Divisions were very clearly told to respect the languages. The book by Verrier Elwin, *A Philosophy for NEFA,* is very relevant, and is a compilation of a series of letters and directives which were given to us in interactive sessions in which the whole situation was discussed. Jawaharlal Nehru said that the NEFA needed a special approach. He had the vision. He consulted Dr B.S. Guha who was the Director of Anthropological Survey of India. He invited Dr Verrier Elwin who lived among the Gonds and Bhils, to the extent that he married a Gond lady and was expelled from the British Mission. Verrier Elwin started wearing *khadi.* So, the Deputy Commissioner and the British Collector wrote against him. He was sent by the British on a mission to preach Christianity, but he became a Buddhist. He certainly gave up his British citizenship. Jawaharlal Nehru picked up Elwin, who was very great scholar from Oxford University, and made him an Advisor for Tribal Affairs. So, Guha and Elwin were there. Then, the two people from the ICS were picked up as Advisors to the Governor. The first Advisor was Kanhaiya Lal Mehta who has written the book *In Different Worlds, from Haveli to Head Hunters of Tuensang.* Later on, he was the Ambassador in Turkey. The second Advisor was Nari K. Rustomji, who also wrote his experiences in *Enchanted Frontiers: Sikkim, Bhutan and India's North-Eastern Borderlands.*

I would now like to talk about the urge among the tribal people for guns and gun licences. Possession of a gun was a matter of power and prestige. So, every tribal wanted a licence to have a gun. I told them that I did not have the power to give gun licence because it was the frontier area. I would have to make enquiries. Even today, in an independent Sub-Division, the Tehsildar cannot issue a licence; the District Magistrate has to do so and he did so after the police and other enquiries. The tribals would illegally get guns from across the border and carry it with great pride and prestige. Whether the gun worked or not, and was useless, made no difference. A tribal would carry it and declare with pride: 'I have got a gun'. A school boy may have no licence, but would write down his name on a chit in Hindi or English, and come before me. He would take out the chit and say that he was a gun licence holder, a very important man. Peter James used to write, see and sign on those chits; that was flaunted as an authority. A young tribal would keep the signed slip of paper in a bag. He would collect the signatures of successive political officers in the hope that someday he would get a formal gun licence. Then we decided that we must have procedure for issuing of gun licences, especially when we did not have any police to maintain law and order.

Local Politics

Shillong was the headquarters of the Government of Assam. The journey from Delhi to Shillong took three nights by train and on the fourth day one went across the River Brahmaputra at the Pandughat Ferry. There was another train service running on the southern bank of the Brahmaputra upto Dibrugarh. Beyond that, one had to travel by a road which could handle only one-way traffic. There was lack of knowledge and lack of interest in the remote tribal areas. A sense of geographical isolation and lack of knowledge prevailed over the administration and that, combined with post-partition problems, prevented the nation from attending to the specific needs of the North-East. The Foreign and Political Department was attending to the partition related issues, and there being no dedicated Ministry for Tribal Affairs in the years following independence, as it exists today, affairs of that part of the country were somewhat neglected. The specific provisions on the Scheduled Castes and the Scheduled Tribes came in to force only after adoption of the Union's Constitution.

The British never wanted to associate the local people in their administration. The Government of India Act 1935, too, had no provision for that. After independence, till 1954, the Government of India did not do anything about that anomaly, and the old system continued. The political officers remained in Dibrugarh across the Brahmaputra from where they would visit the NEFA once a year to keep the administration going. But such visits became more frequent after 1949, when communist regime was established in China. As the Chinese started moving westwards, Jawaharlal Nehru had sensed something from the reports coming in at that time. The Indian Parliament was apparently unaware of the Chinese moves. We probably had our own problems of partition and riots, famine and food shortage in Bihar and other states, to be able to keep focus on this matter.

Tribals were mostly unaware of the general elections of 1952. Only the leaders were aware because they often visited Assam. None of the political leaders of Assam ever thought it wise to visit Pasighat. Even the Chief Minister, Gopinath Bardoloi, never went there. The reason for the NEFA's isolation may have been its remoteness. Besides, neither the state nor the central leaders thought it important enough because there was no voting. The Agency was administrated by the Central government, and so, the tribal people had no representation in the Legislative Assembly of Assam. That was a cause of dissatisfaction. The Agency was called as a 'Partially Excluded Area'. Even in primeval forests, the classification was as 'Reserve Forests', 'Classified Reserved Forests' and 'Unclassified Reserved Forests'. Jawaharlal Nehru was the first to visit the NEFA. In 1962, after the Chinese aggression, for the first time, B.P. Chaliha came to Bomdi-La in the Kameng Frontier Division, where I had moved in after Tezpur was evacuated. I had once embarrassed the Deputy Commissioner, Tezpur Division – Rana K.D.N. Singh, a good friend and colleague – by asking as to why he didn't visit areas under his jurisdiction more often.

So, the evolution from direct central Administration to statehood took about 20 years. The Agency became a Union Territory for sometime, and finally attained statehood. There were many areas in the country which were similarly administered; Delhi, for example, remained a Union Territory for long. There was a feeling – a view to which I, too, subscribed – that certain areas should be treated as Union Territories and directly governed from the Centre. Statehood was all right, but it needed a special approach to administer the remote regions because the developmental needs and socio-political situations were diverse. Today, Arunachal Pradesh, which was one of the most peaceful places, is having problems with the so-called outsiders and resisting the Chakma community from settling down in the state. They feel that inflow of 'outsiders' would deny them their advantages. Of course, I have a different view and have my strong reservation on this issue.

When I look back, the major achievement was that we were introducing development very slowly. I still believe that perhaps it could have been even better if we had not been slower in response to the evolving local aspirations. However, the Chinese attack hastened the process. In hastening, sometimes issues get complicated. When large scale movement of troops takes place in any area, naturally some forests would be cut and tension would take place. If land was acquired by the Defence Ministry for opening a school, there would be a court case. So in the beginning, there was some tension. But the Army personnel were educated on how to deal with the tribal people. As matters settled down, I found that the villagers gave their land very willingly. The tribal people responded very well during the Chinese aggression and supported various developmental activities. Even before the aggression, I myself never had any problem in getting land for schools. One just asked the villagers and they would offer a site. They would supply bamboo, rafters and everything else from local produce that was needed for the construction. All that one had to do was to have the corrugated galvanised iron roofing sheets airdropped. There being no roads, our architecture was influenced by what Dr Elwin had advised us: "Bhai, do not suddenly start sending heavy building materials. Who would carry these? Those poor girls?" Of course, bamboo floors, walls and roofs of palm leaves had to be renewed every year.

We, too, lived in locally made huts for 10 years. I remember, apart from the snow-bound upper reaches of the Kameng Frontier Division where there were slate roofs, in the lower altitude areas there were only bamboo huts – whether these were for the District Magistrate or the Political Officer or the doctor who lived there. Even the hospitals were constructed on bamboo stilts; if a storm came and the structure withstood it, fine. If not, then one made another structure.

Development work on education and healthcare was followed by the introduction of the cooperative movement. It was very much like the old republican practices changing over to decentralisation. The *Panchayati Raj* was already in force in a sense, and we did patronise that. As for the language policy, since the locals did not have a script, it was decided that the *Devanagari* script would be introduced in those areas. It was to be done over a period of time, not immediately. There were discussions. The teaching had to be either in English or in Hindi. However, to nurture local languages, local language officers were appointed.

Jairamdas Doulatram, Governor of Assam, 1950-56

Jairamdas Doulatram was a thorough gentleman. He wrote copious notes and would ask for translations, for example, of every song the tribals sang. He was certainly very dedicated. He visited the NEFA more often than others. So, he came once to Along, and we had a prototype aluminium hut where he was accommodated. The aircraft could not take off, and so, he was stuck for three to four days. Everyday, he used to call a local priest and talk to him and take notes. He also gave a lot of dictation in English. His typewriter used to make so much noise! Doulatram was very popular among the people. As the Governor, he could not visit the remote areas more than once a year. So, he invited the tribal leaders to the Raj Bhawan in Shillong. His successors who did so included Sir S. Fazl Ali (1956-59) and General S.M. Shrinagesh (1959-62).

I remember the last head hunting was done in 1956. Some boys went across a village and brought human heads. So, Jairamdas Doulatram called me and asked me to take the boy with me to Pasighat. The boy was a Longkhai Pangsha, the only survivor in that village when his parents and others were killed in tribal fighting. He had to be removed from that village and brought to Pasighat, which was a different language area altogether. I had just married, and so, we let him stay in my house. We put him in a school and gave him clothes to wear. He used to dine with us. I used to take him to the school. He was a little overgrown, tall and handsome fellow, but he could not be admitted to Class IX. So, he was put in a lower class. Later on, he gradually educated himself before being sent back to his people.

Jairamdas Doulatram was very dedicated to the people. He asked me to look after the first graduate of that area, Dayeng Ering, who was a member of the Lok Sabha (1957-70), and Union Deputy Minister for Food, Agriculture, Community Development and Cooperation (1967-70). Ering and his wife belonged to the Minyong tribe, and an upper caste. The lady was very ill, her arms were twisted by polio or arthritis. So Jairamdas Doulatram asked me to ensure that the couple had help. The Minyongs had a peculiar custom. They went through child delivery in standing position. Dayeng Ering's wife was expecting a baby. My mother-in-law agreed to help her in delivery. But at the last minute, they did not inform us. They called their own priests and women, and under the trees, the baby was delivered, quite safe. Ering's boys have grown up now and are local leaders; their mother died recently.

Dayeng Ering was the number-two man in the government hierarchy in Pasighat Sub-Division. He was full of enthusiasm and ambition. He used to write letters to the Prime Minister, directly. After some time, I asked him not to do so. He replied: "I would not do it in the future. But I would like to be relieved so that I can take up a political career". I said: "That is fair enough". So, we relieved him. He was made a Parliamentary Secretary and then he became a Deputy Minist r in Delhi. I must also mention that the young tribal people had started a stud nts' movement even before political parties came there. They formed the 'Adi Mi hing Students' Union'. The government was very much unnerved by that, appreh-ensive as to what this students' union would end up doing.

Dayeng Ering was a very good human. Years later when I returned from Afghanistan, I had no place to stay in the Capital. In the Central government, one cannot get accommodation overnight. His wife could not come to Delhi because she was always ill. He told my wife, "Sudha, Mamo, here is the key of my house. As a Minister, I am always touring and I have nobody to cook, so you please stay there". I was with my three daughters. He gave me the key and gave me a room at 25, Ashoka Road (New Delhi).

Earlier, he had started living at 25, Ashoka Road, as somebody told him that it was a very lucky house and he might become a Minister. Jawaharlal Nehru was personally very fond of him and brought him as he wanted to encourage the young people. Dayeng Ering joined the Congress Party and became a leader. He used to wear *khadi* and *achkan (long coat).* Whenever he visited the NEFA, he was received with great affection and expectations by the local people. He is still remembered with very great affection for his work in Pasighat. He was always there to assist me in performing my work.

Growth of Insurgency

Insurgency in the North-East was confined to parts of undivided Assam. In the hills there was no insurgency, except in Nagaland, and then in Manipur. The first insurgency started in Nagaland. It was in the time when General Shrinagesh was the Governor.

The 'Naga' is a very broad term. Actually, there are several tribes which include Wanchus, Tangkhuls, Aos, Angamis and so on. So, they had started claiming even parts of Tirap as a 'Naga' area. Even now, there is a boundary dispute between Nagaland and Assam. Naga tribes wanted to be separated from Assam. They believed that the Assamese were dominating them in terms of language, territory and forest rights. Naga areas were was loosely administered, the tribal chiefs controlling the religious and traditional affairs. So, the British kept them as museum pieces, letting them live in their own undisturbed ways.

There was certain kind of romantic feeling attached to the British Deputy Commissioners. J.H. Hutton stayed there for several years, a record time, I think. Then, Charles Pawsey, J.H. Hutton and Inglis were a few names which were legends in that area. They were the first contact of civilization with the tribals. But even if they desisted from interfering in the traditional customs, they propagated Christianity with great zest. The Bible was translated into their language and there were priests who made persistent efforts to convert people to Christianity. Tribes were made to feel that they were somewhat different from the rest of India.

At the time of independence, the tribals thought that the old system of administration would continue. Furthermore, there was a deliberate attempt to administer that area, even after independence, as a 'Crown Colony' under the excuse that in World War II, the Japanese Army had advanced up to Kohima. When that did not happen and independent India asserted its sovereign rights, it was then that the secessionist insurgency started. There could have been mistakes in our policy too. When U Nu, the Prime Minister of Burma, came to India, Jawaharlal Nehru and U Nu went to Kohima in March 1953. There was a usual meeting with the tribal chiefs. There, some of them turned around and started beating their buttocks. It was a very bad, undignified way of tribal protest. That shook the government in New Delhi very badly. It was in front of the Prime Minister of a foreign country, after all.

The Pasighat area had remained untouched by all the secessionist tendencies. Pasighat was an Adi-Minyong area which was on the other side of the Ang River, a tributary of the Brahmaputra River. The Adi-Minyongs were a very peaceful people. But rest of the NEFA, except the Tirap area on the border with Burma, was affected. Provoked by anti-national mentors, various diverse tribes which are clubbed under the sobriquet of 'the Nagas' started inventing claims which were totally bogus. There is nothing common between say, a Tangkhul Naga and other Naga tribes. Naga was a loose term. I remember, the people from the Tirap area wore their hair like the Tamil Brahmins with half shaven front or a fringe of hair around with a knot on the crown of the head. They would sit on the haunches and do the morning prayers. Their language was intelligible. It was not Sanskrit. Most others had a fringe of hair – like what one sees in the photographs of Jawaharlal Nehru. So, demand for a Nagaland was a separate case altogether. Naga's fight was with the Assamese because none of the political leaders of Assam had time for them. It was the Governors who would always maintain the linkages. Thus, it was easy for them to see themselves as different and a separate nation, even if that idea was not substantial.

The geographical isolation of the NEFA from the rest of the country was one very big factor in giving rise to the secessionist tendency. The tribals' resistance to change was another. Change had to be brought about in a manner acceptable to them. In that respect our policy was humane, unlike the Americans who just finished the Red Indians. Here, at least the indigenous inhabitants have joined the mainstream of our culture and plural society. The Adis of today may be wearing different clothes, but the virtues and the other practices of the tribal areas are still there. There is still very little crime in Arunachal Pradesh. There is no drunkenness. As for the Nagas, they wanted a territory of their own. So a separate state of 'Nagaland' was formed comprising the Naga Hills and the Tuensang areas. But the demand for independent Nagaland was totally unacceptable. It is a tendency which rises when the Central government is viewed as weak, as it is in the case of demand for 'Bodoland'. The word 'land' is in itself divisive; that was not realised at the time of creation of Nagaland. Later, not a 'Mizoland' but 'Mizoram' was created – wherein 'Mi' means man and 'ram' means hill – 'men of the hills' so to say; 'Zou' is also a hill.

The cause of insurgency could not be a single one. A series of factors contributed to it. When the tribals started coming out, they asked: "What is this? You people are living in very good houses, why can't we?" So, they started demanding more and more development. With more development came more awareness of the disparities, protests and some violent incidents. The Army was being accused of human rights violation. For example, father of one of my very distinguished colleagues, Dr Thaphlieper Haralu, a *Padma*-awardee and an IAS officer, got killed. His sister, Bano (Nikki) Haralu is a commentator in the All India Radio and Television, and served in the Ministries of Information and External Affairs. This was a thoroughly good family, but a mistake was committed. It was like just the other day when the Americans in Afghanistan killed 17 local people. I do not think it was deliberate, but it was unfortunate.

As matters went wrong, ambitious mischief makers tried to excite the people. There may have been some wrongful killings when firing had to be resorted to. Therefore, the answer was to take slow steps. There were negotiations; even now, that is going on with Thungaleng Muivah. Their main instigator and leader Z.A. Phizo used to claim that Subhas Chandra Bose had told them that they would be allowed to remain independent, autonomous or whatever, and his followers swallowed that banality. I told their leaders very clearly: "If you want to be Indian, then you are welcome; otherwise you are welcome to go to London and have a scotch whisky with those who are financing you. How can you say that Mahatma Gandhi had promised autonomy or a Naga state outside India and Burma? Anybody can say that Mahatma Gandhi said this or that".

The demand actually is over autonomy. India is a vast, varied and plural society and, therefore, the only way is the democratic way in which there is no danger of exploitation and conflict. Thus, the only salvation lies in democratic decentralisation. But every institution resists that. The Parliament does not want to give powers to the state governments. The state government does not want to give power to the District *Panchayat*. But there is another angle. If Nagaland was in the heart of India, like Madhya Pradesh, nobody would be so concerned. But it is a border area. Therefore, if it is vested with wide powers and then if the State Assembly passes a resolution stating that "We will join Burma", then there would be constitutional crisis; Kashmir can also say the same thing and so can Ladakh and Rajasthan. Didn't the Travancore State decide to do so when Sir C.P. Ramaswami Iyer advised them: "You are independent, why should you join India? You have a coastline, you have forests... you have everything". So there is a contradiction, a dilemma between Central control and decentralisation. That is why India has so many problems to deal with, for which there have to be people of wisdom, foresight and pan-India vision to take care of it. I remember, when Tribhuvan Bir Bikram Shah, the King of Nepal, escaped to India, Jawaharlal Nehru gave him asylum. At that time, some political parties opined that Jawaharlal Nehru made a mistake by not assimilating Nepal into India. But Nehru had the wisdom to refuse to listen to such counsel.

A number of factors contributed to the insurgency which has to be tackled with great patience. Firstly, the political leaders did not want to go to the NEFA. Not many MLAs and MPs visited that area. In my time, Dr H.N. Kunzru and

K.M. Panikkar did. Of course, K.L. Mehta, our Advisor, used to come often. But among the political leaders, apart from Jawaharlal Nehru, nobody of any consequence came in the NEFA before the Chinese aggression. U.N. Dhebar came once, but that was much later, after the Chinese aggression. One can argue that if development had been brought at a faster pace at that time, there would have been more trouble. We were at least trained in a way that we respected the local customs, the people's attitude, and their immediate concerns... and therefore, we never had any trouble. I never took any escort as I travelled in those areas.

While I was posted at Pasighat, a major event in my personal life was that I got married. I travelled with my wife and my children were born and brought up in Pasighat, Bomdi-La, Yatung and Gangtok – there being no possibility of sending my wife to Delhi. A hospital was there in Pasighat but there was no electricity, and a child was born...just like anywhere in the villages of India. We stuck to that area and the tribal people used to come to visit us very often. My wife used to teach in the government school. There was no provision for an honourary teacher but we had to find improvised arrangements and the government knew that. She used to walk to the school. Of her students, two of them became Chief Ministers, and one or two became Members of Parliament; they still respect her very much.

CHAPTER 6

UNEASY YEARS IN TIBET

Tibet and Sikkim in 1956-59

I was posted as India's Trade Agent in Tibet from 1956-59. On receipt of the posting order, I arrived in Delhi. It was not only for briefing; when one was posted abroad, one could not go directly from post A to post B, he had to report at Delhi. Even today, when Foreign Service officers go, say from Bonn to Tokyo, they first come back home and then proceed to join the new post. That is the system. At that time, there was a trade agreement between India and China. By this agreement, India indirectly recognised China's claim over Tibet. Thorough briefings regarding our policy on Tibet and the nuances of diplomatic relations between India, Tibet and China was, therefore, called for.

I reached Delhi after three or four days, and reported at the South Block. None of the officers whom I met – from Foreign Secretary, Joint-Secretary and down to the junior most Under-Secretary or Section Officer who handed over the posting-order to me – had been to Tibet; no one knew much about Tibet. The only person who had some indirect knowledge having served in Peking was T.N. Kaul, a Joint-Secretary at that time. But he had very little time to brief me. I could not even meet the Foreign Secretary. Today, when one goes on such an important mission, the Foreign Secretary or the Foreign Minister briefs him/her. I had no occasion to meet Jawaharlal Nehru for that purpose; I had a glimpse of him though, when I accompanied the Dalai Lama, who was on a visit to India. With very little knowledge of Tibet, I proceeded to Gangtok enroute to Tibet, to join as head of the Agency at Yatung.

This was my second visit to Delhi. During this visit, I met Harivansh Rai Bachchan, the Officer-on-Special Duty (Hindi) in the Ministry of External Affairs from 1955 to 1965, who had been my teacher at Allahabad University. He had also taken our tutorial classes in English. I went and saw him in his room, without any appointment, and he was surprised. The first floor in the South Block had the offices of the top functionaries of the Prime Minister's Office. He was on the second floor, in a very non-descript cubicle. I greeted him and said that I had been posted to his Ministry. He did not know that. I asked what the nature of his work was. He said: "I do translations. I also write in Hindi". That meant he had nothing to do with diplomacy or foreign relations as the other functionaries like Sumitranandan Pant had. Pant was actually posted to the Embassy in Nepal. I think Bachchan was very unhappy because the only work that he was asked to do was prepare 'letters of credence' and drafts of treaties. When an Ambassador was sent out to a foreign country, he had to offer his credentials from our President to the foreign Head of State, and then read out what was a kind of a command or a commission. That is a very well-worded, formal letter, known as the 'letter of credence'. I do not think that Bachchan was associated with any political work of the Ministry of External Affairs, or in analysing the reports, events and discussions.

Bachchan gave me his blessings when I touched his feet. He showed a lot of interest on Tibet. But he was not associated or consulted on diplomatic matters...he merely acted as a translator. Jawaharlal Nehru was too busy to consult him, but the Indian Civil Service (ICS) officials of the Ministry did not think it proper to consult the academics. Another teacher of mine who went to the Foreign Service was Dr Tara Chand. He was an expert and an authority on Modern History of India. He went to Iran because of his knowledge of Persian and History, and was very successful. So, he was appointed an Ambassador. Bachchan could also have been so appointed but, maybe, he was too young at that time to be appointed as an Ambassador. He was given the rank of Deputy-Secretary straightway, and did not have to start as Under-Secretary.

The Foreign Service Department was not mature enough at that time, and that there were only a few ICS officers who did not opt for District Administration, and so could be drafted into the Foreign Office. Few officers of the old Indian Political Service, about three or four, had also been inducted. Among these, Iskander Mirza went to Pakistan (who later assumed power as the President of Pakistan) while Mirza Rashid Ali Baig, the famous husband of Tara Ali Baig, remained in India. Balraj Kapur, Indersen Chopra and Jagan Nath Dhamija were others in Foreign Service. Dhamija was the Ambassador in Afghanistan from 1960 to 1964 when I worked with him. But at the time of the posting, I could meet none of them. I only met an Under-Secretary who gave me the posting order and whatever information he had. Also, there were no 'station reports' which offered guidance regarding equipping oneself with clothes, routes, journey and various other information. Then, when I met Apa B. Pant, the Political Officer in Sikkim and Bhutan from 1959 to 1961, I had some inkling of the current events in Tibet. T.N. Kaul had briefed me: "Keep your eyes and ears open, and keep us informed of the developments".

The nature of the job of a Trade Agent, as it implies, meant that he promoted India's commercial interests. This was a peculiar Mission. The Ambassador of India was in Peking (now Beijing), which was several days' journey from my location. Technically, I was under the Ambassador of India in Peking. The 'Political Officer of India in Bhutan and Sikkim', a title that we inherited from the British, had his headquarters in Gangtok, the capital of Sikkim, which was a protectorate of India. Gangtok was probably the most accessible place from where he operated his Mission and journeyed to Tibet. One Agency was established in Yatung, which was a very beautiful, picturesque valley, 9,000 feet above sea level and near the tri-junction of Bhutan, Sikkim and Tibet.

The Mission in Lhasa was established much before independence. Earlier, it was known as the British Political Mission. The British Political Officer, resident in Gangtok, and the Head of the British Mission in Lhasa had direct access to the Viceroy who used to consult them directly. After the departure of British and after the Agreement of 1954, it was converted to a 'Consulate General of India'. I do not think that the Political Officer in Gangtok was ever consulted by the Government of India before negotiating regarding the new status of the Mission with the Communist Government of China. All negotiations were held in Peking and that was why some of the Members of the Parliament were very unhappy about the major decisions taken by, I think, K.M. Panikkar and T.N. Kaul – who were there. T.N. Kaul must have been a First Secretary at that time.

Another element that surprised me was the fact that the Government did not continue the Mission at Lhasa after India's Independence. Nobody had asked them to withdraw. This had baffled me. I put this question to my British counterparts – the British diplomats – whenever I interacted with them in Delhi or outside. Only the Tibetans told us that perhaps the British lost interest and wanted India to establish its own Mission. After the Agreement of 1954, if India wanted to hand over the 'dak' bungalows (mail staging posts), then these could have been transferred to the Tibetans. The Tibetan Post Office was then under the control of the Government of the Autonomous Region of Tibet, formally it was a province of China or under Chinese suzerainty though.

While in Delhi, I did not know the ground realities in Tibet. I did not even know what the other Missions in Tibet were. Nobody told me, and in a week's time, how much could one learn? A normal training should have included a perusal of the old files. There was no Training Division, training officer, or a Human Resource Development (HRD) department in the government. These days, even if one joins a new company, there is an HRD manager to brief him; or when one joins a district administration today, the District Magistrate is there to guide him/her. When a Foreign Service officer is attached to a Division and when he is issued with a posting order, he goes through not only all the records, but also the history, language and various details connected with his assignment. here was no such preparation then.

When I landed in Gangtok, I was told to wait to be put on duty because the Dalai Lama was there. One of the officers of the Ministry, P.N. Luthra, was already there. Chinese diplomats were also there, and they were staying in the same house. The Dalai Lama stayed in the Palace Monastery; as was the custom, he could not stay anywhere else. Sir Tashi Namgyal, the Maharaja of Sikkim (1914-63), was a great *bhakta* (disciple) of his. Every morning, the Dalai Lama did his *parikrama* (holy circumambulations). He and his entire group were the guests of the Maharaja and the Government of Sikkim. Rumours notwithstanding, is it not true that our Political Officers in Gangtok, including Apa Pant, used to interfere in administrative matters and denounce the local administration. At that time, in 1956, there was no question of interference.

I had two tenures in the Sikkim region, in one of which I was confined to Tibet. What I did not know, but was apprised by the Maharaja and the Maharani before I left for Tibet, was that they were related to the nobility in Tibet, and that the Maharani had her properties there. Thus, even if I was India's Agent, I was to represent Sikkim's interests in Tibet. Accordingly, the Maharani used to ask me about their many palaces and servants in Tibet. The *Diwan* (Chief Minister) of Sikkim from 1954 to 1959 was Nari Rustomji, who was later the Adviser to the Governor of Assam from 1963 to 1966, and then the Chief Secretary of the Government of Assam from 1966 to 1971. Rustomji was extremely popular with the people of Sikkim. As the Diwan, he used to dress like a Sikkimese. He was an officer of the Court and of the Government of India. He was paid by the Government of Sikkim, although he was an ICS officer. Sikkim was also like any other state, except that it was a protectorate of India.

In Gangtok, the Political Officer's job was to also train young people of Sikkim to come up to a certain level of professionalism. Sikkim had very few policemen, and they did not have their own army. The 'Sikkim Guards' were raised much later. At that time, the Maharaja had a small police force because there was no need for much policing while external security was handled by the Indian Army; it was not stationed inside Sikkim though. The Army garrison at Darjeeling was headed by Lieutenant Colonel Raghubir Singh Brar, who was a remarkable man.

After the Agreement of 1954, the Indian Army escorts which were stationed to guard the Mission at Lhasa, and the Agencies at Gyantse, Gartok and Yatung in Tibet, were withdrawn. He visited Gangtok once or twice a year to meet a small company of about 30 to 40 men of the Indian Army who guarded the Residency. That was all. Even in Tibet, the only Indian Army presence was just in guarding our treasury.

Sikkim was a protectorate of India. We were like the head of the Indian family, and that was our job. The Political Officer had a very good rapport with the Maharaja. Earlier, the British may also have been acting in the same manner. Sir J. Claude White, after whom the 'White Hall' is named, was the first British Political Officer. At the time of Nari Rustomji, the Legislative Assembly was constructed and gradually, the evolution towards statehood had commenced. The Maharajkumar, being the Head of the Transport Department, was one aspect of that development.

Except for the period of transit, I did not spend much time in Sikkim. That was a brief interlude of six to 10 days, and not more. But every time I passed through, I met the Maharaja as a courtesy and he offered me his car and also blessed me. Our Political Officer for Sikkim and Bhutan, Apa Pant, with whom I spent time during my training period, used to discuss many matters with me. He was stationed in Gangtok and, therefore, his interaction with the local leaders was much more than with the leaders of Tibet. The Political Officer used to visit Lhasa, a 21 days' journey, once in a year to meet the Dalai Lama and the Tibetans. He did not interfere in Tibetan matters as such. Whenever the Tibetan leaders passed through Gangtok, they met the Political Officer and exchanged their ideas and gifts. If there was any message from His Holiness to the outside world or to the Government of India, they carried it. Otherwise, Tibet was autonomous.

Trade Agencies in Tibet

In Delhi, the brief given to me was to look after India's interests, to keep my eyes and ears open and to inform the Government of India of all the developments going on. One does not have to be a spy for that; the job of a diplomat is to promote the interests of his country. As stated, the briefing was not as thorough as it should have been. There was no special directive. Therefore, one had to learn on the job by oneself. There was hardly any staff available to me. There was one whom I designated as the Vice-Agent and who was my number two man; and there was one doctor.

As per the Agreement of 1954, there were three Trade Agencies, one each at Yatung, Gyantse and Gartok. The Agency at Yatung was the most important because it was en route to Lhasa from Gangtok via Kalimpong. Kalimpong was another trade-mart and the Chinese had established a Trade Agency there on a reciprocal basis.

During that period, I met the Chinese Agent at Kalimpong. I also met the Chinese Ambassador in Delhi before proceeding, as that was customary. He called me and my wife for lunch, and that was followed by a meeting with the Chinese Consul-General in Kalimpong. There was also the Agent of Bhutan in Kalimpong. The Agent of Bhutan was not stationed at Gangtok, the Capital of Sikkim, but carried on all negotiations between India and Bhutan from Kalimpong which is in West Bengal, India. There was no other diplomats in Gangtok. Presently, there is no Chinese Agency at Kalimpong. Perhaps that should be the first step when we reopen our Mission in Tibet.

The Government of India has not released the official records from 1914 onwards regarding Bhutan, Sikkim and Tibet. These are still classified. The normal way would be to follow the British practice, which stipulated that more than 25 year-old records were to be declassified. The current records, of course, must be secret and one must not have access to these. After coming back from Tibet, I wrote a report. When I wanted to have access to that report, I was told that all records relating to 1914 onwards were classified, and that these had not been sent to the National Archives of India. These were still held in the Ministry of External Affairs. Even in the Ministry, there was an embargo. These can not be read without obtaining permission. So I could not get even routine information regarding the Indian Frontier Administrative Service, of which I myself was a member! Actually, there are no political implications. For example, the debate whether there should have been an Indian Judicial Service goes on. There was nothing secret about the reports of the States Reorganisation Commission, and it was available for reading. No doubt, citizens should have access to treaties and documents relating to Sikkim, Bhutan, Tibet and the Himalayan Region from 1914 onwards just as we do, and have access to those before 1914 as well.

The Dalai Lama

When I reached Tibet, I was accorded a very warm welcome. At that time, the Dalai Lama was on his way back to Tibet after having travelled to Delhi, fed up of Chinese high-handedness. The Tibetans asked me: "Where is the Dalai Lama? What is happening to him?" I replied: "He is a guest of India and has now reached Sikkim, and is on his way to Lhasa". They heard me very eagerly. They were very happy that I brought this news. They were under the impression that the Dalai Lama might stay back in India. Two years later, that was what happened, obviously because he must have been in a very difficult position. What, after all, was the use of staying like a prisoner Tibet, when one could not perform even *pujas* (worship) and other rituals due to constant interference from the local Communist rulers? Once there, I realised that our relations with Sikkim were entirely different from what prevailed in Tibet.

The Chinese had promised that they would upgrade the road from Lhasa up to Nathu-La, but that road was not ready. The Dalai Lama had to go on a pony from Gangtok to Nathu-La. He travelled to Siliguri by train and then to Gangtok by road. He must have stayed in India for at least three to four weeks, I cannot remember exactly. When I arrived in Gangtok, he was there. For my briefing, I stayed at the Gangtok Residency for sometime, when there was an internal debate in the Kashag (Tibet Cabinet) regarding the Dalai Lama's date of return to Lhasa. The Chinese had sent two of their diplomats to the Indian Residency in Gangtok to keep abreast on the Dalai Lama from Gangtok. Dalai Lama was escorted up to the Nathu-La Pass. I did not come to the Pass to see him. There was no requirement of a protocol except that he had come from my country. I do not think that the Chinese would have permitted or liked it even. Once in Tibet, the Dalai Lama was placed on a very high pedestal. He was a cherished and protected symbol, and it was not at all easy to meet him except by a formal appointment. There were elaborate rituals in which outsiders had no place. Maybe the Chinese officials had come up to the Pass to receive him and then turned back – I do not know. The Maharajkumar of Sikkim went along – on a pony and not on a vehicle. He halted at Changu Lake where he did his prayers. When he returned, he announced the release of all the lands from the control of the state.

Communist Chinese indulged in elaborate propaganda to criticise the feudal system of administration in Tibet where the monasteries took away a portion of the farm produce as a tribute, as a tax. The rationale for this practice was that one-third, or every third child, whether a boy or girl, joined the monastery. If it was a girl, she became a nun, if a boy, he became a monk. So, if one third of the produce was given to the monastery that meant that the family was only supporting their own child. After all, the monasteries did not have extensive properties like our temples have. Tirupati, for example, has a very huge Trust. The income from Tirupati is in terms of gold ornaments, money, crores of rupees, and so the government has appointed an administrator to the Trust. Similarly, in Tibet it was traditional that every farmer contributed from his produce to support his own daughter (maybe a nun) or a boy (maybe a lama) studying in a residential public school, and going through training on any discipline. The farmer's produce was merged in a common stock from which everybody was fed so that no one could say that one's rice, bread or butter was superior or inferior to the rest.

The Chinese alleged that the monks lived like lords. Not at all! Their officers did so, not the monks. There was a Monk Magistrate and there was a lay

Magistrate. The position of the Monk Magistrate was higher than the other. Dzong means a fort or what one may call a district headquarters. So, every district had a Dzong, which was an important part in the monastery. The Monk Magistrate lived in the monastery and his position was the highest in every public function. Monk Magistrates and the Monk Police were there to ensure discipline and control the traffic. Every monastery had its own lands and Press. The Tawang Monastery had its own Press. Lhasa had its own Press. So, the system was that the monks kept on learning as in a school. After that, everybody did not become a Professor or even a Bachelor of Arts, but they were graded as monks. So, they occupied their respective positions. Most remained to work for the monastery, even sweep floors – like in Roman Catholic Church where nuns do all the prayers, the chores, and managerial work too. That was the system.

Intensely hostile Chinese propaganda was the reason why the Dalai Lama deliberately asked Jawaharlal Nehru to let him reside in India. Nehru had apparently replied: "There is no problem in giving you shelter if you want to stay on here. Today, we would call that as 'political asylum', but at that time, Jawaharlal Nehru did not refer to it as such. But when a spiritual leader, or any leader for that matter, leaves his people in a time of distress and trouble, then he would soon be forgotten by the people. A leader must stay with his people. Mahatma Gandhi came to India and stayed here. If he had gone back to the Union of South Africa, then he would have had more legal practice. The same was with Jawaharlal Nehru. He came back from England to live and suffer here.

Dalai Lama followed that dictum and went back to Tibet. He must have known that some Cabinet Ministers who had arrived in Gangtok had sent messages for him to return to Tibet. Finally, the Tibetan Cabinet must have agreed that the Dalai Lama went back because he was a constitutional monarch. He was so advised by his Cabinet advisors – referred to as the 'Tutors' – who were travelling with him. There was the Senior Tutor and the Junior Tutor of cabinet rank, who advised Dalai Lama on matters relating to religion and faiths, rituals, protocol, and similarly, defence, currency, coinage, territory, judiciary, external relations and the rest of it. They must have sent messages of Dalai Lama's return. The scene was electric throughout; whatever the Chinese propaganda was, I could see the people just rushing to prostrate on the roads as Dalai Lama's procession went by. They would come down from the rooftops because nobody could be positioned higher than him. One could call it a security measure, but that had always been so – just like in the days of the Indian maharajas. In this case, it was done out of deep respect.

The Trade Agency

As I recall the broad features of the India-China Agreement of 1954, the Passes through which the traders and pilgrims could go across to Tibet

Autonomous Region of the People's Republic of China were defined. Indirectly, the five principles of *Panchsheel* were initiated in the Preamble to include mutual respect for each other's territorial integrity, non-interference in each others internal affairs and so on. Indian traders could go there without a passport. I and my family had Indian passports because I was a diplomat and accordingly, I had immunity from arrest, and had the use of 'diplomatic bag' and other facilities. The Indian Trade Agent had a distinct status and overtime, the post had acquired extra-constitutional powers by custom and convention. In the past, the British Trade Agents must have travelled on British passports. They were, in any case, the overlords. Major George Sherriff was the Head of the Mission in Lhasa from (1943-45). Many of them were either ex-Armymen holding Army ranks or from the Political Service. The Foreign and Political Department, directly under the Viceroy used to control them. In India after independence, the Ministry of External Affairs did that.

In Tibet, my main job was to promote and look after India's interests. The dak-bungalows had already been handed over to the Tibet administration. There was not much of Indian property left. The Chinese were systematically settling in the Hans of pure Chinese ethnicity into Tibet for various developmental works. The detachment of the Indian Army had been recalled. Besides three or four persons – two clerks, a wireless operator and a doctor – we did not have any office staff from India, all others were local recruits. Tibetans, who were employed by us, were questioned by the Chinese authorities day in and day out. Even my own cook had to go for questioning; after dinner at night, he would be called by the Chinese Political Commissar. The Chinese had established a sub-office of the Foreign Bureau of the People's Republic of China mainly for issuance of passports and visas, like we have the Ministry of External Affairs and its offices in the States.

The questions related to their daily movements when indoctrination took place... as to how good the Chinese were, how good the People's Republic of China was. They also used subtle propaganda. There was Mao Tse Tung's 'Red Book' which the Chinese ingrained into the Tibetans. The Tibetan language was not taught in schools; they had started teaching the Chinese language there. Chinese dress and goods were flooding the Tibetan markets. Indian goods which were sold included bicycles, blue jeans from Kanpur and Calcutta, (now Kolkata) tea from Assam, copper and silver brocades from Banaras (now Varanasi), and a few other items like *Thanka* paintings for display in monasteries. Petrol and all the steel, corrugated iron and tin sheets for roofing purposes, also came from India. Maybe cement also came as there was no local cement factory. Later on when the jeeps came, they used to be dismantled and taken to Tibet.

Tibet was as primitive as any other part in that region, except they had a high degree of culture. Spiritually, the Tibetans had reached great heights... as they did culturally, in their language and music. Industrially, Tibetans were very poor. Theirs was a pastoral economy. The *yaks* (local all-purpose domestic animal) used to graze in vast pastures. In certain valleys, some barley would grow and also some fruits, mushrooms, etc. In my compound in Yatung, as soon as the snow melted, I used to get natural mushrooms – which are now Rupees 100 to 200 per kilogramme. Yatung is located in the Chumbi Valley, on the borders of Bhutan, Sikkim and Tibet. This was the first big town in Tibet.

There were Indian traders in Tibet. There were nearly 100 shops in Yatung, which was a big bazaar according to their standards. In Lhasa, there were some Ladakhis; Indians were mostly Ladakhis and the Khachis (Ladakhi Muslims). There were also some Chinese Muslims from western China – Hawhow, Hopalingpas and Khachis. The Ladakhis were Indian citizens and they travelled on 'Indian Trader Certificate'. Traders and border residents from Sikkim and Bhutan travelled on the same Indian Trader Certificate by Nathu-La and Kalimpong routes. Bulk of the traders used to go across either from Nathu-La or Jelap-La pass. These two were the recognised routes from the Sikkim side. There were other routes from Shimla and Uttar Pradesh. The Barahoti route in the Garhwal-Kumaon area of Uttar Pradesh has many more passes to go across into Tibet. These were also used in a limited way.

The three Trade Agencies were located at Yatung, Gyantse and Gartok. The post at Gyantse was vacant for sometime because R.S. Kapoor, the officer there, had gone to Germany. Till the time he returned after several months, I held concurrent charge at Gyantse and visited it sometimes. Phari was a village in-between my jurisdiction up to Gyantse. Gartok was an itinerating Mission. It was a unique situation in which the Trade Agent of India went from one route and came back via Uttar Pradesh, or went from Uttar Pradesh and came back via Shimla. He came to Gangtok to give his report to the Political Officer. So, was a unique kind of a Mission – a mixture of trade, commerce, cultural exchanges, and diplomatic responsibilities.

In their private capacity, the Chinese officials used to visit my house very often because the diplomatic corps in Tibet was very small. There was a Mongolian representative whom I did not meet, but I met the Bhutanese and the Nepalese representatives. Of course, the Chinese were the overlords. For all purposes, Tibet was independent from the time the Tibetans had expelled the Chinese Amban (imperial representative) after a clash between Tibetan Garrison and the Chinese. So, for 50 years, till 1949-50, the Tibetans had their own coinage, territory and government that were the attributes of sovereignty. They used to negotiate with the British through British India. On Independence, India inherited that Agency. Had the British decided to stay, we could have had our own Mission and functioned from one part of the building which could have been handed over to us. But the British did not wish to continue. Had there been a Mission of a powerful Western country like the United Kingdom, then the Chinese would have thought twice or at least would have been under pressure to leave Tibet undisturbed. But that did not happen. The result was that when Tibet was being taken over – or "integrated", as they claim – by the Chinese Communists, nobody supported them. Of course, India supported them directly or indirectly by allowing the Tibetans to escape to India. Even today, these refugees are free to do what they like as long as they avoid open political activism.

China's takeover of Tibet had started off, I would say, from 1950 onwards. For the next six years, the Chinese moved slowly and systematically. I did not have any doubt in my mind about the Chinese intent. That was why I opposed the entry of thousands of gallons of petrol that used to come from India. There was some resistance to the Chinese takeover. The Americans excited the Tibetans and I am quite certain that the Central Intelligence Agency funded all the dropping of the arms etc. to the Tibetan rebels. But armed insurrection cannot succeed unless one has superior arms. One of the mistakes that the Tibetan leaders made was that they started firing at the Chinese troops. Chinese were looking for such an excuse, and the result was that they subjugated Lhasa. So, the autonomy of Tibet became a myth at that time.

Chinese in Tibet

The Tibetans were losing their political power completely. The Chinese took possession of the dak-bungalows constructed by the Government of India. We had voluntarily withdrawn our troops from Tibet. The Chinese Army was building up in a big way. That was very indicative.

When I went to Lhasa, the Chinese showed me the developmental work that they were carrying on. I was quite surprised to see parts of NEFA and Sikkim being shown as parts of China, where our developmental work was being suggested as their doing! I had been to NEFA in 1956, and had come from Pasighat. I had personal knowledge about the Siang Frontier Division which was being shown as part of China. When the Chinese guide indicated to me the locations on the maps, I had to inform him that I had been to the places he was showing me. So, I smiled and told them that I was there. I wrote to the Government of India in my report that I was a bit astonished to find that the development which I had undertaken was being claimed by a Chinese official as their achievement! The

Chinese redrew their maps in 1954 showing Sikkim as a part of China, but the Government of India did not react.

No reply used to come in those days. Only monthly reports came to a District Magistrate or Collector. But the MEA did take notice. Policy matters were initiated by the Under-Secretary based on reports from the Ambassadors. So I got a letter from B.K. Acharya, the Joint Secretary who was the Head of the Division that dealt with China, and Tibet as a part of China. With just the Foreign Secretary and then the Minister above him, the Joint Secretary was a very high rank. I reported that I did not find the Chinese very friendly. My analysis was that the Chinese intention was not good. The Chinese were not only putting obstacles on the path of the Indians, they treated us very badly, charging us as imperialists and pro-Americans. The Marwari traders and their *munims* (clerks) who were very simple people with modest education were harassed. They had nothing to do with politics. But even if the Indian traders were harassed, they got their dues and there was no problem of payments. The Chinese started buying a very large quantity of petrol straight from them – over a thousand mule-loads used to cross the borders and proceed to Tibet. I felt that all the goods that were coming from India went to the Chinese hands.

Tibetans were very poor. We could see them in rags. There were no schools. No English books were available. We had one small school inside the Indian Mission in Lhasa. The Chinese protested against our running of that school. Leave aside Hindi, even when we taught English to the Tibetans, the Chinese would try to teach them Chinese instead and not the Tibetan language. They did not open any schools at all. I used to show the Tibetans a few informative films. The Chinese objected to that too. I told them: "I am not asking your people to come to my school. The children of my own staff and my daughter have to study. Where would they go? This was my school. I did not invite anybody and did not charge any fees. We have only one or two people – my wife and the wife of a peon – to teach".

I reported to the government that I found out that the Chinese were building up their military potential and, therefore, steel and petrol should not be sent to Tibet. I did not say that food should not be sent. The report must have gone to the Ministry of Commerce but I do not know what happened. After a month, I got a letter from B.K. Acharya, the Joint Secretary, in which he said: "We find it a little strange because what you have recommended goes against our policy. Would you reconsider this? India would like you to reconsider this matter". Every month, I used to send a report, as did every Ambassador and Mission Head. They also wrote to Apa Pant, the Political Officer. He must have got a copy of my report, as it used to go through him to the Ambassador in Peking with one copy endorsed to New Delhi. There, the Joint Secretary must have thought that the reports were serious, and so, must be sent to the Prime Minister.

Then I contacted Apa Pant, who said: "You come and see me". So, I went on a four-day journey to Gangtok. This practice was called 'consultations'. It was like that when there was a crisis, the Ambassadors were invited to New Delhi and then they were sent back after consultations. In our case, there was no other communication. There was no telephone contact. Either one physically went or resorted to cipher messages, which was a very long process. In such primitive conditions, wireless sets worked on a petrol-driven generator. So, it was easier to reach Gangtok and talk it over.

Apa Sahib asked: "What is your view? Do you want to reconsider the matter?" I replied: "I still feel the same". He said: "Then do not be defensive about it". He must have been getting his own assessment from Bhutan and other sources. I told Apa Sahib: "It does not require a spy to see that all the military installations are pointing towards Sikkim, towards India. Why should a friendly country put the Army on the borders? They should put the Army on some other side". We did not have our Army in Sikkim. My own guards in Tibet had been withdrawn, I had no guards at all. About 20 people and a Lieutenant Colonel of the Punjab Garrison used to come from the military station at Darjeeling, that too only for the guard of honour on the Republic Day and the Independence Day.

So, I wrote to MEA again and stated that I still felt the same way. When I wrote that report, the Foreign Secretary had no option but to show it to the Prime Minister. The Prime Minister must have been seeing other reports also, maybe from Peking. So, he decided to visit Tibet and I was asked to sound the Chinese that our Prime Minister himself would like to visit Tibet.

A Daughter Born

At the Indian Mission, we had a doctor but no dispensary. Originally, there was a big dispensary and a school. It so happened that the doctor was on leave in India. So, just a compounder was there, but there was no facility for surgery.

When my wife was pregnant, we started a fortnightly pre-natal check-up. At first, the Chinese said: "You send her to our hospital with someone escorting her and we would certainly look after her". So, she went there for various tests. They were very polite but did not want me to come along. It was a military hospital. When she went there the first time, she saw a nurse with a stun-gun. Stun-gun was a very delicate instrument with hardly any safety lock. It could go off even with a slight jerk. The doctor also had a pistol. Doctors and nurses were Chinese, and there were no Tibetans. Later, they said: "Sorry, there is no need to send her because at the time of delivery, we will not be able to look after her and help her in any emergency". The situation was very unusual. So, I asked the government as to what I was to do now when the Chinese had virtually declined any help. I said that it was very unfriendly act to an accredited diplomat, and for an unarmed lady going to their hospital to have weapons all around her. It would make anybody sick – whether he was an Indian or a foreigner. A strange reply was communicated through the wireless. The advice stated: "We strongly advise Mrs. Sudha Johorey to fly to Darjeeling in India". They seemed to have no idea as to how Sudha Johorey would fly to India, the nearest airport being four to five days' journey away. There was no airfield in Darjeeling or in Gangtok either.

That was in 1958 when my daughter was born. My wife went out of Tibet with great difficulty in the month of March or April when it was snowing. One rides a pony to climb a pass as walking was difficult. When coming down from a pass, one could not use a pony as there was danger of falling down a precipice. But my wife could not even walk down. So she was strapped to the pony and brought to Gangtok with great difficulty. Apa Pant's wife, Nalinibai, a gynaecologist who had studied in the Royal College of Surgeons, advised her 48 hours total bed-rest. After two days of rest, my wife travelled to Madras to join Kamala Devi Saksena, my mother-in-law who lived in Perambur. Kamala Devi Saksena was the wife of Dr R.S. Lal, who was the first Indian Superintendent of the Almora Jail when Jawaharlal Nehru was incarcerated there. My wife took a flight from Silliguri to Calcutta, and then from Calcutta to Madras. There was no direct flight or train to Madras in those days. After four to five weeks, the baby was born in Kalyani Hospital in Madras – with the strangulated neck caused by the long journey down from the hills. My daughter survived and came to Tibet when she was 22 days old, but even that was done at grave risk.

Disaster at Gyantse

In implementation of the India-China Agreement of 1954, we were asked to withdraw our troops from Tibet. So, we did that. Unfortunately, one day before the withdrawal of the last troops from Gyantse, they had a party. The Tibetans also came to that party, but no Chinese were invited. At about 1.30 am or so when everyone was asleep, there was a flood. Suddenly, some lake burst in Bhutan and the whole garrison at Gyantse was wiped out. The Indian Agent Pemba Tsering and his wife also died. This happened before I reached there. Pemba Tsering was given the title of Raisahib, and was the last British Agent and the first Indian Agent. His daughter was studying in Darjeeling, and so she survived. Only one Major McFarlin survived. The horses which were tied were all dead. Maces, silver crockery, cutlery, etc. were all lost. Even the wireless operator died. There was no time for rescue.

The news reached the dak-walla's (message-carrier) wife in Yatung bazaar through the 'pony express', as the mail was popularly called. The dak-wallas used to come to Yatung from India via Sikkim, where they used to exchange the mail bags that arrived from Gyantse. At 12 noon, they would sit down to have the ritual tea, exchange scarves, do the puja, and then the dak-walla would return. One day, the mail bag did not arrive and for two or three hours beyond the usual time, nobody came. The dak-walla's wife was waiting, as she always did on the road near the Agency to attend to the horses, spread the carpet, offer the ritual tea and then, do the puja three times. She said that it was a very bad omen that the dak-walla had not come. She took a horse and began a search. She covered a journey of about four or five days in just two days, and reached Gyantse. She changed horses every ten miles. She found that there was nothing left of the garrison camp. At the same time, we got worried when the telephone and wireless at Gyantse kept on ticking and there was no response.

Indian Properties in Tibet

In those days, the post offices also had telegraph lines, but there were no wireless sets. Telegrams, at the second stage of development, used to be composed by codes consisting of 'Dots' and 'Dashes'. Our telegraph lines and post offices were all constructed by the British Indian government. It was our property. Similarly, the dak-bunglows and such premises were the property of the Government of India. I do not think the Government of China gave any compensation to the Government of India when we handed over our properties in Tibet. Whether we asked for it or not, I do not know. We just handed them over because I do not think we knew how to exercise power or the art of diplomacy. At that time, we had little experience in dealing with the foreigners or with the Chinese, except having some cultural contacts with them.

Jawaharlal Nehru had spent a lot of time abroad, studied there and knew world history. But down the line, who were the successors of the British rulers. Senior members of the ICS in the Secretariat or in the field were invariably consulted on policy matters. But the Government of India did not associate non-career diplomats with important foreign assignments. On the other hand, Sir Stafford Cripps, for example, who was not a member of the British Foreign Service, yet was asked by the British Government to negotiate with India. We did not even consult the people from the academia. Now, we are learning the hard way to prepare our officials to negotiate with due foresight.

From old records, it can be seen that when the Great Game was being played out in Central Asia, Russian Political Officers were always in touch with the top state hierarchy at St. Petersburg, Leningrad or Moscow. Similarly, the Viceroy of

India always consulted the Indian Political Officers in the Frontier States, though he might not have been monitoring the Indian states so closely. The Himalayan Frontier was a very important region, with sensitive centres like Gangtok, Peshawar, Landi Kotal, Kathmandu and Kabul spread all along the Himalayan belt. I had the pleasure of staying in and seeing those places. Governors of these areas were very highly trained British officers; they were the elite and the most respected representatives of the Empire. They were all Empire-builders; maybe from their attitude, life and devotion to duty, they were like *sanyasis* (hermits).

There were two opinions about their conduct. Some were very ruthless. One must have read about Sir Francis Younghusband who conducted business with more force than was necessary. On the other hand, some of them were much respected for their benevolence. Charles Pawsey, for example, stayed in Nagaland for a long time, and knew the local language, customs and other social practices. Sir Claude White, who constructed the British Residency in Gangtok which is now the Raj Bhawan, was an engineer, and that was why the people named it the 'White Hall'. Sir Charles Bell who was a Political Officer in Sikkim from 1908 to 1921 authored the 'Bell Series' on Tibet.* Even today, these are the most authentic books on Tibet.

Before proceeding on a political assignment, a young officer should go through all these records and make time to educate himself. But things were moving very fast in those days. Jawaharlal Nehru himself said that the typewriters could move later on, meaning thereby: "*Bhai, jao kisi tarah*" (brother, proceed anyhow). So, my first posting was in Siang and second posting was in Tibet. Jawaharlal Nehru had a vision of the Frontiers and saw that matters were moving fast in the region. He had his advisors, of course. As I stated earlier, there was a purpose behind the 'Forward Policy' at that time. After all, when independence came, they had to know the situation they were in and what their line of thought was. But we were unaware as to what was happening in the Ministry of External Affairs on the Tibetan front: I faced this disconnect even during my second tenure.

China's Growing Unease

There were growing instances of anti-India hostility shown by the Chinese officials, Han settlers and their cohorts. I have already described earlier about my wife's experience. Then there was the Mansarover Yatra (pilgrimage) to Tibet undertaken by Indians over thousands of years past, just as they do today. They,

* The principal books by Bell are : (i) *Tibet : Past and Present* (1924), (ii) *The People of Tibet* (1928), (iii) *The Religion of Tibet* (1931), (iv) *Grammar of Coloquial Tibetan* (1939), (v) *English-Tibetan Dictionary* and (vi) *Portarait of the Dalai Lama* (1946).

too, suffered Chinese hostility and anger. I believe when Raj Kapur went there, he was stopped by the Chinese. After the Dalai Lama left, the Chinese held a demonstration against me, actually in a sense against Indians. They shouted slogans like, "Down with the Indian Imperialists", "Down with Nehru" and "Down with Johorey"; that was the first time ever in my life that I was bracketed with Jawaharlal Nehru! I was quite surprised and asked them as to what they were shouting for. The demonstrators were all Chinese. Hostility was there even before, but after the Dalai Lama's exit, it became very open. There was a fire in the bazaar. It was caused by the Chinese or somebody else but they locked up a few Indians on frivolous excuses. So I exercised my right as my government's representative to have legal access to them. But the Chinese would not allow that. They said: "You come and we will discuss". There were no lawyers. Then they said: "No, no, we will handle it". I said: "What are you people doing? I will have to defend them". After three to four meeting sessions, the Chinese released them.

Attitude of the Chinese officials towards the special relationship between Indians and Tibetans was that of unease, bordering on hostility. This attitude is best depicted by two episodes. On 17 July, 1954, at about the same time when floods hit Assam, the Indian Agency in Gyantsey was washed away by sudden floods caused by a cloudburst. That is very unusual where the rainfall was only two to three inches in a year. A lake in Bhutan had suddenly burst. The Agency was housed in the Gyantse Fort, a traditional mud-brick construction. So when the fort collapsed, the Indian Agent and his wife were killed. That was the last day of the withdrawal of the troops as a consequence of the 1954 Agreement, and many of our horses slated to move out were killed. We shifted the Agency to a small house on another piece of land owned by India. Then we made plans and an estimate of the cost for a new building. Habib Rahman, our famous Chief Architect, made a special design based on Indian architecture. One of our engineers came and we started the work. The labour was Tibetan. We could not import labour from India because it was too cold for them to work in this location. The Chinese started to frighten, but not injure, the Tibetan labourers by provocative firing of machine gun on the pretext of range practice. They asked the Tibetan labour not to work for us. We had no control over Tibetans, and so they would often run away. Then, our engineer also died in Yatung. I cannot recollect whether he was sick or something happened to him. A Chinese doctor was called but he could not revive him. So, the whole project could not take off. Then, our relations went from bad to worse. I do not know whether the Chinese finally gave permission to build the Agency or stopped the construction, but we did not proceed further. The design of the whole project may still be lying in the archives.

The second episode is related to the famous Indian film star Raj Kapoor and his team who wished to go to Mansarover. The party went to the border and was kept waiting for about three days. Raj Kapoor pleaded with the Chinese officials: "Chou En Lai (the suave and popular Chinese Premier, now spelt as Zhou Enlai) invited me to come here and so I have come. Please let us proceed". The Chinese official told him to wait till he checked up from Peking. After a wait of two days and after they checked up, Raj Kapoor was allowed to proceed to the Mansarover Lake.

There was no doubt in my mind that the Chinese were very hostile in the sense that they were preparing themselves for a show-down, and taking full advantage of our policy of open trade to get as much resource, material and logistics support as they could. They were also trying to subvert the border population and trying to block our contact with them. That was their plan. If I invited any Tibetan leader to my house, he would be questioned the next day by the People's Commissar who was like a Political Officer – a man who had all the powers. He once invited me to see a Commune to impress me. I used to tell them that our country was democratic and I have a right to differ. Our method was that whether we agree with anything or not; once a task was given, as a dutiful civil servant, I would carry it out. They used to find this very strange.

Dalai Lama's Visit to India

The Dalai Lama's visit to India during the 2500th birth anniversary or *Mahaparinirvana* of the Buddha was a landmark event. The Dalai Lama was invited, but the Government of China apparently told that Panchen Lama, the next high ranking monk, should also go. The Dalai Lama was received with great honours. I was attached to his party to visit a few places. The Dalai Lama visited Kanpur to see the aircraft factory, the Hindustan Aeronautics Limited. Arjan Singh – the senior-most officer – who later went on to become an Air Marshal, invited Dalai Lama to sit in the cockpit of an aircraft. Meanwhile, the Panchen Lama, stating that he also wanted to sit in the cockpit, occupied one seat. But since it was a two-seater, he had to eventually come down. There were similar problems of protocol between the Dalai Lama and the Panchen Lama. For example, there was only one Circuit House in Agra. So, the Dalai Lama stayed in the Circuit House and the Panchen Lama was put in some hotel which he took as an affront. He thought a hotel was a secondary place. So, he went and slept in the train, as I was told. He was angry, and so were the Chinese.

The Dalai Lama is the supreme pontiff and had both spiritual as well as temporal powers. In the Tibetan Cabinet, he was assisted in religious matters by the 'Tutors', who were all high grade lamas. From the age of nine, the Dalai Lama kept himself secluded. He could not even live with his mother, and no women entered his chamber. His mother and other women visited him only for worship and puja. He was kept totally *brahmachari* (celibate). The Panchen Lama was also of very high rank. In India, *Kushak Bakula* is a very high ranking lama in the hierarchy of Buddhists. The other very high ranking lama, higher than him, is the head of the Rumtek Monestary in Sikking, His Holiness, the *Gyalma Karmapa*. 'Gyal' means a King and 'Gyal Karmapa' means supreme. Dalai Lama is also a Gyalma Rinpoche or the King Rinpoche, who is a 'Supreme Incarnation'.

The Chinese made it very clear that they put the Panchen Lama as an observer so that the Dalai Lama did not go beyond a certain limit. The Chinese forced the Panchen Lama on us. So, we had to accept him; how could one not host the Panchen Lama, or any other lama for that matter? The Dalai Lama met the Prime Minister and other Indian leaders. Mostly, he confined himself to seeing the religious leaders and places. He was also shown the development projects. He also went to Sarnath and to South India. He went to Andhra Pradesh, the home of Shanti Deva, who was one of the authors of *Prajñâpâramitâ*, the book of transcendental wisdom comprising of several volumes, whose original manuscripts were lost in India but then rediscovered in Tibet. In ancient times, four or five Buddhist gurus had travelled to Tibet from India; Gautama Buddha was not the only Buddha. Later, when the Muslims invaded India, many of them crossed over with their books and their religious knowledge and stayed there – Ashwaghosa from Bengal, Shanti Deva from Andhra Pradesh, Atisha Dipankar from the Bihar area and many others. Thus, most of those scriptures were found in Tibet...some were still found in the Indian monasteries as well.

When the Dalai Lama was in India, he asked for political asylum. Jawaharlal Nehru talked to Mao Tse Tung who promised to grant autonomy to the Tibetans. But he put off the implementation of the agreement for autonomy. The Dalai Lama was crestfallen. That was why he did not fly back to Peking (now Beijing). He deliberately chose to go back to Tibet by land route. Repression of the Tibetans started after that, when the Tibetans refused to go by the Chinese propaganda to show that the lamas indulged in feudal exploitation of the masses. Maybe, some of the local lords, whom one could call *zamindars* (landlords) did exist, but there was no slavery. It was not as bad as among certain tribes in the North-East. These local lords spent time playing the Chinese game of Mah-jong and practiced feudalism, but they were also attached to the social customs. Like the Indian *zamindars*, they took care of their ryots like paying for weddings in poor peasant's or servant's family. There was no doubt that there was theocracy and feudalism, but it was not as diabolic as the Chinese liked to show.

CHAPTER 7

TURBULENT TIMES IN TIBET

Chinese Impositions on Tibetans

Tibetans were among the most peaceful people in the world. Here in India, we had political parties and an open Parliament, whereas in Tibet there was open debate on religious matters. These debates were held in Tibetan monasteries, but there was no political party. There was just the civil administration and a unique brand of civilisation. The constitution of Tibet was unique. One may call it theocracy, but it was of a different kind altogether. One could not really compare the Tibetan polity with any other. One-third of the Tibetan population was beholden to matters of 'after-life'. Girls joined the nunnery and boys went to the monastery. It was a voluntary custom.

In the Tibetan economy, a portion of agricultural produce was given to the monastery for their upkeep and maintenance. One may call it taxation in modern terms. Tibetans had their own currency, coinage, legal system and independent relations with the neighbouring countries like Mongolia, Bhutan, Nepal and British India. Even China had a delegation; it was headed by the *Amban* who was like an Indian Political Agent. So there was some kind of a relationship between the Chinese Amban and the Tibetan government; it was somewhat similar to that between the Viceroy of India and the Indian Princes. While the Central Government of Tibet was based in Lhasa, the Governors ruled from provincial capitals. The *Dzong Pangs* were the District Magistrates. *Dzong* means a fort housing a monastery where all records are maintained. Indeed, it was a unique civilisation.

Tibetans were economically very backward. With my experience, I realised the deplorable condition of the Tibetan economy. The Government of India argued that if we did not supply them cement, steel and other materials, they would be thrown into the arms of the Communists. My response was that the Chinese were already in full occupation of Tibet, and ruled them with the help of armed force. Even if the Chinese Army used the petrol supplied by India, they were not dependent on us. They were not going to starve if we stopped our supplies, but they were just taking advantage of supplies from India. They had also started levying tax from the Tibetans. They did not pay them wages for the labour used in construction of roads and buildings. They imposed Chinese language and altered the demography. No newspapers and public meetings were allowed in Tibet. There were no international newspapers in Tibet, only Chinese newspapers and circulation of some Red Army news. There was no freedom of movement in the Chinese system. When Jawaharlal Nehru went to Peking and tried to move from one place to another, even he was restrained. Then, when the Dalai Lama came to India, Chinese observers followed him to keep an eye on him.

The Chinese started developmental work along with imposition of Communism in Tibet. That was why everyone – every peasant in town – was invited every evening to the "Commune Meetings". There, the Chinese would propagate about Mao Tse Tung's greatness and the USA's nefarious foreign policy. Tibetans knew that there was no question of Chinese giving them any autonomy. They were treated harshly. Sometimes, they were even flogged. That was why the Tibetans were very upset. China's developmental work did not assuage their anguish; after all, the British had done a lot of developmental work in India, and yet they were asked to leave. Actually, there were two contradictory reports about Chinese rule over Tibet. One was what the Chinese claimed: that they were doing a lot of developmental activities and liberating Tibet from the clutches of feudalism and poverty. The second was the reactions of the Tibetans who were absolutely convinced that the Chinese behaved like an army of occupation. They were suppressing all cultural and religious freedom, not to mention political freedom.

Jawaharlal Nehru's visit to Tibet in 1958

There was a Sub-Office of the Foreign Bureau of the People's Republic of China (PRC) in Yatung, something like a mini South Block (in New Delhi) in Tibet. When I first mooted the subject of Nehru's visit, the reaction of a bureau official was: "How could we make a suggestion like that when even their own Prime Minister had not visited Tibet?" He further stated that there were no roads, and there was the question of security and various other administrative problems. He did not use the word 'civil war' but, in fact, the agitation among the Tibetans was going on and they did not want us to see that. They were cracking the whip upon the Tibetans. They were trying to set up the Communes which they did not want to be seen. I replied very clearly that I could not advise our Prime Minister not to come. That would be his decision and that of the Government of India's; I was only communicating it for our mutual convenience so that we could work out the details. I even went to the extent of saying that if they did not want Nehru to come, they could refuse him. We left it at that and did not discuss any further. I communicated to the Government of India that a visit to Lhasa was out of question. The bureau official had categorically stated so. Then a decision must have been taken at the level of the Prime Minister. The King of Bhutan had also invited Jawaharlal Nehru to visit his country.

Actually, Jawaharlal Nehru wished to visit China in 1957 but on the request of Mao Tse Tung, postponed it to 1958. This was six months before Jawaharlal Nehru's arrival in 1958. It took a long time to prepare a Prime Minister's tour to Tibet – all the information, food-habits, accommodation, transport, security, who he would meet; all these were fixed, maybe that these details must have been decided after consulting Peking. Then the invitation was sent, and the dates were finalised.

Finally, once the programme was received, we discussed where Jawaharlal Nehru would stay and so on. Consequent to the India-China Agreement of 1954 on Tibet, our own buildings, post office, dak-bungalow and barracks were vacated, and the Chinese had built fortifications of the People's Liberation Army – a hospital and some administrative buildings. The dak-bungalow was vacant but virtually in ruins, and the post office had been handed over to the Chinese. The barracks outside our compound had also been given away, but we retained a portion of it because we still had a dozen odd mules and horses after the rest had been were withdrawn. There were no Indian troops and no police. Our own muleteers who brought mail from Gangtok as per international mail convention changed over at the Indian dak-bungalows located enroute. There were no security officers with the Mission like we have today. I conveyed the invitation from the Chinese, offering Jawaharlal Nehru to stay in the Chinese fort at Yatung.

When the programme and the dates were fixed for the visit of Jawaharlal Nehru, the Sikkim Durbar tried very hard to complete the road up to Nathu-La with the help of our Central Public Works Department (CPWD). The road design and construction was under the charge of one Mr Mathur, the Executive Engineer at CPWD, and completed under the guidance of the Maharajkumar of Sikkim P. Thondup Namgyal – the last Chogyal, who himself was the Development Commissioner. Prime Minister Jawaharlal Nehru could come up to Nathu-La and Changu Lake by a jeep. Then the party would change over to horses. Finally, it was decided that the Prime Minister and his party would stay in our Agency House which was a small building... somewhat like a dak-bungalow, with four rooms in a row. I added a small room and bought a small generator, and brought it from Calcutta to provide for lighting. A small two bed-room accommodation was thus prepared for the Prime Minister.

On the question of security, I informed the Chinese Foreign Office that we did not need their security staff within the Missions compound. The Chinese reluctantly agreed to that arrangement. I think they must have sensed the dangers of contact with the Tibetans. I argued with the Ministry of External Affairs that if Jawaharlal Nehru stayed in a Chinese fort, then the Tibetan leaders would have no access to him. The Tibetans would be very unhappy, and they would be more comfortable to meet him in my house. Jawaharlal Nehru decided to stay in the Agency House.

On the way, Nehru wished to visit a highly respected 92-year old lama in his monastery. I had earlier met this lama in connection with my search for the *Vimana Shastras* (books containing the ancient art of flying). We carried out a rehearsal. I had informed the Chinese officials that when Jawaharlal Nehru came, he would visit the monastery. The Chinese official asked why the Prime Minister wanted to visit this monastery. I replied that there was a local practice about the entry into Tibet by foreign Heads of States, and that Jawaharlal Nehru was referred to as Pandit Rinpoche from Kagyu. He would be granted temple honours, and the monastery band would receive him as he passed through their area. Therefore, Jawaharlal Nehru wished to visit the monastery. I told the Chinese that if they wished, they could ask Jawaharlal Nehru not to come. They did not answer in a yes or no. We then sent them a minute-to-minute programme.

Nathu-La

The Maharajkumar of Sikkim drove up to Nathu-La with Jawaharlal Nehru, with the Indian flag flying on the jeep. Then they went back. Nehru was punctually received at Nathu-La, and I was there. The Maharaja of Bhutan had sent four horses because Nehru was also going to Bhutan. The Chinese would not allow the Tibetans to give their horses. There were a fixed number of Indian flags but no Tibetan flags. Besides, there were no flags at all along the route. These are matters that have a message; these indicate the degree of relationship, and the level of the protocol. Normally, a Head of the State is given an inter-services guard of honour, and each country had its own protocol.

Accompanying Jawaharlal Nehru was Jagat Singh Mehta, who was the Deputy Secretary in the MEA, New Delhi. There was Apa Pant and his wife, Nalini Pant, who was a doctor, and Major Ken Sarker of the Army Medical Corps, who was a doctor but did not wear any uniform. Then, there was Parameshwaran, the photographer and one of the stenographers of Jawaharlal Nehru. Apa Pant had arrived one hour before the arrival of the Prime Minister. Of course, my wife was there to receive him. That was all, a small party. I and my wife had come from that side to receive Jawaharlal Nehru.

At Nathu-La, the Chinese did not follow any protocol as such. They did not present Jawaharlal Nehru with any guard of honour. There were two reasons for it. They did not want Nathu-La to be indicated as an international border. This is my analysis now, in hindsight. It was very odd. When Jigme Palden from Dorji, the Prime Minister of Bhutan (1952-64), came to Bomdi-La, we treated him as a Prime Minister and the Head of State of a friendly neighbor. Although Jigme Dorji was a good friend and a very informal person, he did not want any protocol formalities. The Chinese also did not welcome Jawaharlal Nehru with the traditional offering of scarves. Of course, the Chinese soldiers were there as an escort to prevent chances of any untoward incident like waylaying etc. It was for security reasons, but there was no guard of honour, no matter how small. I was there, of course. I did my Indian style namaskarand received him. I had my own horses. Jawaharlal Nehru was given the leading horse. Apa Pant, who had also come, was given another. Jawaharlal Nehru did not take notice of all the lack of protocol. He was beyond the mundane and frivolous niceties of protocol. He was a man of the masses, and was not disturbed by such petty though meaningful actions of the Chinese.

When we started off for the monastery – despite the Chinese disapproval, of course – Jawaharlal Nehru saw the lama band from a distance. It was very picturesque. He dismounted and rested there for 10 to 15 minutes in deference to the tradition, and to accept the monastery's honours. The Chinese, too, went in with me to see the monastery. They did not remove their shoes when they went inside. So the Tibetan monks were very unhappy, even though they would not be rude like our *pandas* (keepers of religious practices). If one goes to Benaras (now Varanasi) and violates the rules there, he is certain to be given a stick by the *pandas*. But here I could see the agony on the faces of the Tibetan monks.

The Prime Minister's party did not halt on the way. Normally, it was two to three days' journey to Yatung, but he covered it in one day. The pony express took two days. After this one halt at the monastery, when he came down, we found that the Chinese had sent a very special open car for him. It must have been an imported car. Indira Gandhi and one security officer sat in that car. I did not sit in that car but I briefed Jawaharlal Nehru, before he got into the car, to look at the mountain slopes on either side.

When an Indian Army regiment served in a particular field area, they would commemorate the event by carving out on the high, rocky mountain walls, whatever was the insignia; for example, the Punjab Regiment's ship. It was an old tradition of the Indian Army: wherever they went, they left a mark. The Chinese had blackened these out a night before the Prime Minister's arrival in the Chumbi valley. I noticed that when I was going to Nathu-La from the Tibetan side. There were all these black patches –insignias blackened by tar. On the way, as we were talking, I pointed out to Jagat Singh Mehta: "You see the black patches on the mountain-side, all the insignias are blackened out so that there is no trace of any Indian presence".

After Apa Pant sat in the car, I told him very clearly: "Sir, I have been sending reports about the Chinese behavior... but I am disappointed at the lack of any response from the ministry. Leave aside my personal comforts, but what the Chinese did was a direct affront to India. They have even insulted the lama by entering the monastery without removing their shoes". He did not say anything. I had told him that when he went along the journey, he would find out more of this attitude.

As we neared Yatung, there was a bazaar. Jawaharlal Nehru could not go visit it because the car took a different route. At a distance of about one kilometre of flat ground, he came out of the car. Then he took a horse and suddenly charged into a gallop, and nearly caused an accident. While going upslope, one has to move slowly, like a holiday stroll... but at a gallop, it is a different story altogether. The Chinese Colonel, who was following me right from the beginning, could not keep up to the gallop and was left behind. Jawaharlal Nehru's horse was number one, and reached earlier. Even the Consul-General was left behind. Apa Pant was there, of course. We reached the Agency House earlier than others.

Yatung: Tibet

On arrival at the Agency House in Yatung, Jawaharlal Nehru immediately changed from riding kit and breeches into *sherwani* (Indian close-neck jacket) and *churidar* (narrow, pleated pyjamas), and wore his trademark red rose. He asked as to how far the bazaar was, to which I replied that it was less than a 100 yards downhill. He started walking, and we went down to the bazaar. Earlier, I had told every Indian to wear a cap because if the Chinese arrested them, then we would know. So they were all with their caps on, even the *paanwala* (betel leaf seller). The moment he entered the bazaar, all Indians and Tibetans rushed towards him; somebody touching his hands, somebody prostrating flat on the ground and somebody offering him flowers. The Indians were very well-disciplined as they stood there. Colonel Lu came with us too. He had been a Garrison Commander and Chief Political Commissioner – somewhat equivalent of senior Central Intelligence Agency official. He asked me: "What is going on? We did not have this in our programme, why have you come here?" I replied: "How can I tell him what to do. I cannot tell our Prime Minister what to do or what not to. He is your guest and his security is your responsibility. So you tell him to go back". Colonel Lu could not prevent the Tibetans from approaching and getting near Jawaharlal Nehru. Some of them were even crying. Their sobbing and tears were more eloquent than any formal parlays. There was Tibetan disapproval of the Chinese at every stage.

Then, Jawaharlal Nehru came back from the bazaar. In the afternoon, there was a reception to which I had invited only the Indians. I did not invite the Chinese. In the evening, there was a mini-banquet, and I sent the list of all my guests to the Chinese Foreign Office, so that they could not claim that we had surreptitiously called anyone. At this banquet, Dsarong Dza Dza – the retired Defence Minister of Tibet who was our very good friend – also came. His daughter was married to the Prime Minister of Bhutan. She used to come every year and stay with us for a week, before going to her place in Lhasa. They were very nice people, real aristocratic, nobility, well-educated in Darjeeling. They spoke both, English and Hindi. Nehru joined us after all of us were seated. In that small room, there was just one sofa and not a very big one at that; naturally, the Prime Minister was sitting on it; Tan Kuan-san sat on his left. The banquet party started. About 10 minutes after that, Dsarong Dza Dza came in. He was a tall man, educated, and trained at the British-Indian Army School in Quetta, which was like the present Staff College located in Wellington, in South India; senior military officers were trained mid-career in Wellington. He had long hair and used to wear a *pugri* (turban) with all his medals. This time, of course after retirement, he came in his standard Tibetan dress, and made an entry with a seven-foot long scarf. Naturally, all of us stood up; that was the protocol observed for a Head of State. Jawaharlal Nehru also stood up to receive the scarf. Immediately afterwards, Nehru nudged Colonel Lu and Tan Kuan-san to sit with him. There were just two seats, and so, another chair was brought.

Jawaharlal Nehru talked in Hindi. After the party was over, Dsarong Dza Dza stayed back – he enjoyed his drinks and dinner. Nehru was very happy with the visit, and he told them so. That was one opportunity for the Tibetan leaders present to tell Jawaharlal Nehru very clearly as to how the Chinese were committing atrocities, and how the Sino-Tibetan 17 Point Agreement was being violated. The Agreement vis-à-vis the Indians was that we could engage in free trade up to Lhasa, and that the Tibetan nationals could go to Rawalsar and Amritsar (sacred place for the Sikhs) besides the Barahoti Plains, Rishikesh and Simla for business or pilgrimage.

When all the guests left, Jawaharlal Nehru went to his room, changed into the *churidar pyjamas* and *achkan*, put on his dressing gown and sat down. He then called Jagat Singh Mehta (later on Foreign Secretary), Apa Pant, Dr Major Ken Sarker of the Army Medical Corps and myself, and said: "Everybody tells me to get tough in Tibet. What am I going to get by being tough? In 1950, when Chinese came to Tibet, we had a famine in Bihar". These were the exact words of Nehru: "We had a famine in Bihar. They asked us to send a brigade. When we cannot tackle the problems of food or poverty, why send a brigade there? As it transpired, many among the Tibetans were lukewarm in seeking our support. From military point of view, even air-dropping a jeep in Lhasa would have given some advantage to our Mission there. At that time, we had 22 men of the Punjab Regiment there who, from their position on a hill, could have easily held up a thousand Chinese troops from that height". Jawaharlal Nehru continued to reflect: "If tomorrow the people of India vote for communism, I would not mind it. But I shall not have violence". What he meant was that if Chinese were meant to occupy Tibet by force, he would not have it. He was a Socialist and gave a vent to his anger.

I was a junior officer. Jagat Mehta, the Deputy Secretary who was a couple of years senior to me, was a witness to the historic visit of Jawaharlal Nehru to Tibet. He was earlier a teacher in Allahabad. Apa Pant, a Maharashtrian Brahmin, was educated in England and learnt Sanskrit from his father. The Raja Sahib of Benaras and ApaPant were among the few princes in India who were Brahmins, whereas the princes of Kolhapur were Marathas. I did not know the distinction between these because Marathi is a language patronised by the Brahmins. But they were all learned people. In my innocence, I had once said to Chintamani Deshmukh, known to most as 'CD', "You, after all, are a Brahmin in the Cabinet". He had replied: "A Deshmukh is not a Brahmin. Deshmukhs are Marathas". This time around, I took the opportunity to inform Jawaharlal Nehru that one of my proposals to build a compound wall around the Mission was disallowed by the South Block. I said: "Sir, I am living with my family. I have a one year-old daughter. The second one is on the way. If the Chinese construct a latrine next to our building, how could I conduct my business here? So, I should be allowed a compound wall".

Coming back to Jawaharlal Nehru, he was very thorough in his desk work even while on tour. He was punctual to the core. Even after a function, he would dictate his notes. The next morning, his staff was ready but the stenographers felt completely drained out; they were not used to the high altitude. First he wanted to know as to what all was happening. While briefing him regarding the important programmes of the next six days, I gave him the news that Feroze Gandhi had a heart problem. There was also the news of a death. When I gave him the message stating that Dr Bhagwan Das was no more (he passed away on 18th September 1958), he looked out and wrote down in his own hands: 'DTO (Date, Time and Origin) Yatung, for Sri Prakasa (son of Dr Bhagwan Das), and sad to hear that the grand old man is no more. The inevitable has happened. Much love from far off Tibet – Jawaharlal Nehru'. I gave the message to the wireless operator. This paper remained with me when I returned from Tibet. I kept it as a memento. Years later, I gave the handwritten dispatch to the daily National Herald for an article titled *India's Public – A Nehru Legacy.* I had some sentimental attachment to that nationalist newspaper.

The Chinese must have received all the reports of how Jawaharlal Nehru arrived in Yatung ahead of schedule and the confabulations which was held during my banquet. These developments must have been annoying to them. The sum total of all these happenings was that the Chinese reaction was not only very cautious, but they also became suspicious of our intent. All our reports from Lhasa, Yatung and Barahoti areas talked about the Chinese military build-up. The next day, on 1st October – China's National Day – the Chinese hosted a farewell reception in his honour. That made me visit the Chinese Foreign Office on two consecutive days, one as the head of the Diplomatic Corps. At the Chinese Republic Day Reception, Jawaharlal Nehru sat at the main round table along with the Chinese. I also sat there. The norm was to move from table to table. The Political Commissar said: "*Gembe*! (cheers), it is the Seventh Republic Day of China and seven years of peace in the spirit of *Hindi-Chini, Bhai, Bhai*". Jawaharlal Nehru returned the toast, and said: "Yes, seven years of peace. For the next seven years also, we hope there will be peace". But that was not to be! Next day, Jawaharlal Nehru left for Bhutan.

When Jawaharlal Nehru returned from Bhutan, we received him at the Tibet-Bhutan border beyond the Asam Sha Bridge which was inside Bhutan. I showed him some of the clippings which I had received from the newspapers from India. There was George Patterson's report on Jawaharlal Nehru's visit. Of course, the International Press must have come to know that Jawaharlal Nehru had gone to China and it was feared that there would be a showdown on security. Whether the idea was inspired by the Chinese or not, I do not know... but it was stated that he was undertaking a very risky mission when the Khampa Tibetan rebels were active against the Chinese expansionism into their homelands.

Overall, the Chinese reaction to Nehru's visit was adverse. At that time, China was building up its military power in Tibet and purposefully proceeding to establish their full administrative control.

Dalai Lama's Escape

The Dalai Lama was going to be conferred with the *Geshe* (Lharampa) Degree. That was the highest honour – somewhat like a doctorate on divinity. Hundreds of people were gathering to offer him scrolls and presents. Presents were items of religious use; one of these was a huge lamp made of gold. The Khampa Tibetans were the first to reach Lhasa, the capital of Tibet, to participate in the ceremony. Tall in stature and known as brave fighters, they were people from the Kham Province in eastern Tibet. The Khampas had been the first ethnic group to rebel against Chinese occupation of Tibet. Their rebellion started in the Kham province, which is the eastern-most province of Tibet and the western-most province of China. Khampas formed Dalai Lama's personal bodyguards, and they were the people who actually escorted him and his people later on – when they escaped from Lhasa to India. They were also very brusque in their manners. When the Khampas gathered in thousands, the Chinese got worried that there might be a showdown. Even a spark ignited by possible Chinese misstep would have created a flashpoint. Such was the situation at that time. The Governor of Kham asked the Chinese *Amban* (representative of the Government of China in Lhasa) to offer the traditional welcome scarf first when the Dalai Lama arrived for the ceremony. Some films are available of that ceremony.

Then one night, when a *puja* (worship ceremony) was going on, the Dalai Lama escaped. We did not know about it; none of the foreign diplomats did. Our Consul-General also did not know about it. Dalai Lama was escorted by his own people. One day S.L. Chibber, the Consul-General of India in Lhasa, heard gun-shots being fired. So he came out to see as to what the matter was. Our staff also came out and found themselves under a crossfire between the Chinese and the Tibetans. Chibber told me about the incident,which I then informed the Government of India about. We did not know as to when the Dalai Lama escaped or what was happening. All we knew was that firing was going on. All the employees of our consulate stayed indoors; no one came out.

Dalai Lama did not come via Gangtok, which was the best route to India. He came directly through the Khenzamane-Tawang route. Located in the North-Eastern India(now known as Arunachal Pradesh), the great monastery at Tawang had, in the past, produced a Dalai Lama; therefore, it was an important Buddhist institution. Dalai Lama took the route from Lhasa to Tawang may be because the Gangtok border at the Nathu-La-Sikkim-Tibet tri-junction was heavily fortified by the Chinese. Tawang, on the other hand, had significant Indian presence. Being rather difficult, it was not a normal route to and from Lhasa. The journey used to take several days. Dalai Lama's party may have taken about 8 to 10 days to reach Tawang; I do not know any more details about that event.

Jawaharlal Nehru welcomed the Dalai Lama; he was given a warm welcome all over India. Tamil Brahmins and other religious leaders prostrated before him. The Chinese were unnerved by the tremendous reception that he got in India; there was no doubt about that. The Tibetans felt that India, the land of the Buddha, was a safe haven where there was scope for freedom and preservation of their culture.

The Chinese reacted in two ways. First, they started propaganda amongst the Tibetans stating that the Indians had kidnapped the Dalai Lama, put him in jail, and were ill-treating him. That worried me because it could lead to some misled Tibetans to turn violent. Then they staged demonstrations against me and India, which was also a cause of worry. Chinese soldiers and some Tibetans, including some of my own erstwhile servants, participated in such demonstrations. Some of the Chinese soldiers wore Tibetan dress but they could be easily made out. Obviously, it was the Chinese Army which organised the demonstrations. The crowd was made to march past in front of my compound and demonstrate against the Government of India.

CHAPTER 8

MORE TURBULENT TIMES IN THE NORTH EAST

Bomdi-La: China Attacks

After my tour of duty in Tibet, I returned to India in 1959. After an interlude of about four months, I was posted again to the NEFA on the Burma (Myanmar) border. I assumed my charge as the Political Officer of Kameng Frontier Division at Bomdi-La in 1960.

Reports of the Chinese build-up kept coming in, whereas we had yet to start with building roads into our mountainous border areas. The first one to be built was the Gangtok-Nathu-La road when Jawaharlal Nehru was visiting Tibet; the existing track was not even 'jeepable'. I had then reported to the authorities that the condition of the road was bad, and was told by Apa Pant that both the Prime Ministers had spoken to each other; that the Chinese had promised to build the road up to Yatung while the Government of India would build one from Shiliguri(the railway head in North Bengal) to Gangtok(the capital of Sikkim). Accordingly, as mentioned earlier, the road from Gangtok to Nathu-La(that is to the Tibet frontier) was constructed by the Central Public Works Department (PWD) in collaboration with the local PWD, while the Chinese built the road from Lhasa to Yatung. Today, the road to Gangtok-Nathu-La is a very good road, a National Highway.

The road from Tezpur to Bomdi-La was already under construction. So when that road was completed, Jawaharlal Nehru visited Bomdi-La in 1961. Earlier than that, Major General B M Kaul and General P N Thapar(Chief of the Army

Staff) had also visited the area. The Prime Minister of Bhutan had also come because the road to Bhutan was being aligned through the Indian side. At that time, there was no direct route into India from the Tibet side.

On National Days like Nehru's birthday and Gandhi Jayanti, the practice in that area was to join in in the cleaning work, planting of trees and some feasting. In the monastery, they held prayer meetings and there was a cultural programme in the school. All that was going on normally when, without any warning, the attack came. As the war broke out, the instructions to the civil administration were to render all assistance to the army. Meanwhile, the army arrived and then, naturally, we rendered them all the facilities that we could offer. The entire population rallied round. The boys and girls vacated the hostels and took up to carrying loads of the army from the dropping zones to the defences and bunkers. The local population gave anything that the troops wanted – food, shelter, local bamboo, etc. There was no restrictions on anything that was to be given to the troops. But some people developed cold feet and reported to Delhi that they were not getting porters. B N Mullik, Director of the Intelligence Bureau, sent a Special Officernamed Charanjit Singh to check whether the civil administration was cooperating. I said: "I cannot accept the allegation that the army was not getting porters. All these Tibetan refugees are there in addition to the local porters".

I used to visit the dak-bungalow to attend to routine matters when one morning, a wireless message came stating that the Chinese were digging up trenches close to the Indo-Tibet Border. A jawan of the Assam Rifles Forward Post had sent a wireless message: "*Kataron Mein* (danger!), Red". There was no army deployed on our side of the border at that time, we had only our para-military force, the Assam Rifles. The message further said: "*Dhoom dhaam aa raha hai* (hearing report of firing)". The next morning, we found that the Chinese had over-run our positions and come up to Tawang. Tawang, one of our Sub-Divisions, was partially occupied by them. The Chinese aggression had started. Longju and some other smaller skirmishes had already happened. Now, the Chinese were moving forward. But the information of the actual attacks came when I was in Bomdi-La in October 1962. Tawang was occupied by the Chinese in October 1962, and after some weeks, Bomdi-La fell on 17th November 1962.

The Tawang monastery was like a huge university. It had its own printing press, its own agriculture, its working force, scholars and hundreds of monks from all over the adjacent areas. On 16th November 1962, the news came that the vehicles which carried rations to the Tawang evacuees – who had been housed in a place referred to as 'Tawang Zone' – were stopped by the army. I wondered as to how anybody could stop movement of these rations. I thought that may be the drivers had been frightened by Chinese firing. I went there and found that the military post at Tawang had fallen. Even in Darrang, the Chinese were expected any time.

My Superintendent of Police(an Indian Police Service {IPS} officer of the Intelligence Bureau), and a very fine chap, had just returned from Tezpur. He said: "We have been reporting China's moves, but nobody would listen to us. But if you come along with me, maybe the General (B M Kaul) would listen because you are the head of the civil administration." So, I went to the Dirang Dzong, which was the Headquarters of the Army Division. After the loss of Tawang, they had moved to Dirang. The brigade in Tawang had fallen and its commander, brigadier John Parashuram Dalvi, was presumably captured (which was substantiated later). Few days earlier, he was with me; he was going home on leave. But when news came of the Chinese advance to Tawang, he flew back to his HQ. In Bomdi-La, he had breakfast with me and played with my children. I went to Dirang on 15th November 1962, and I met the General Officer Commanding (GOC) of the army, along with the Superintendent of Police. I told the General two days prior to the fall of Bomdi-La that the Chinese might come from Mago Chuna side. He took no notice. Then, the last meeting I was in was in Dirang – which was about an hour or two across the Bomdi-Lapass. Dirang Dzong was the Block Headquarters where there was a magistrate, a doctor and a school. A Block consisted of a primary school, a health centre and agriculture extension workers. The Block Development Officer (BDO) was also the magistrate of the area. It also had the monastery where, in the past, the lama was the leader of Dzong. When Dirang fell, the lama of Dirang Dzong could not come out. He sent his people away, but was himself captured by the Chinese and made to dance and sing Chinese praises.

Brigadier Gurbaksh Singh, the Brigade Commander at Bomdi-La(the son of Sir Sobha Singh and brother of Khushwant Singh), was a very good friend. I had given him the Circuit House to stay in. The Brigade Headquarters was at a walking distance from my house. When the fighting was going on, we would meet in the morning to have breakfast together, and to exchange the information of the day. Whatever information I gathered, I would update him about it all at night. One day, the supply trucks was stopped from coming to Bomdi-La again. I went to resolve the matter but by then it was dark, and the trucks had to turn back. I decided to go and see Gurbaksh. He was in the camp itself, and said: "Things are bad. We should meet again after two hours. You come to my place." By that time, the firing had started and some shells fell here and there. The attack on Bomdi-La was on. Then, the Sela Pass was bypassed from both flanks, and the Chinese were trying to break-in. They had not yet actually entered the Bomdi-La town.

In the evening, when Bomdi-La was about to be overrun, the Brigade Commander told me: "I would be leaving now, and you must leave too." My loyalty was to India but as a part of the civil administration, I had no firm immunity against prosecution by the Chinese. If any soldier was taken prisoner, he was to be treated as a Prisoner of War and treated under the provisions of the Geneva Convention. If a Political Officer was captured, he could be tried for anything – including refusal to fly the Chinese flag. We did not have the 'War-Book' at that time; normally, every District Magistrate knew that the instructions in that book were to resist the enemy; we had our very clear instructions under the 'Defence of India Rules'. But presently, the events moved very rapidly and instruction came for all officials to evacuate, and not be captured to prevent anti-India propaganda obtained through torture. That kind of thing had happened during World War II. In Ross Island of the Andamans, the Japanese had captured the civilian administrator and tortured him because he had no immunity. A Prisoner of War could not be treated cruelly, but others were.

My orders were very clear that I should stay in Bomdi-La as long as the army was there. But if the army had to withdraw, I was not going to administer vacated areas and take orders from the Chinese Commissar. So, I withdrew from Bomdi-La. Instruction from the Commissioner was that I should proceed to Tezpur. I argued that I need not go to Tezpur...that I could escape to another Sub-Division which was at a distance of 10 days' journey, and where the Chinese could never reach. But at that point, our contact was cut off. I was the last to leave. I asked the women, children, leprosy patients and the local leaders to leave first. One of the leaders was Shabdrung Lama, a very important and high lama of Bhutan who escaped one day before I left. I did not burn the District Treasury becaus it would have been an act of distress to burn one's own treasury and one's own f ag. I took that decision at night at 9 pm, while the civil administration functi ned till midnight – the post office, hospital and the school; we had closed the sc ool earlier because the children were helping out against the utter confusion.

At midnight when I asked, the Brigadier said: "I am leaving now; you take your own decision." I said: "I am not going to salute the Chinese flag. If you are here, then I will stay." So, I took the decision at about midnight to evacuate the treasury. It had several crores of rupees. It had 40 boxes of currency, coins, gold, opium, confiscated goods and books. So we put the label 'Army Vehicle' on the two jeeps, and then George(my Treasury Officer), Thomas from some other branch and one clerk went down with the treasury, along with two guards from the Central Reserve Police (CRP). They left for Tezpur at midnight and must have reached next day. The journey to Tezpur took about 12 hours. I had lost contact with them after they'd left.

When Brigadier Gurbaksh Singh said that he was leaving, I asked him: "Are you not going to fight?" He replied: "How can I fight? General B M Kaul is giving direct orders to my companies and battalions. The Brigade had three battalions comprising of the Rajputs, Sikhs and South Indians. I think the Gorkhas were also coming in. There was utter confusion. So, as he left, I lost touch with him. He asked me to do him a favour. The next day was his daughter's birthday. So, I went to the post office which had a facility for wireless telegram. There were no telegraph lines; our telegram was through the wireless. So I gave the Post-Master five or six rupees, and sent a telegram: "Happy Birthday from Daddy – Gurbaksh Singh". I told the Postmaster to close the set after clearing the telegram, and he did that.

The Institution of Sabdrung Lama

At this point, it would be interesting to mention about the Shabdrung Lama's institution that was prevalent in Bhutan. The Shabdrung was a Buddhist school of thought, and the position of Shabdrung Lama was almost similar to that of the Dalai Lama in Tibet. Gradually, the Shabdrung grew to be a very powerful person. Then, there were the internal rivalries and jealousies – like in any other organisation.

When the last Shabdrung was gone, the new Shabdrung was 'discovered' in the area where I was serving – the Kameng Frontier Division, which is now in Arunachal Pradesh. Being born outside Bhutan and not living there, he was not welcome to Bhutan because Bhutanese high lamas thought that he, too, would go away as the Dalai Lama had. The Shabdrung Lama was very small when the Chinese attack came. So, before Tawang fell, his followers evacuated him. He was then a boy of eight or nine years, and was carried on the shoulders by the nuns and monks. All of them were evacuated from Tawang, but where to, I do not know. Later on, he went to Benaras. Whether he is formally 'installed' as Sabdrung or not, I do not know, but certainly he is not in Bhutan. The Government of Bhutan would not welcome him because they are now modernising the State. They do not want a rival centre of power. At that time, the common man of Bhutan was in awe of the Shabdrung – like the Pope, whom every Catholic worships. So, the institution of Shabdrung at the moment could be non-existant.

Evacuation to Tezpur

At about two in the morning, the orders came that only women would be evacuated because there was no transport. Vehicles that were going down were taking evacuees from Tawang; and in the same vehicles, the Indian troops were coming in. The men had to walk, but the women were carried in cars with their little baggage. Tenga, our immediate destination, was about an hour's journey down the valley. Dr Pal Chaudhury and Pema Wangdi, our interpreter, were with me.

To digress a bit, Pema Wangdi's son Prem Khandu Thungon became a Minister of State in the Government of India when Sheila Kaul was his Minister. Prem Khandu Thungon was from a very good Chief's family; they were the Tongos of Shergaon and Jigaon, the two unique tribes of the Monpas. Monpasare not found anywhere else in the world. Their unique characteristic was that the unmarried girls had to keep long hair, and were not allowed to cut any hair. They were a very colourful, very fine people. They had the habit of covering their face with their hair.

So, Pema Wangdi, myself and Jogesh(my driver) started off in one jeep. Dr Pal Chaudhury was not well, and took the other jeep. We came to Tenga Valley. Then Pema said that his tribesmen were left behind, and trapped in Jigaon and Shergaon. So I asked him to go, and I gave him a letter of authority. He used to wear a brass plate with the Ashoka Lion on it and a red sash of his office, like one would find on High Court peons. It was an old British practice. The brass plate had the inscription of "Kameng Frontier Division". His salary was same as the village chowkidar's, but that was not important. The official letterhead had "Political Officer, Kameng Frontier Division" printed on it. I wrote: "Pema Wangdi is our head interpreter with a gazetted rank, and is a very important leader in his own right. He is the owner of two villages. He is going to evacuate people from his villages and he should be given all assistance". But because he was very fair, had sinking eyes, round face and fringe hair, soldiers still caught hold of him; even if he spoke in Hindi and showed my letter, they accused him of being a spy, undressed him and beat him up before letting him go. Anyhow, he went to his two Sherdukpen villages – Jigaon and Shergaon – to evacuate his clan, their women and jewellery, and their mules and horses. We met after two days.

Bomdi-La was about 9,000 feet above the sea level and Tenga Valley was about 6,000 feet, a descent of 3,000 feet over a winding road. The Tenga Valley was a very large valley, where there is a cantonment now. So these people left at about two in the morning. By the time I reached the valley, it was just about getting bright. There, I found a team of the Ministry of External Affairs, led by Rashid Yusuf Ali, who was then Deputy Secretary in the MEA. With him was one American correspondent and a foreign television team, but they did not go further as Bomdi-La had been occupied by that time. Yusuf Ali asked me: "K.C. what is happening?" I said: "Bomdi-La has fallen now. You cannot go to Bomdi-La. But I will go and see if there is anybody left". I sent back Yusuf Ali and his party. On return to Bomdi-La, I found Dawar, the District Agriculture Officer, asleep in his house, unmindful of the Chinese attack. He did not know that everybody was leaving. We had a meeting in my house. My office was very close to my house and I had asked all the Heads of the Departments to have their dinner with me. Dawar was probably sleeping and did not come to the dinner meeting. Anyway, I discovered him and asked him to leave Bomdi-La.

The Chinese had occupied Bomdi-La at eight in the morning. As I could not proceed further, I came back to the Tenga Valley, helping people evacuate by clearing the road from boulders and a damaged tank. There was much confusion among men of the Border Roads Organisation and the Assam Rifles in the Tenga Valley. By the time I came back, the workers of the Border Roads Organisation and the prisoners started fleeing. The villagers' morale was very low. They said: "If the Indian Army was withdrawing, what would happen to us?" Brigadier O M Mani, the Chief Engineer of the Border Roads, was in Tezpur. Colonel Siddhu, who was the Task Force Commander, asked me for further orders. I told him that I could not give him orders;that he should talk to the Chief Engineer and let me talk to my Commissioner. So he allowed me to use the wireless set. P N Luthra, who was the Commissioner of NEFA, had shifted from Shillong to Tezpur. He asked me: "K C, what are you doing?" I told him that I was trying to go to Kameng and Kherewa Sub-Divisions, which would take me 10 days. I added that the Chinese would never be able to get to Kameng and Kherewa, which were on the eastern end of the Bomdi-La District. Tawang had already fallen. Bomdi-La, the District Headquarters, was attacked on the night of 17th November 1962, and evacuated. So, two Sub-Divisions and the District Headquarters were lost to the Chinese, and I was started movingsouth. P N Luthra said: "The orders are that you come to Tezpur". He had given me orders, and I had explained my position.

So from Tenga, I proceeded to Tezpur. Pema Wangdi had left and no jeep was available. I did not have a radio. Marching to Tezpur, I came to a place called Forest Camp where I met Lalchand Lama – my Deputy Forest Officer, who was living comfortably with his wife. He gave me the first report that an elephant had been shot dead. That elephant wore a nice little chain which made tinkling sounds like a little girl's *ghoonghuroo*(ankle bracelets). That chain also had the identification number of the elephant because it was a government property. Although it had a chain, they thought the elephant was wild; in panic, they shot it dead. People were very upset as they considered it a bad omen. Lalchand Lama was a Mizo, and being a custodian of the forest, was very upset. He was an Indian Forest Service (IFS) officer. He did not know about the Chinese advance because the bungalows of the Forest Department had no telephones in those days. There was only one wireless, which was with the army... and one line was in my house. I asked him to go ahead to Tezpur.

It took me about two days to reach the post at Chacko Camp, normally a 12 hours' march, where I spent a night. By the time I reached Chacko Camp, the Chinese had started firing. There were a lot of casualties and the pioneers of the

Border Roads Organisation had to be withdrawn from there. The whole night, I was trapped at Chacko Camp and reached Tezpur only the next day. The Treasury Officer had left for Tezpur with the treasury. There was no space in his vehicle, and so, he had left my suitcasecontaining some woollen clotheson the road. When I found it, it was burning.

When I reached Tezpur, I enquired about my treasury. I had asked my treasury officer to go to the Deputy Commissioner's office and hand over the treasury, and to not take orders from anyone else. Then, I found a whole heap burning. I felt very sad because that meant the officials in Tezpur had set fire to the treasury. There was no trace of my Treasury Officer. He did not hand over the treasury in Tezpur. He apparently took the initiative, and went to the Brahmaputra ghat, hired a boat, and crossed with all the treasury boxes from Bomdi-La. He took an intelligent decision and acted with courage. I was saved the disgrace of my Bomdi-La treasury being burnt by somebody else. He left the jeep at the petrol pump somewhere near the station. We went with one person. The Deputy Commissioner of Nagaon was R L Paramashivan, an IAS officer. My treasury officer deposited the entire treasury under the custody of Paramashivan. This was across the Brahmaputra. Then, I went to the Deputy Commissioner's office. I camped in the Circuit House. There was total panic in Tezpur, and officials were going away to the south of Brahmaputra. I did not find any of my staff in Tezpur. The officials of Tezpur had just thrown the coins in the pond, and children were trying to fish out the coins in the pond. The Tezpur treasury was burnt by the Deputy Commissioner, but not the Bomdi-La treasury. As I said earlier, Bomdi-Latreasury was carried to safety across the Brahmaputra, and deposited with the Deputy Commissioner of Nagaon.

Confusion and Consternation

Bomdi-La was a prestige issue. Jawaharlal Nehru had been there a year earlier, in 1961. So the defeat and fall of Bomdi-La became a symbol of our nation's loss. As a matter of tactics, had the Chinese bypassed our defensive positions and descended upon Tezpur, they could have been cut-off at Bomdi-La and would not have been able to withdraw or escape to Tibet. That was the reason why they did not advance to Tezpur; they did not even reach out to Bhalaphung. Had the Chinese ventured to stretch themselves up to Bhalaphung or down to the plains of Assam and our brigade had held on to its defences at Bomdi-La (which was a domineering position, no matter what)... so long as we had the will and the ammunition, the story could have been different. The Chinese did not have tanks; they came on foot whereas we had some Stewart tanks. The Chinese, therefore, wisely terminated the aggression at the Chacko Camp which, as the crow flies, was about 10 to 20 kilometres from Tezpur – and then withdrew.

Loss of Bomdi-La was a very big shock. The people of Bomdi-La were one of the most culturally advanced people, whereas other tribes in NEFA were still in a Stone Age phase. Bomdi-La was a seat of the Buddhist traditions, and had the distinction of having nurtured a Dalai Lama. Traditionally, Bomdi-La had always been a part of India. However, as reported by an Indian Political Officer, R Khathing, they were not so interested in participating in our post-independence development schemes as they were in their religious-political game. So, the shock of loss of Bomdi-La caused the local administration and the State government to panic. The Governor of Assam (1962-68) was Vishnu Sahay. Later, after he had retired, I put this question him. He said that the order of the Home Ministry was for everybody to be evacuated to the south of River Brahmaputra. That decision was taken in New Delhi, not by the Governor. In Tezpur, there was utter confusion because there was panic among the population. The Chinese were advancing. Thousand of refugees were coming in.

Journalist Kuldip Nayar who had accompanied Lal Bahadur Shastri, the Union Minister of Home Affairs, to visit Tezpur at that time, reported that there was utter confusion at Tezpur and that people were thoroughly demoralised. He also had mentioned in his book, *Between the Lines,* that he heard some announcement over loudspeakers stating that the Government of India was no longer responsible for citizens' lives and properties. I can tell from my personal experience that there indeed was confusion in Tezpur, but I did not come across any such announcement; it could be true if a man of Kuldip Nayar's eminence said so. The Tezpur treasury was destroyed and the coins were dumped in a pond. This practice was repeated in every town in the vicinity, and that caused the local children to take out the coins and play with them. Tezpur officials did not give space to keep our District Treasury. They asked George, my Treasury Officer, to burn the boxes. George said: "I take my orders from my Political Officer. I cannot take orders from you." He then took a decision, even without any escort, to take a boat, cross the Brahmaputra and go to Nagaon which was the seat of the Deputy Commissioner and Collector. About 40 boxes were put in rickshaws and taken to Nagaon. Even if a handful of people had known about the two crores rupees in the rickshaws, they would have stabbed the Treasury Officer and looted the money. But every rupee was accounted for. George handed over all our district treasure to the Deputy Commissioner of Nagaon and took a receipt. That was the sense of integrity of our officials in the civil administration. George told the Deputy Commissioner of Nagaon: "My Deputy Commissioner is still on the way. Whether he would come here and when, I do not know." We had lost touch with each other.

In the face of a chain of tactical reverses, the Army withdrew while denying the road axis to the enemy to slow down their advance, but the 'scorched earth' policy was not followed. There was no recourse to burning of crops in the villagers' fields. As regards the rumour that there were plans to blow up the oil fields of Digboi, which was way down in the plains of Assam, I do not know what instructions were given by the Government of India to the local Deputy Commissioner.

The Chinese advanced in the wake of the Indian Army's decision to withdraw. That was the decision of the army; it is on the Commander's orders that soldiers fight on till their positions is overrun or they are killed or captured, or they have to fight to the last man. Of course, there could also be a tactical withdrawal from here to there while a running fight continued. It is possible to argue that if the Indian Army had not withdrawn from Bomdi-La (which was a dominating ground) and had the Chinese bypassed Bomdi-La, then they could have been encircled and trapped. There was also an opinion in the defence circles that the Chinese had stretched themselves to the plains, and that the Indian troops could have encircled them and cut off their line of retreat. So, half way through to the plains, the Chinese did not think of going beyond the Chacko Camp. Then they withdrew behind the Indo-Tibet Border, the McMahon Line.

I remember that President Sarvepalli Radhakrishnan flew in. I got a message that the President was touring to see my area to boost up people's morale. There was no airfield in Bomdi-La; there was only a Dropping Zone. There was no question of his landing; the announcement was only to boost the morale of the civil administration.

Tezpur in November 1962

Once there, I stayed back in Tezpur because I was visiting various refugee camps. A scheme for rehabilitation was drawn up, but the government staff did not get anything – not to my knowledge anyway. Only the population was given certain benefits from the rehabilitation scheme but it was not much. Everyone suffered in the war, so how much compensation could we give? One of my officers, who was coming to meet me, was killed. We never found his dead body. The farms and other properties were damaged. But for devastation of agricultural crops there was no compensation. No outright compensation of the kind which a Railway Minister announces after an accident used to be given those days. My personal properties were lost. In the army, if one loses one's kit in battle, there is some compensation; soldiers who are killed in battle get some nominal relief. There was no rehabilitation, only a transit relief camp functioned. Rehabilitation was undertaken after people returned to Bomdi-La after the Chinese withdrew. In Tezpur, it was only a holding operation in the sense that only food was given to them. They remained in the camp, awaiting their turn to return after the ceasefire. Later, the Five-Year Plan was revived, and that brought some relief.

I heard about the ceasefire by China only when I reached Tezpur. After the ceasefire, I was more like a migrant administrator, and not an evacuee. So, my camp office functioned with a few staff members who were there. Every day, early in the morning, I used to go to Misamari and Nagaon – both south of Brahmaputra, and helped to keep the displaced people together in the school buildings which served as relief camps. People were in great panic because they had left their property behind. Thousands of Monpas had arrived. Not all the people of Bomdi-La had come. Only some leaders and students did so. Some parents were separated from their children. Some people had fled to the jungles. So, my role was only to keep up their morale and arrange food and medical help for them. There was hell of a crowding in those camps, and people were in a very dejected mood.

In the civil administration, we joined in regular search and rescue operations. We started searching for the Indian soldiers who were trapped. Many of our soldiers and villagers had escaped into the jungles to avoid being captured. Three helicopters were used for that purpose during my stay in Tezpur. One Badal Mukherjee and my wife, who knew the area well, joined in the search. I rescued about 14 people in one round and 12 in another. Those were very challenging operations. People were hiding in jungles, not knowing where else to go. Once the helicopter landed, we would shout: "Please come, we are Indians". We rescued a number of people, including two or three officers, in those sorties. One of my pictures came out in the newspapers to report that about 40 people were rescued, who would have otherwise perished without food. Air Marshal M M Engineer of the Indian Air Force, who was in-charge of this operation, asked me for guides and possible routes. So I went in the first helicopter while Badal Mukherjee went in the second. The third helicopter did not return for a very long time. We were worried about it falling into the hands of the Chinese who were still around, but it came back safe.

Then, Jawaharlal Nehru came to Tezpur. Earlier, Indira Gandhi had come when Tawang fell but could not go forward and spend the night in Tezpur. Nehru wanted to evaluate the situation. There was a crucial meeting in the Circuit House. Officials from the Government of Assam were there. Rustom Beheramshah Vaghaiwalla (an ICS and Commissioner of Upper Assam {Hill Areas}) and P N Luthra (Commissioner of NEFA) were there. Jawaharlal Nehru sat and behind him was B N Mullik, Director of the Intelligence Bureau. I do not think there was any

Minister of the Government of Assam in that meeting. I cannot recollect seeing Fakhruddin Ali Ahmed in Tezpur. He and the other Ministers were in Shillong. In that meeting, there were no army people... none at all. There was only the civil administration staff of Tezpur and Bomdi-La, and some people from Delhi.

Then, when Jawaharlal Nehru asked, Rustom Beheramshah Vaghaiwalla gave his story. He gave a long story of how brave he was and how he controlled the traffic and this and that. Jawaharlal Nehru kept on listening. Then he asked me: "*Tum batao* Johorey *bhai, kya hua?*" (Johorey, you tell me what happened). He had been in Tibet with me earlier, so we shared a good rapport. He was in a very pensive mood. I said: "My administration worked till midnight, and when the Brigadier told me that he was leaving, I had no orders as to what to do. I had no War Book with me. I did not burn my treasury but brought that over, and evacuated the local leaders while some people were left behind in the jungles. We evacuated the hospital and gave all help to the army. The army could not say that it did not have porters or accommodation."

Then, the Commissioner, or someone present, mentioned that the view of the army was that the population had been subverted. I said: "Sir, I cannot accept this charge. The perception that the local population was subverted is totally wrong." I said that it was possible that an odd person turned a spy; how would one know? There was one Phuphu Dolma who used to sell tea. On my way, I also had tea in her tea-shop because there was no dak-bungalow in Chacko Camp. We knew Phuphu Dolma and her mother very well. She also used to sell carpets and many other things. People must have said that she might be a spy. That was totally wrong. Lord Emery's son became a much-hated 'Lord Ha Ha' when he was arrested by the Germans during World War II and made to sing their tune. When the Japanese occupied Port Blair in the Andamans, guards deserted while the British Commissioner was taken prisoner and tortured. I also stated that there was no question of my staying back and be taken a prisoner by the Chinese. So, I took my own decision to evacuate when the army said that it was not going to fight the Chinese. I thus told them my side of the story. Jawaharlal Nehru, in his wisdom, listened to the whole story and after the meeting was over, I was told to stay there, and not to go to New Delhi.

A very sad story relating to the evacuation of Tezpur was that of the Deputy Commissioner Dr Das. He was a PhD in agriculture. I was told that he went to see off his wife at the airport when she broke down seeing all the people fleeing to Calcutta. The tea-gardenwallas had booked the aircraft which would take them from Tezpur to Calcutta. There, she said to Dr Das: "You come with me to Calcutta and come back in the same aircraft." So, he apparently boarded the aircraft. By the time he reached Calcutta, all the flights of the civil aviation was frozen. There was fuel only for the Air Force planes, and nobody could fly to Tezpur. He was stuck in Calcutta. There was also the traditional Bengali and Assamese rivalry in Assam. It is an old one because after the partition of Bengal, parts of Bengal went to Assam and Bihar. All the intellectual elite, doctors and lawyers in Assam were Bengali-speaking. That was the reason. So, the Calcutta Press wrote in bold letters: "Assamese DC Runs Away". They did not realise that the Deputy Commissioner was a Bengali. The Assamese were very angry because they said: "*Amader* DC *Polaiche. Polaiche*" (our DC has run away). To my mind, the Deputy Commissioner committed a mistake. He should have applied for leave before leaving the station. A Deputy Commissioner, Collector or a District Magistrate was not supposed to leave his jurisdiction without permission. If he was on leave, hen the next man became the Deputy Commissioner. A district cannot be w thout a head. Just as the King never dies, the motto being 'Long Live the King', s also a district cannot be without a District Magistrate.

When the Tezpur-treasury was burnt, the government was very angry. In their wisdom, they sent a man from Shillong, Rana K D N Singh, as an Additional Deputy Commissioner of Tezpur. Singh – who was my batch-mate and a very good friend – came two days before the orders for evacuation of Tezpur came. We did not know who gave the orders to evacuate to the south of the Brahmaputra, but apparently the Union Home Ministry did. The orders were for the army, and not for the civil administration. People saw no sense in staying on when the army itself was going away. The Corp Headquarters at Tezpur was not a fighting force. It was like a Secretariat. A Secretariat could always be moved from New Delhi to Ghaziabad. It was not the operational entity.

So, when the people saw the Corp Headquarters vehicle moving out, they started running away. People from the tea garden also started leaving. Some people say that there was looting in the tea gardens. God knows whether it was true or false. I did not see any. Anyway, there were thousands of people in the Misamari Railway station, so I went to the station. The then Minister of Railways Shah Nawaz Khan, who was a former INA man and a hero of sorts, was also there. My driver said: "*Ham to ja raha hain abhi, yeh aap le jaiye army ke paas patrol hoga, ley jaiye*" (I am leaving, you take the car and get some petrol from the army). I went to buy petrol. The pump attendant said: "*Harey Ram! Aap kaha se aa rahe hain? Bomdi-La?*" That man, a purbaiya, then said: "*Main bhi bhag raha hu, kitne chahiye? Bhar lijiye*" (God, you are coming from Bomdi-La? Take as much as you want). I wanted to pay him. He said: "No money. I am the last man". So whatever petrol was there, I filled it up. There was a mental hospital. Dr Bordoloi let off the patients of mental hospital because they were without food. So, all the mental patients were roaming in the streets. It was complete chaos. The Tezpur administration had totally broken down. There was a state of panic in Tezpur. I stayed in the Deputy Commissioner's house because there was no place to stay. I also went to a tea garden, and met my British predecessor, Gregory, who was the secretary of the tea garden.

Return to Bomdi-La

The ceasefire took place on 21st November 1962. I only learnt about it after I reached Tezpur. Earlier, my plan was to leave the staff, treasury etc. and go back to Bomdi-La. But there was no going back because the Chinese were in occupation. I remained in Tezpur, and stayed in Deputy Commissioner's house because he had already left. There were all kinds of rumours about the Chinese presence here and there. The Chinese occupied Bomdi-La for about a month. I must have stayed for little more than 10 days in Tezpur before my re-entry to Bomdi-La. I used to meet my officers who were all there, waiting to go back and discuss the situation.

One fine evening, I was asked to return to Bomdi-La. We were told to arrange some transport and go back there. So my wife Sudha and I, one doctor named Dr Subhash Sarkar and one engineer named K L Mazumdar returned. The four of us represented the Government of India in Bomdi-La. The ceasefire was a unilateral announcement, and the Chinese must have indicated that we go in when they had pulled out. Under the circumstances, we did not return to Bomdi-La with our troops. If the Indian Army entered while the Chinese were still in Bomdi-La, there could be a fight. So, it made sense to ask only us to go there. It was a practical decision after I had opined that the population had not been subverted. A Deputy Superintendent of Police (DSP) of the Central Reserve Police Force, and a truck load of about 11 constables, accompanied us. I had a lot of cooked food prepared. As we reached the Tenga Valley, the DSP had a serious headache and felt very sick. So I asked him to stay back.

I used to fly a flag on my car. In those days, the District Magistrates were allowed to fly flags by the order of the Government of India because there were no Ministries in the North-East Frontier. With me were two other vehicles; one with some ration-items, food, etc. and another with the Press people – including George Verghese, Amal Home from Calcutta, Kasturi Srinivasan of The Hindu and Hildred Hill. Hill was an unusual journalist. He was suffering from polio and had a lot of gadgets on his leg, and so he walked with great difficulty. I was told in the morning that these people would also go in with my party. I was the leader of the party. I protested to Vaghaiwalla, the Commissioner. I said: "Sir, what is this? Why are you sending these Press people? On the one hand, you say that these people are against us and so we will get adverse publicity; and on the other hand, you want to take them when there is the tendency to show off." Vaghaiwalla replied: "No, the Parliament is very angry and wanted first-hand report. They have said that no amount of public handouts would do. So, the Prime Minister has decided to send the Press." I said: "Then you send your own Public Relations Officer." But the Commissioner said that was an order from New Delhi. "You let the Press people go and report whatever happened. Let the Press see for itself, even if it is too bad," he replied.

Had the population been subverted, we could be the first target. We had no protection against that eventuality. It could have been a rebellious situation because the public could say that we deserted them in their time of need, and now we come back because of a favour from the Chinese! I, therefore, wondered about the kind of reception I would get, because the Chinese had been there for one month. The people might demand that we go back. What would I do then? I cannot open fire. It will be a hopeless situation. I would have no access to higher authorities. I would be in the field. Who would I talk to? There was no Minister there; Jawaharlal Nehru was in New Delhi.

On reaching Bomdi-La, we went to my house, 'Kameng Sadan' – the Deputy Commissioner's house. By that time, the sun was just about to set. So the decision was taken not to hoist the flag at night. As we reached Bomdi-La just before the sunset, hundreds of people who were hiding in the jungles saw, from the hilltops about two kilometres away, the Indian flag moving along with four civilian vehicles. In the Deputy Commissioner's house, we found out that the furniture and all fittings had been looted. So, for the night we slept on the floor. That night, the Press folks wanted to cross over the Bomdi-La Pass. So I said: "Whoever wants to go can go there; but if you get lost, do not blame me. What is the use of provoking the Chinese? On their side, the Chinese might create some incidents. Anyway, you will see nothing at night. So, you are free to go, I cannot stop you. But I have given my advice already."

The next morning, my wife organised a general cleaning up of the kitchen area. There were chicken bones left by the Chinese soldiers on the night before, and so it was all very filthy. I had a Gurkha cook to clean up the place. He, like the other Gurkhas, was very neat. It was bitterly cold. The Gurkha did not light the *chullahs* (oven) without fully cleaning them. So as he put his hands in a *chulha,* he found what turned out to be gelatine sticks. Fortunately, I came to know and found gelatine sticks, detonators and plastic explosives in the iron stove of the kitchen. I cleared that *chulha*; as an old Sapper, my knowledge of engineering was helpful. In any operation, the first thing that the Sappers did was to either remove the mines or lay these if withdrawing. So very gently, we removed those explosives and put them aside.

In Bomdi-La town, many people came to my house. Old women were crying... weeping, touching my wife's hands and feeling me, as if I had come back from the dead. That was a very touching scene. I think some of them were even detained by the Chinese. I told them: "*Theek hai, ruk jao, aaram karo, shanti se, abhi to koyi Chinese nahin hai. Woh to bhaagne wale the* (it is alright, live without fear, in any case the Chinese were to run away). So they went back to their hamlets. The next morning, we had a flag hoisting ceremony. I hoisted the flag for which I had made sure to carry my *achkan* (official long coat).

I showed to the Press the hospital that the Chinese had damaged. I said: "A hospital should not be looted. I mean, one may take the medicines away, but why damage the syringes and throw them on the floor. I will never excuse the Chinese for the damage done to the hospital". They also looted the library and my personal property. They had taken away all my personal crockery, cutlery, a few of my dresses, my souvenirs, carpets and the utensils. Of the government furniture, only a few chairs were left behind. Similar was the case in the school. The Press must have written all these in their dispatches. When our own dispatches reached the MEA, the spokesman made it public, and noted as to how the Chinese devoured all the cows and pigs from our Government-run farms. Then the Chinese came out with a rebuttal. Whether they looted the villagers or not – I do not know – but all public property in Bomdi-La was looted. They did not find the treasury, but took away the generator.

Livestock of the people was taken away. But the People's Liberation Army followed the Communist methods. They made them sing the song 'East is Red', sang with them and filmed Tseng Tsaring, the *Gaonbura* (village headman) of Dirang Dzong in ceremonial dress. I later defended Tsang Tsaring. I asked: "What is the point of casting aspersions? If one were to be captured, what could one do? If a few people sang with the Chinese, they did so out of fear. Will they not be forced to sing the Chinese song?" Many of our ground-level administrative officials had continued to function in the occupied areas, but the Chinese had nothing to find faults with them as they normally do to discredit their opponent. We, of course, had every reason to complain that they intruded in our area; it was totally wrong and that was why they had to go back.

The Chinese were far-sighted. They claimed that they cleaned up the places they had stayed in inland, and made many such pious pronouncements. In one instance, when one female American reporter asked as to why the Chinese did not discuss their conduct, they came out with a Press statement stating that theirs was the only example in history when all the captured weapons had been returned.

After a few days, we went to Dirang Dzong to look for A V N Paul, my Additional District Magistrate. The Chinese, who were still there, handed over some weapons to us and in a very sarcastic way, said: "These are all the weapons that your American friends have given you, and you do not even know how to use these". The weapons were all packed. They took away some weapons and returned some. They also returned our prisoners. We received about 20 Prisoners of War, including one Lieutenant from the Madras Regiment. There were no men from the International Committee of the Red Cross there. Our men went there and brought the prisoners back.

Immediately after my return to Bomdi-La, I started getting hundreds of letters from various friends and relations of my officials, and also from the soldiers' relations. I sent many search-parties who brought all kinds of information. They also brought many weapons of dead Chinese soldiers; as in Walong, our soldiers, too, had fought very well and many Chinese soldiers were killed. My photograph had been published in the front page of the *Anand Bazar Patrika* of Calcutta with the headlines: "The Indian Flag Flies". For the first time, I found my name in a leading newspapers. Our generation was very conservative. We kept away from the Press. There was an official government spokesman. But for the first time, I was exposed to the Press. Meanwhile, our villagers and search parties had found many Chinese weapons when they were searching for our people, living or dead.

The Chief Justice of Assam High Court and Lalji Mehrotra's son, Justice Gopalji Mehrotra, came and camped up. I put him in the Circuit House. The Chief Justice visited the courts. Then, he wished to come to my house. I said: "Sir, I will come to you." He said, "No, no, I want to talk to you." He came with his wife. He said, "Look, my brother's son-in-law, Major Yogesh Tandon, has been missing. Please do something about it." I promised to do my best. There was also the request of the Mehtas for information about Lt Col B N (Baij) Mehta. Prior to China's attack, his wife had been invited by us to teach at the school where my wife Sudha was teaching; when she had helped in organising a road-side camp. Since Bomdi-La was a non-family station, I had obtained informal approval of the General Officer Commanding to invite her. But we could not find these officers.

Visitors Calling

After the war, many political leaders visited that area. It was the Prime Minister's decision to invite the political and other leaders to do so. Five very important leaders came. One was Jayaprakash Narayan who came with his wife,

Prabhawati. Narayan spent a night in Bomdi-La. Dr Rammanohar Lohia also came, spent a night, and went up to Dirang Dzong forward areas. Then, Pratap Singh Kairon came to Tezpur and met our own refugees from the villages of the forward areas.

Pratap Singh Kairon acted fast. He asked me: "Sahib, *aap ko kya chahiye?*" (what do you need?). I replied that it would be good if he sent some blankets. In my presence, he telephoned the Chief Secretary of Punjab. He said: "Please send by aircraft, a thousand blankets and a thousand *gutkas* (religious books of the Sikhs). The *Gutkas* were for the Sikh troops and the Sikhs living in Tezpur. Blankets were needed for the villagers in the forward area who had lost everything to the Chinese, and needed to be rehabilitated. Pratap Singh Kair then asked me to show him where the firing took place? I showed him the bullet marks on my house, the Circuit House and the damaged hospital.

Dr Rammanohar Lohia did a very funny thing. He wanted to break the 'Inner Line Regulations Act' of 1873. Tis Act was enacted by the British to protect their own interests, and stipulates that every citizen(even my wife, who was not a government servant) must take permission from the Government of India to visit the NEFA. We continued with it because we did not want a flood of cheap goods going there and ruining the tribal crafts, language, attire, dances, and their unique culture. The authority to grant permission was delegated to the local Deputy Commissioner. Lohia's point of view was that he was an Indian citizen who was going to Indian territory; if it was not a military area, why should he not be permitted to go? So the Deputy Commissioner said, "We will give you permit, no problem, Sir." He replied, "No, I do not want a permit. I am against that restriction on my movement." So he was technically arrested, given lunch and sent back. He was not ill-treated. Even today, like in Kashmir, the erstwhile NEFA(presently Arunachal Pradesh) continues to fall under the Inner Line Regulations.

On his arrival, I sent him to a village. I myself did not go. I said: "You talk to the villagers. If they say that the Government of India was bad, then they would tell you SO." So, he went to the school where the children chanted 'Gandhiji *ki Jai*' and '*Jai Hind*', and the National Anthem was sung. They put up a small play and then, they chanted 'Nehru *ki Jai*'. Lohia immediately asked: "*Kyon bolte ho,* Nehru *ki Jai? Main abhi ja raha hoon*" (why are you praising Nehru? I am leaving). One villager asked: "Where will you go? I will kill you if you leave. Nehru is our leader. *Tumi koi jabe, kete jabe, Ami katibo* (I am going to slice you)." He was very angry. The Block Development Officer (BDO) who was with him laughed and said to Lohia: "Please, do not take this seriously. They only know Jawaharlal Nehru and Mahatma Gandhi. For them, they are India. They are going to sing and you must listen. You cannot go. It would be an insult if you do so. The children of the village want to sing in your honour." When Dr Lohia returned to Delhi, he complained about this incident.

Jayaprakash Narayan was very sober and very dignified. I put him in the Circuit House. He stayed the night with us and met some local leaders. In the morning, his wife came and sat with me and my wife for a long time. He was not ill at that time, but he used to take *triphala* and others medicinal herbs. Apparently, he was quite happy because I got no feedback against the administration. Later, I asked Saran, one of very close relations of Lal Bahadur Shastri who was working on his thesis on Jayaprakash Narayan, to collect the notes he left in Bomdi-La.

I met Bimla Prasad Chaliha after my return to Bomdi-La. He was a giant of a man, a huge man! Chaliha was the Chief Minister of the whole of undivided Assam. Chaliha, Gopinath Bardoloi and other Assamese started talking loosely, saying that NEFA meant 'No Entry For Assamese'. They unnecessarily dragged us into a controversy because we had started spreading Hindi among the people of Tawang, who themselves actually wanted to learn the language in the first place. The Prime Minister had also mentioned that, and so, a controversy was fuelled. The Assamese view was very narrow-minded. Geographical isolation was there, no doubt, but one could not build a bridge on the Brahmaputra in a day. Influx of Bengalis added to some kind of alienation among them.

Chaudhury Ranbir Singh toured the area and said that people were happy there. He was one of the last few surviving Members of the Constituent Assembly,* and a great man. He was in Lahore Fort Jail in the undivided Punjab during the 1942 movement. Some years back, as the Chairman of the Freedom Fighters' Association, he had invited me to go with him to its session in Indore. At that time, the Congress Party was in power. C K Jaffer Sharief, the Minister for Railway, came to address the freedom fighters. It was a big conclave. I took active part in what was the last big conclave of the freedom fighters. I am also a permanent member of the Freedom Fighters' Successors Association.

General K M Cariappa also visited. He came to the Recruiting Centre and Cariappa gave a talk in his own way to all of us lined up. He asked the women to produce strong children. He was against family planning programme of the Government of India. He said: "*Bharat swatantra hai; aap log ek dam bachcha paida karo*" (India is independent, so get on with producing children). So, all the women laughed. Cariappa was extremely popular. A Coorgi brought up in a

---

* Chaudhury Ranbir Singh died on 1 February 2009 in Rohtak, report *The Hindu, 02.02.2009.*

Western environment, he used to talk more like an Englishman: "*Koich ko nahi jana, mar jayega ham log yaha, koyi chodke nahin jayega,*" (do not go anywhere, we will die but not leave)he stated. He may have given his impressions to Nehru orally.

Indira Gandhi, who had no position in the government, visited as a member of the Congress Party and the Citizens' Council. She came up to Dirang Dzong in a helicopter. I have not been able to see her report. Biwi Amtus Salam, a Gandhian worker, also came. When Indira Gandhi came to Dirang Dzong, Biwi Amtus Salam wanted her to inaugurate a Gandhi Ashram. Normally, there could be no such programme in a Gandhi Ashram amidst dead bodies lying all over the place. Anyway, we agreed. The Governor, Vishnu Sahai, and Indira Gandhi arrived in one helicopter. We welcomed them with burning incense sticks and a scarf each. When I asked the Governor, he said: "*Theek hai, karne do*" (let them do what they want). But as soon as Indira Gandhi reached the spot, she said: "*Nahi, nahin,* inauguration *nahin karenge*" (no, there would be no inauguration). At that moment, there was a sound of a shot being fired and a bullet went through one of my Magistrate's feet. I got very worried. Luckily, there was no Press on that day. Otherwise they would have said that somebody had shot at them. It was not a shot by any sniper. It came when a garbage dump which had unused bullets left in was set on fire. There was a dead soldier's helmet lying there and Indira Gandhi picked it up. I had no camera, else I would have taken a photograph. I do not know if somebody had photographed her at that time.

Indira Gandhi went up to Tawang and came back to Dirang Dzong. She was very touched and remained there for two hours. There Tseng Tsaring, the village headman, advised her: "Madam, you see, when a Juniper tree or a Pine tree grows between two boulders, whichever boulder is stronger, the tree takes that shape." He was the same person who had been accused of siding with the Chinese because he were shown dancing to Chinese propaganda song; the photo was published in their magazine, *People's War*.

New Delhi did not encourage or allow the journalists to visit the NEFA. The first journalist to visit Siang was Prem Bhatia. He came with the State Reorganisation Commission and visited the Balek group of villages in the interior of Pasighat. For some reason, that area was open to journalists and political leaders.

I think the mission of the Indian leaders was to assess the mood of the people because the charges were being levelled against the government that we had lost the war with China because of two reasons. One was that the 'Forward Policy' was a bad decision. One of the very senior officers of the Indian Police Service at that time was of the view that B N Mullik misled Jawaharlal Nehru on the

Forward Policy. But exactly what was the Forward Policy? It was just to show that India was entitled to open up a post office or a school in her forward areas. That was no provocation to the Chinese. If we claim Tawang to be our own, why should we not open a high school in Tawang? Earlier, before independence, only Tibetan was taught by the lamas. Then, after independence, people wanted to learn science and technology. So, it took about six years for the Forward Policy to get started. It was started in 1954 when India raised a special cadre, the 'Indian Frontier Administrative Service' (IFAS), for the administration of the frontier area. It was a policy in the right direction. We could not leave an administrative vacuum or keep the people of Tawang as specimen in a museum. How the area developed was again a separate question; it took so many years. But I am still convinced that the Forward Policy was the right decision. It was claimed to have offended the Chinese. In reality, the Chinese wanted some excuse to attack. Even if bits of Tibetan language and religion spreads to Himachal Pradesh, it does not make Himachal Pradesh a part of China. This was our view.

Generally, the visitors' assessment was that the public was not against the Government of India. The war was lost just due to bad tactics. This charge that the border population was disloyal was untrue. The same allegations had been made in Kashmir, where armed raiders from Pakistan were sent in September 1947.

The Henderson Brooks Report

When General Himmatsinhji who was sent to take stock during Sardar Vallabhbhai Patel's time submitted his report, he queried as to why India should claim upto McMahon Line or if the boundary should be delineated short of it. Surely, it was the right decision to cover the administration right up to McMahon Line, and the people chosen to undertake this task were volunteer civil servants. So, there was no complaint against the civil administration or the army. There was hardship and a number of people suffered there, but not as badly as in the state of Jammu and Kashmir. There was no opposition from the local people to any move by the army. In fact, local people, including students and women, were carrying loads of ammunition from the helipad to the army units before, during and after the war. They completely cooperated with the army. The tribals never questioned anybody.

We lost the war with China in 1962, and we should accept it. Why did we lose the war? It was not because the population was subverted or that we were capturing somebody else's territory; we were just not prepared. The Chinese started building up in Tibet in 1950, and then started moving ahead slowly. In 1956, they had deployed their Frontier Guards. We were also sending Survey Parties to our forward areas. One member of our Survey Party was killed in the Siachen border area. So, it is not a question of provoking. Had we left our forward areas in a vacuum, then the Chinese would have occupied those areas and we could not have dislodged them. After all, one has to defend his home from unauthorised entry and has to be alert to guard it – that is the analogy. In 1960 when I returned from Tibet, a decision was taken to set up a cantonment in Tawang. I recommended that we build not temporary huts but permanent ones –the former gave an impression that our stay was temporary. The Chinese are building pucca buildings on the other side. As to why the war was lost is a different issue. That is where the 'Henderson Brooks Report' comes in, which neither I nor anyone else can refute. Even the overwhelming superiority of the Chinese and as to what the central cause of the debacle was may be a point of debate. Brigadier J P Dalvi's book, *Himalayan Blunder,* gives his assessment.

The Government of India has not made the Henderson Brooks Report open to public. I have a feeling that he must have given a very damaging assessment of the Indian Army's performance. Lieutenant General Henderson Brooks arrived without any appointment and I met him. That was after the Henderson Brooks Committee was appointed. I knew that Committee's report was making rounds. He came to my office. I took him to the camp of the Assam Rifles. I said: "You talk to the *jawans* and ask whatever you wish to."

The Henderson Brooks Report must have brought about a professional analysis of the war, with no political side of it. The political angle was discussed by the people. Brigadier Dalvi and others criticised Jawaharlal Nehru. There were different views on V K Krishna Menon and his role. Being a strong Leftist and with professed leanings, did he underestimate the Chinese threat or did he inadvertently weaken our resolve? Did he express any doubt about our territorial justification based on custom, usage and the McMahon Line? Was he for the Chinese? God knows what he was for! Then, critics often quote Jawaharlal Nehru's words while leaving for Colombo: "I have told them to throw the Chinese out." Frankly, I have had no access to the Henderson Brooks Report. But whatever had come out in the Press, it was more of an attack on the policy of the government. So, I have a feeling that being a serving General, Henderson Brooks must have found holes in the planning for the war or in defending against the attack.

After the war, Lieutenant General S H F J. Manekshaw took charge. The first thing he said was: "Gentlemen, we are going to live, fight and die here. Every officer will carry 40 pounds on his back, his seven days' food. There will be no loot from the local villages." The Indians Army behaved extremely well with the local people. So there was no question of people going against us; I served in the North-East for 10 years, from 1954 onwards since the time the

Forward Policy started, and there was not a single case of highhandedness. The army, in fact, joined us in the work of development. They were very cooperative. When I asked our soldiers not to cut bamboos, they paid for every bamboo. But my advice to them was that they should not build houses with bamboos. Just as I used to get corrugated galvanised iron sheets and construct pucca buildings, they could show the Chinese that we were going to stay there in the NEFA as well. The local people should also know this.

Padma Shri and Time Out from NEFA

As an impact of the war, development of NEFA was accelerated. But it had to be a steady process. If the NEFA was suddenly let open, then there would be a flood of outsiders and adverse fallouts. Look at how the Americans had treated the Native Americans tribes; they nearly finished off the Red Indians. Our advisors on Tribal Affairs, Dr Verrier Elwin and Dr B S Guha, asked us be humane and have respect for the tribal languages, and their faith, and religion. But that did not mean that we would allow head-hunting or murder to go unpunished. So we had to work through the existing institutions and we were trying to do that.

I administered the area for three years, till September 1963, when I was transferred – to Afghanistan. I had finished my tenure at Bomdi-La for over three years. One can call it normal or abnormal that I was sent to the Secretariat in Shillong. IAS officers move between districts and Secretariat. So, I came to he State Secretariat in Shillong. That was when my Padma Shri award was announce. Then, because of my experience with the North-East Frontier tribes, the Ministry posted me to Afghanistan.

I had not been to my village and home in Badaun for many years, as there was no opportunity to do so. By this time, my father had died and my mother was in Allahabad. All my five brothers and five sisters had dispersed. They wrote me several letters when they saw my name in the newspapers. I really wanted to go and see them. So, I asked the Chief Secretary: "Why don't you give me leave for 30 days, I have not taken leave for three years." I was granted leave for 30 days. The award of Padma Shri was a high point in the achievement of a young officer from Badaun, a sleepy place nobody had ever even heard of. The people of my village pleaded to me: "Why don't you come here, you have your zamindari. Why don't you join politics?" I had become a small-time hero after the Padma Shri award. They knew about my father's law practice, and that I was a law student. One of my brothers had become a Civil Judge. So they felt that I could carry on the family tradition.

CHAPTER 9

THE AFGHANISTAN EXPERIENCE

Diplomacy in Afghanistan

I was posted to the Indian Embassy in Kabul after the war with China, and remained in Afghanistan from 1963 to 1966. That was the time when Prime Minister Daud Khan resigned, and King Zahir Shah took this opportunity to attempt a major constitutional reform. I served with two Ambassadors. The first was Jagan Nath Dhamija, who was the ambassador from 1960 to 1964 – at the time when Mohammad Daoud Khan was ousted.* Then, by the time I reached, Daoud was already out. I was the number two. I was the First Secretary of the Political Consul, and did all the political and commercial work. The second ambassador was General P N Thapar, the former Chief of the Army Staff (1961-62), who resigned after the China War debacle. General Thapar was given this assignment because Jawaharlal Nehru had qualms of conscience when the General was singled out for the debacle. This was told to me by Thapar himself. He remained the Ambassador in Afghanistan from 1964 to 1969. There were two major events during my tenure: One was the signing of the Indo-Afghan Trade Agreement, which was a major economic deal; the second was the visit of Dr Zakir Husain, who received a standing ovation wherever he went.

Politically, economically and culturally, India's stock was very high in Afghanistan. Dr Zakir Husain was the only foreigner invited to address the University of Kabul. Dr Zakir Husain had brought with him a brief draft of the speech he wished to deliver. He called and showed it to me at night. My wife and I had learnt Persian from a tutor, so I knew Persian but was not as good as

* On 10 March 1963.

Thadani(the official interpreter who also did corrections). We had two interpreters, but the second interpreter had left. Thadani, the full-time interpreter, was brilliant in Persian. Dr Zakir Husain took much pain and rehearsed his whole speech of about 45 minutes to leave a deep impression on his listeners. They gave him a standing ovation for several minutes.

There were only 22 embassies in Kabul at that time. The USA had a very large mission. In addition to diplomats in the embassy, there was a significant presence of the US Aid officials. The US Ambassador, John Milton Steeves, was an old India hand. He surprised me by greeting me in Hindustani! Apparently, he had taught in the American missionary colleges, of which the most famous were the Ewing Christian College (Allahabad), the Christian College(Madras)and Forman Christian College (Lahore). The Americans were friendly and forthcoming, particularly in asking us for technical staff in Aid programmes. They were also quick in responding to Jawaharlal Nehru's appeal to world leaders in the wake of Chinese aggression.

The first thing, we got a message and also the news that Khan Abdul Ghaffar Khan was coming to Kabul from his exile somewhere in Cairo. Instead of going to Pakistan, he decided to come to Kabul and remain in exile. He was a very distinguished national leader of undivided India, and a member of the Congress Working Committee. The South Block (Central Secretariat) located in New Delhi did not give me any instructions, but it was my own decision to go and meet him because he was my hero during the Quit India movement. Normally, as per protocol, an Ambassador would not call on a controversial visitor unless it was a State visit. I received him at the airport, and greeted him with a namaskar. Some Indians were also present. The Government of Afghanistan was not represented, but their ex-Prime Minister and some other leaders were present to receive him. King Mohammed Zahir Shah (1933-73) offered to accommodate h m in his own palace, but the Frontier Gandhi said: "No, I am just a faqir." The palace was 30 kilometres outside Kabul. Finally, he chose to stay in the family estate of King Mohammad Amanullah Khan (1926-29).

When I went to call on the Frontier Gandhi on an appointment, he was very warm and cordial, and immediately gave me time. He was seated on a *charpoy* (cot) and offered me tea in the true Gandhian style. He had a khadi *jhola* (satchel) with him. He took out tea leaves, made tea and offered it to me. He also gave me some biscuits and *roti* (Indian bread) to eat. He kept on asking me: "How is everything in India?" This was my second meeting with him. I first met him when I went from Allahabad to Pratapgarh Railway Station to meet him. He was on his way to Bombay in August 1942 to attend a meeting of the All-India Congress Committee, which took the decision on Quit India. When I reminded him of

Allahabad, he said: "Yes I remember." One of the main topics he talked about was the 'Partition', which he said was very painful. He was very sad and critical about the turn of events. He was, of course, an advocate of Pakhtoonistan. "We tried very hard to prevent the Partition. The Congress was in power there, and there was no question of a referendum. But *hamein to aapne bherion ke havale kar diya*" (you threw us to the wolves). Still, with all the suffering that he had gone through, there was no bitterness in him. He did not say anything against the British or the Pakistani regime, but observed: "*Unki mat mari gayi hai to kya kar sakte hain?*" (what to do when they have lost their mind?). I saw a kind of compassion in him. Normally, a man would be very bitter at his age. He was quite old and frail, but very pink in complexion, physically fit, and mentally alert.

He had come alone. His son Wali Khan (who was in exile), came later on, after the first few days. Next week, I met him again to tell him that Madalsa Narayan wanted to visit him. He said: "*Arey woh kitni badi ho gayi hogi ab to. Woh kya* politics *karengi? Unhone to sirf bakri charaane ka kaam liya tha.* (Oh, she must be all grown-up by now. What will she do in politics?She just took care of Mahatama Gandhi's goat). *Haan theek hai, usko bata dijiye main miloonga usko* (Yes, I will meet her)."

So, I informed Madalsa Narayan that she was welcome and fixed an appointment. When she came, I accompanied her and sat for an hour. Again, it was more of a goodwill visit. Then, my third meeting was when Pyarelal, the Secretary of Mahatma Gandhi, came to meet him. Pyarelal was not in politics at all. At that time, I also met Khan Abdul Ghaffar Khan's son Wali Khan, who had arrived by then. He remembered Sankho Chaudhuri* and asked about him. He did not talk about the revival of their party, the 'Khudai Khidmatgars'. But he was very critical, disappointed and hurt that the Indian leaders agreed to the Partition against his advice. Pakistan was lost, but he was very, very sad over that. But the circumstances were such. One would probably remember that when Jawaharlal Nehru was the Vice President of the interim government before independence, he visited Peshawar in the North-West Frontier. At that time, the powers that be arranged some kind of firings in that tribal area just to shake him up. The British tried to bomb certain areas to excite and intimidate the tribals from favouring India. Later, I was told that Wali Khan was invited to Pakistan.

Political Situation

King Zahir Shah ruled over Afghanistan from 1933 onwards. He became a constitutional monarch after the reforms initiated by him after Daud's resignation.

---

* Indian Sculptor (1916-2006).

Apart from being a monarch, he was also a very senior leader. The tribal loyalty was still there, and everybody respected him. He did not interfere much in the government.

Mohammad Daoud Khan was the Prime Minister from 7th September 1953 to 10th March 1963. When I reached Afghanistan in 1963, Daoud had resigned from his post. Although the political atmosphere was hot on the question of Pakthoonistan, he resigned because of pressure-tactics from Pakistan, and as I have a feeling, in connivance with the CIA who arranged that. I was told by the senior leaders that the King had decided to have a government of commoners, and none of his Cabinet Members were to be related to him. Of course, others among the nobility could be there. Daoud was the King's direct blood relation. He may have resigned on this issue or because of differences of opinion, or on the question of Afghanistan's neutrality.

As regards the idea of 'Pakhtoonistan', the Pakhtoons live on both sides of the Durand Line, and are of the same race, religion, culture and tribal affinities as the Mohmmadzais, Durranis etc. are. The Durand Line was an artificial partition effected by the British rulers of India to mark their area of influence, leaving Peshawar to the Indian Empire (now Pakistan), but the cultural cross-flow was least interfered by them. It was like the Mall Road in Simla which the British controlled, while on both sides, it was a princely territory. So Daoud had his doubts about the validity of that Line. But that was not the reason for his resignation.

The Pakhtoonistan question used to be discussed among the people. Every year, they used to have a flag-hoisting ceremony to mark the 'Pakhtoonistan Day', but it was not a public holiday. It was celebrated with pomp and show, and speeches were made openly. But after Daoud's departure, it took a back seat. It became a ritual, and agitation took a back seat except at the time of the India-Pakistan war of 1965. Badshah Khan was, of course, very clearly pro-Pakhtoonistan, but he did not say that a sovereign Pakhtoonistan was possible at that time. The Afghans wanted Pakhtoonistan not as an independent State, but as a part of Afghanistan because culturally, they are an overflow of the same stream. But that could be said about northern Afghanistan also, where the people had more in common with the Central Asians than with the inhabitants of the Kabul Valley.

Daoud was definitely a good friend of India. He was not a Communist as was borne out later on. The Americans got him killed as they thought he was a Communist while the Russians thought that he was pro-American. Daoud was a great admirer of Jawaharlal Nehru. I met Daoud once or twice. I first met him at the airport when he went to receive Khan Abdul Ghaffar Khan. He was not in the government but he came readily. That showed his attitude towards Pakistan.

Daoud was like a Marshal. We used to call him, 'Sir Marshal Daoud'. He certainly supported India, and voted with us in the United Nations.

There was no military coup. A new government was formed because the King decided to give power to the traditional 'Jirgas' (assembly of tribal leaders). Dr Mohammad Yusuf became the first non-royal Prime Minister from 1963 to 1965. His team comprised of young and educated people, some German-speaking, some French-speaking and one or two English-speaking. That was another unique thing about the Afghans. They were educated through French, German and English mediums. When they met in the Secretariat, they talked in their own language, of course. Dr Mohammad Yusuf was a commoner. He was an engineer and spoke German. His was a non-communal government. They started the developmental process and received aid from the United States of America.

A Constitution was framed. The country was reorganised into 24 provinces and Governors were appointed for each province. Two Jirgahs were made; namely the 'Wolesi Jirgah' and 'Meshrano Jirgah', the Lower and the Upper Houses respectively, and that formed the Afghan Parliament. These were like our Lok Sabha and Rajya Sabha. There werea few strong Leftist even – a female member named Anahita, and maybe one or two more. They administered constitutionally, and that was welcomed by all. But there was open dislike of Pakistan.

In the Pakistan embassy, there were no Bengali diplomats. There was one Bengali who was also sent away. There were no Pathans. There were only Punjabis. Even the military attaché was a Punjabi. One solitary Bengali clerk who remained had no diplomatic status. The Inter-Services Intelligence of Pakistan did not seem to exist. The Government of Afghanistan and its Press did not encourage any anti-Indian activities.

When the Pakistani flag was pulled downin Pakhtoon areas, Pakistanis tried to pull down the Afghan flag in the Afghan Consul General in Peshawar. Kabul retaliated by being hostile to the Ambassador of Pakistan. In fact, the Pakistani Ambassador moved about in our car with the Indian flag flying many times – he was that frightened. There was a complete social boycott; no barber would go to the Embassy of Pakistan, and water and electricity was cut off. The Pakistani Ambassador was not invited to any functionuntil Dr Mohammad Yusuf came to power. Later on, Pakistan changed their Ambassador and replaced him with a Pathan. When they introduced Urdu in the University of Peshawar, Pakhtoon students were very agitated. They said: "Our language is Pushtu whereas Urdu is a foreign language. You can teach Punjabi, you can teach Bengali, but why Urdu?" So, there was some clashes between the Pathan students and the government police. That was the situation.

Talks were going on for demarcation of the Sino-Afghan border. The pre-Partition India, China and Afghanistan border tri-junction, and the Wakhan Corridor – an area that lies between India and Afghanistan – was delineated in favour of Afghanistan. When the Chinese delegation came, the coordinates had to be given. So, because of our border disputes and at our instance, the Afghans made a statement on the geographical coordinates of that tri-junction, implying that the adjacent area still belonged to India – even if, defacto, it was with Pakistan. That shows their deference to our own sensitivity, and significantly showed the depth of our relationship. Although it was supposed to be a quiet diplomacy, our friend Humayun Kabir came and gave a ress statement saying that the Afghans were our friends, and cited the Wakhan example. The Afghans were a little upset about it. In those days, they had to maintain a balancing act. They had to live with Pakistan. They had to live with the USA. American money was coming via Pakistan.

Dr Yusuf's administration was effective but neutral. He did not resent any country. His government started off in a big way. The American Aid Mission was increased. The Russian aid also started pouring in. The sugar mill was made by them. There were very few good roads in Afghanistan. There was one highway to Kandahar, another to the Soviet frontier and the third connected Peshawar. The Solang Tunnel towards the Russian frontiers was built with the Russian aid. The Kabul airport was made with Russian help. The road was also financed by the Russians. The famous Kandahar International Airport was built entirely with the assistance from the USA.

Indian assistance came through a Technical Assistance Programme. The Government of Afghanistan requested for 16 teachers from India; when they arrived, there was a lot of anti-India write-up in *The Peshawar Times*, but not in Kabul. Kabul welcomed them. They openly asked us to send many more. We rained their census workers and for the first time ever, a census was attempted to elp in planning based on statistical figures. The literacy rate was very low. Univer ity of Kabul was formed at that time. They did not have any foreign students or oreign teachers, but they started the education of girls – little girls started going to school for the first time. One Indian male teacher, a short statured Mr Sharma, wa quite upset when he was posted to a girl's school. I consoled him: "You sho ld not worry. They have reposed so much confidence in us that they have invit d male teachers to teach their girls." Indians were the first of the male teachers in girls' schools. It displayed a great faith in us, and was an honourific act.

When Jawaharlal Nehru visited, the Afghan women discarded the *purdah* (veil). Jawaharlal Nehru was accompanied by Indira Gandhi as his daughter and hostess. King Zahir Shah decided that in the state banquet, Queen Humaira

Begum and Indira Gandhi would be on the same table. Words were passed on to all the officers to bring their women. When a Head of State comes on a visit, everything is laid down according to protocol as to who would come and who would not come. The Afghan women chose to discard the purdah and came wearing western dresses. Women of royalty, of course, never had any purdah. They attended all the functions and sent their girls to schools.

Villages, in any case, never had the purdah system; it was followed only when the village women came out to sophisticated societies, never in the villages. It was the same as our Rajasthan, where women worked in the fields but they put on a *ghoongat* (veil) only when they came out to high society. Afghanistan's village women used the *burqa* (full body covering), which they call *chadri*, when coming to the city. Our Afghan maid used to put on the *chadri* when she entered the city. When I asked her as to why she did it, she replied that it was to hide poverty. They were so poor that when they came to the urban areas, to the sophisticated cities, they put on the *chadri*. Once inside the house, no *chadri* was used. It was normal to find women working in the field or tending the animals. In the bazaar, one could hardly find any woman with *chadri*.

The Press was free, and used to be critical of the government. Kabul Times was the only English newspaper back then. The Press Corps invited Indian journalists, O P Kalhan and (later on) Promila Kalhan, for example, to work for their Press. Then there were other newspapers like 'Parcham', which was bi-lingual. The Afghans called their Persian language 'Dari'; the intonation was not quite different from Iranian Persian in accent and pronunciation. Persian taught in India is the Iranian version.

There was no violence and no fighting in Afghanistan. There were 40,000 Hindu and Sikh families in Kabul city. They were Afghan nationals of Indian origin. They would come to India on pilgrimage on Afghan passport. Trade was very common, despite the fact that Pakistan tried to create some trouble on the passage of Afghan goods to India. At first, there was the traditional barter trade between India and Afghanistan. Some goods came to Amritsar in transit, and some amount of tea, cloth and other things used to go to Afghanistan. It was a total barter system at play. Most of the Afghan Hindus, Sikhs and Muslims used to come with their carpets and dry fruits. They used to come right from the pre-Partition days, and carried their sales drive right up to Calcutta and beyond. When going back, they would take home sacks filled with tea and cloth. From that side, they would bring carpets, *badam*, *angur* and *kishmish* etc. Then, the 'Kabuliwalas', as the Afghans were popularly called, also started lending money here. They were smart traders who used to lend money and collect it back with interest. This was a traditional trade, active for more than 100 years. Rabindranath Tagore's moving story, *Kabuliwala*, had been written in that context.

Then we signed an agreement at the behest of the Reserve Bank of India. The Afghans protested in the beginning. They said that they did not even know how to write a cheque. Then, we had a full trade agreement with them. In fact, the Government of India gave them aid for a hospital when the Government of Pakistan refused to allow the steel to be transported. It was difficult for us to import steel from Europe via USSR. I do not know how they managed it, but it was done. The economy of Afghanistan was dependent on trade; their major source of income came from export of hides and skins to Europe. Just as we have Indian tea auctioned in Berlin, Western Europe and the UK, fur and carpets used to be exported to Europe and India. Afghan *mewa* (sweet meat) was also imported by India.

In short, the Afghan economy was well on the way to development. Neutrality was paying them. It was a competitive co-existence for the two rival blocks. If there was a certain number of American experts, there would be the same number of Russians too. The Afghani government maintained equidistance from both, and were very choosy in accepting economic aid. The King was, perhaps, holding the purse and may have been behind the scenes, but Daoud was still influencing. But there was no such signs. They did not ask for American or Russian arms, and they continued like this till much later on.

Of course there was utter poverty in Afghanistan, but the price of bread was very strictly controlled. The poor Afghans could afford meat only once in a blue moon. Otherwise, they would eat naan, *angur* (grape) and *kishmish.* The Afghans are healthy people, and there was no such devastation which one sees now. There was freedom of movement, and there was no domination of the mullahs.

The Cold War

The Cold War was going strong in the West. But in Afghanistan, the Russians and the Americans were working together in harmony. They had divided their spheres of influence. The Russian workers were in Mazar-e-Sharif in the northern areas. The Americans were in the western areas adjoining Iran. The Russians, because of their socialist way of life, mixed with the locals more frequently and endeared themselves to the Afghans. The Americans did not do that. They had their own water and other inhibitions; for example, the American engineers would move about in their air-conditioned caravans, and would hardly mix with the Afghans. But the Russian workers would share the *naan* with their Afghan labour. They did not bring in air-conditioned caravans. The Russians were there as soldiers, workers, engineers, technicians and other people. The Americans gave a number of scholarships to the Afghans. They would invite some young Afghans to the USA, train them and bring them back. Some Afghans came back with American wives. There was a very big US Aid Mission there. The Russians did not have a mission like that, but they were working on the Solang Road Project, for which they brought in heavy machinery and skilled workers.

I did not notice any discontent among the Afghans against the USSR or the USA, but they did not mind debating contentious issues. The Americans used to say that the Afghans were neither friendly with them nor with anyone else, but worked for their own interests; the 'Kabuliwalas' were perceived to be very cunning. Later on, differences might have developed, and a large number of people turned to Communism. But for the first five to six years, there was no danger to Daoud's regime at all. When Daoud was out of power, he did not scheme against anybody.

My relation with the Soviet Embassy was good. The Russians were very friendly with us. I met Leonid Ilych Brezhnev in Kabul. We greeted each other, but there were no formal talks. He expressed his point of view and offered any help we wanted. He could speak in Urdu. He had been a diplomat, and visited Delhi later on as well. When Brezhnev and the Russians delegation came, the Afghans organised a game of *Buzkashi*, which resembles Polo. The carcass of a goat is kept in the middle and both the teams come charging, and whoever can lift that carcass scores a point. It is a very tough game, tougher than Polo.

All the equipment in the Afghan Army were Russia-made. The Americans did not bring any arms; or the Afghan did not accept arms from them – one does not know. That was why people believed that Afghanistan was moving more and more towards the USSR, and that was the reason for the USA to think of counter-coup. That was very unfortunate. All the leaders whom I knew were all neither pro-West nor pro-East; they were completely neutral. Maybe a few young people were Leftists. They used to say that Afghanistan was like Switzerland, a land-locked country; that they were non-aligned and had no other policy.

The Afghans always voted with us. There were very good exchanges between India and Afghanistan, despite the creation of Pakistan. Every year, the Pakhtoonistan Day was celebrated in Afghanistan. They never gave up their claim over Pakhtoon areas. If that claim was diluted under the influence of the West, the Russians supported them. Afghans used to say that there were only two countries: Ariana, that is, the Afghanistan of the Oxus, and Hindustan, beyond the Indus. The King's uncle Shahab Ali told me that Pakistan was a creation of British imperialism. King Zahir Shah, of course, kept away from politics, but the Foreign Minister used to openly say the same. That was why they were friendlier with us and very hostile towards the Pakistanis. But the Americans were helping Pakistan to prevent its going the Russian way. Pakistan became a member of the Western power blocs, namely, the Middle East Treaty Organisation (METO) or Central Treaty Organisation (CENTO) and South-East Asia Treaty Organisation (SEATO). The Afghans did not join these blocs. That was why the Americans thought that the Afghans would go the Communist way. Then, the Russians, in their stupidity, attacked Afghanistan. While the Afghans had welcomed them earlier as helping friends in development, they resisted the Russian invasion very fiercely with American help.

The Indian Connection

India had very good relations with Afghanistan, and offered whatever help the Afghans wanted. We sent them teachers and made them a hospital. Dr Zakir Husain, the Vice President, signed a Technical Assistance Agreement with Afghanistan as well. We trained their census workers and nurses. Although the Americans had offered to train them, they would not send their female staff to the USA; not bilaterally though, otherwise whenever any invitations came from the West, they used to accept those. They also sent delegations to the United Nations. Despite the fact that there was Pakistan in between, our relations with Afghanistan continued to grow.

Dr Rammanohar Lohia, a Member of Parliament, visited and met some Afghan leaders as well. His visit was, of course, very interesting. He immediately recognised me. Sarcastic as ever, he remarked: "*Aapne to hamari giraftari karwai thi* (you had me arrested). But I will come and have lunch with you, I will not call on the Ambassador." I said, "No, no, how can you ignore the Indian Ambassador?" Parvathi Krishnan, a Member of the Lok Sabha and a card-holder of the Communist Party of India, also visited.

Another distinguished visitor was Kamaladevi Chattopadhyay, who was the Chairperson of All India Handicrafts Board. She held the rank of a Cabinet Minister. We went together to Ghazni as the Governor there had invited us to lunch. He was an Afghan Sikh, a tall fellow. So, when we went to Ghazni with the Indian flag flying, and the Governor came out to receive us. When the driver got down, the Governor embraced him and asked: "Bhag Singh, where have you been all these years?" Actually, Kamaladevi said: "Are we the VIPs or have we come to a wrong place?" I replied: "No Madam, this is their tradition; they embrace each other, and eat together." The Governor embraced our driver, who was an Afghan Sikh national and a strict vegetarian. We sat on the floor on the carpet to eat; for Bhag Singh, pure vegetarian food was served at the other end. The

Afghan Governor and Kamaladevi Chattopadhyay sat opposite each other on the floor, and had their tea and *khana* (food). They talked about Afghan handicrafts. She wanted to see and get some samples of the handicrafts. She saw their carpet--making centres. In fact, every home was into making carpets. She was very well-received.

P N Sapru came as the leader of a cultural delegation. He was of heavy built, 75 years-old and could hardly walk. The Afghans were very impressed. Indians were their very good friends, and so, they commented, "See how they respect the elders in India, just the way we do!"

I remember the visits of Madalsa Narayan, Shriman Narayan and Kamalnayan Bajaj. Madalsa is the daughter of Jamnalal Bajaj, and Kamalnayan Bajaj is his son. Shriman Narayan was an Aggarwal from the Uttar Pradesh. Jamnalal was from the famous Bajaj family, and was a disciple of Mahatma Gandhi. Kamalnayan Bajaj came twice, because he was a friend of Jagan Nath Dhamija. They were together in Cambridge, besides being politically linked. He used to come and stay with the Ambassador. Other people did not stay with the Ambassador, but Kamalnayan did. He had the habit of inviting a number of Gujaratis, who were basically vegetarians. He used to organise parties and invite a few people, and make *bhelpuris,* 10 to 15 types of *churan chutneys*and Gujarati food in general. He would himself prepare one or two dishes. He would also invite the Afghans, who would be quite amused to see the fare.

In 1965, we got information that the Afghani government had invited Prime Minister Lal Bahadur Shastri to visit Afghanistan on the way back from Tashkent. All arrangements were made. In fact, the Afghans went out of the way to welcome him, and gave him the status of a Head of the State. Normally, there are laid-down number of flags to fly for a Prime Minister, Head of the State, a President or a King. In this case, it was decided to fly flags as for a Head of State's visit. In deference to his wishes, the Afghan King even arranged a completely vegetarian dinner. It was a very good gesture. The Afghans called up and asked my wife whether our cook could take charge of the kitchen of the King and buy all provisions that we needed at their expense. So, we agreed and made the arrangements. They even got *paan* from Benaras, *barfi,* sweets and bananas, and all kinds of eatables.

We advised them that the Prime Minister would not like to climb steps. In another very noble gesture, the King agreed to come down from the podium to receive Prime Minister Shastri. That caused a lot of furore among the Pakistanis there. They asked as to how it was that they did not invite President Ayub Khan who was also in Tashkent. When my Pakistani counterpart asked me, I said that

I did not know about it. He was quite surprised. They were quite peeved because it showed the Afghans' closeness to India. Whether the Russians influenced them or if it was their own decision, I cannot say. But the fact was that they invited us while in Tashkent, the Russians played a major role. So, all the arrangements were made. Lal Bahasur Shastri was to be received at 8 O'clock in the morning with all the pomp and ceremony, and a two-day programme was organised. But suddenly at 3:00 a.m., the news of his death came. It was a great shock. The Afghans felt very sad. They admired him greatly. They had read about Lal Bahadur Shastri's simplicity, which impressed them to no end.

We used to celebrate our Republic Day. Afghans did not call theirs as the 'Independence Day' but as 'Jashn-e-Istiqlal', which meant that they had always been free. We were one of the few foreign nationals who were invited for their cultural programmes. The Pakistanis were never invited. The German and the Indian cultural teams were invited, but not the Chinese or the British. The Afghans, for some reason, admired the Germans. They would also invite the French to a programme of Western and Indian music. Then, the King would inv te the Indian performing artists to the palace and not the others. The Indian artis s were always welcome. Vilayat Ali Khan, while he was alive, used to go there wice a year. He taught sitar to the King's son. Amjad Ali Khan, the sarod playe , also used to come. Fayyaz Khan had been there earlier. Indian cultural tea s were very well-respected and given a lot of gifts. In fact, the King gave one Merc des to Vilayat Khan. When he had arrived in India, there was a problem bec use of heavy customs duty. But the King's gift, one cannot refuse.

Many Indian cultural delegations came at that time. Normally, not many people understands classical music, even in India. But in Kabul, when sitar was being played or a programme of classical music was organised, many of the top people came to listen even if it was snowing. Siddheswari Devi, the famous classical singer, and Yamini Krishnamurti, the famous Bharatnatyam dancer, performed there. The Pathans would sit very quietly, in a verydisciplined manner. I remember, in Allahabad, the moment Harivansh Rai Bachchan came on stage, everybody behaved nicely. But when serious classical musicians performed, students would walk out. But the Afghans and King Zahir Shah himself had great love for classical music. Their own music was more like the Indian classical music. There was Pathan folk music and dance. Among the performers, there was no *purdah*, and boys and girls would be merrily dancing and singing away.

The Afghan King's brother once told me that there were only two countries: Oxus and Indus. The Oxus was Afghanistan or Ariyana, and Indus was Hindustan. And he also said that Britain, an imperialist State, had created the State of Pakistan wedged between Afghanistan and India,which would create more trouble. And that is happening now; there is trouble in Baluchistan. The Afghan King's uncle Badshah Shahab Ali had been to India before, and we had a very good relationship. That was the time when Khan Abdul Ghaffar Khan came, and the war of 1965 with Pakistan took place. He said that he was sure that in 1947, some tribal leaders were misguided by the British officers to invade Kashmir for loot and plunder. At the time of the War of 1965, he assured me and said, "Please tell the Government of India that not one Afghan would support Pakistan." The Afghans remained totally neutral. When Jawaharlal Nehru died, they had *fateha* (the short first sura of the Koran, used by Muslims as an essential element of ritual prayer) in all the mosques. They came to the embassy to condole Nehru's death. Shahab Ali said very clearly that Afghanistan and India were neighbours. Later on, things went off track.

Religious Harmony

There were no religious fanatics then, unlike the Taliban who destroyed the statues of the Buddha. Every village had a mosque, but no fanatics. I was invited to visit the Kabul museum, where I saw the statue of the Kushan Emperor Kanishka with a fiddle; his dress was like a modern *dhoti*. The museum had a number of objects of Gandhara art. Also, I had visited Bamian Valley, which was shown in all the tourist literature. Afghan tourist literature stated that Afghanistan was the land of the Aryans. 'Ariana' was the local name. They always said that the *Rig Veda* was composed 40 kilometres North of Kabul, in a city called Kapisa, and that it was the mother of all civilisations.

The Afghan history books as well as the Afghan tourist literature were full of complete pictures of the Gandhara art, their lineage and their traditions. They used to say that the oldest Fire Temple was also there, and Zarathushtra and his Parsees were called 'fire worshippers'. That is why the area north of Kabul and the Bamiyan Valley was called'Mother of Civilisations'. The Afghans used to say that they were ruined because of Genghis Khan and his grandson, Kublai Khan – founder of the Mongol Empire as well as the Yuan Dynasty in China. These marauders from Central Asia came and destroyed their civilisation. The Afghan King Zahir Shah used to say: "There is no difference between you and me, between an Indian and an Afghan. When the Arabs came, the original inhabitants left Afghanistan and went to India and those who could not go, became Muslims." The Afghans were very critical of the Arabs, who came and destroyed their ancient culture.

There was an Italian Professor, Professor G. Tucci, who had earned notoriety. When I went to the Kabul museum, I asked for some expert sources, historical records and copies of manuscripts. While passing through Pakistan, I visited Taxila, where I saw statues being dug up and lying in the open. Children used to sell them as souvenirs. Professor G. Tucci has done a lot of work on the Kabul museum. So I enquired Professor Muhammad Ali, an eminent Afghan historian, about him. Professor Muhammad Ali reacted very strongly. He said: "That fellow is a plunderer. He took away many of our art-objects and manuscripts, and did not even pay for them. He used to bribe the village chowkidars to obtain them." That way, many objects of art have found their way into museums in the West. Professor Tucci played a double role. Of course, what artefacts remained were very badly damaged.

Gandhara Buddhist objects of art were kept in the Kabul museum. The area from Taxila onwards is called Gandhara, where there are many objects of art. There is even a statue in full figure of Lord Vishnu. The Afghan staff took great care of the objects of art. One of my own servants used to sweep with great reverence the room where we kept an idol of Lord Ganesha. So, they had no inhibitions. Of course, they observed their own fasts and other rituals as devout Muslims. But there were temples and mosques side by side in the streets of Kabul.

The Afghans were always very proud of their Aryan ancestry. They would say that they were the pure Aryans. The Iranians claimed that they were the oldest Aryans. When Emperor Mohammad Reza Shah Pahlavi of Iran (1941-79) was celebrating the 2500th Anniversary of the Persian Empire, we Indians were also invited. He was given the title of 'Arya Mehr', meaning'Moon of the Aryans'. The Afghans objected to that title. They would say that their civilisation was older, and that Dari was the name of the language of the Afghans. They said that Iranians had become Westernised in culture.

Iran and Afghanistan never got on well together. There were no boundary disputes between Iran, Afghanistan and Pakistan, but there was a cultural dispute because Mohammad Reza Shah Pahlavi, the Shah of Iran, was completely Western. The Afghan King also used to wear Western attire but he maintained his neutral stance, whereas Iran was fully in the American camp. Afghanistan was not in any camp, and that was another common aspect of India-Afghanistan relations. Iran and Pakistan, both had joined the Western defence pacts.

Afghans were very chary of Zahiruddin Muhammad Babur (1483-1531). Bagh-e-Babur, as he was called, was buried in Kabul, but none of their tourist literature gave any importance to him. However, the Indians liked to visit Babur's mausoleum, and the place where Subhas Chandra Bose had stayed during his escape to Europe. Bose's place was well-kept. When I asked them why they disliked Babur, they said that Babur was not an Afghan, and that he had displaced them. To them, Babur represented the hordes of uncivilised people from Central Asia.

There were Jews in Kabul as well. On the streets, one would find all currencies, and the black market was called the 'Azad Market', meaning free market. The rates in Azad Market used to be published in *The Kabul Times.* There were 22 families of Afghan Jews who spoke Hebrew. I do not know where they camefrom, but they were free to do trade. They were in money exchange business, and they used to display their coins on the streets from where one could buy any currency freely – Deutsche Mark, Francs, Pound, Sterling, Dollars, and all other currencies. It was a strange phenomenon. Nobody would steal and there was no cheating. Anybody could take any currency, give a cheque and go. In fact, I asked one Jew: "How do you know that the cheque would not bounce?" He said: "No, it never does. We have hardly had one or two cases. In 99 per cent of the cases, nothing has ever gone wrong." People used cash in the open market rates, and got more money for the currency. There was no Central or Reserve Bank. Later, they invited the Indian bankers.

In Daoud's time and even earlier, the Finance Minister of Afghanistan was always an Afghan-Hindu. I met the last Finance Minister, Rais Hukum Chand. He was given a title of 'Rais', which meant nobility or high rank. Then there was a Vyapari Sangh (a Merchants' Association), and the Chamber of Commerce where most of the members were Hindus. They would mix very freely – the Hindus, the Muslims and the Sikhs, and except the Sikhs, all would wear their turbans in a definite style. The Afghans would freely come to Bombay and send their children to study there. The Taliban was a phenomenon that came much later. It started off from Pakistan itself. Actually, some of them were Muslims of Indian origin who went to Pakistan and started the menace. In Pakistan, they are still called 'mohajirs' or refugees, and treated with great suspicion. I think that the students and the refugees who have fled to India would go back one day, and the Afghan women would come out openly against Taliban barbarism. At the present moment, the Pakistani elements are still there, and the years of devastation that Afghanistan has seen is a very long period to be forgotten soon.

Pakistani Tricks

Fikret Belbez, the Ambassador of Turkey, was a very handsome, young man. Turkey was a mildly Muslim country at that time. In fact, it was the Turkish First Secretary Kaya Toperi who came to my house and asked: "Are you meeting the King tomorrow?" I was the Charge de Affairs, our Ambassador being away. He said, "My Ambassador and all the Muslim Ambassadors are meeting the King." I said, "I have not receivedan invitation, and I cannot just go uninvited flying the Indian flag. Then, I swung into action. I rang up the Afghan Foreign Office.

It transpired that the meeting was in the context of the India-Pakistan War of 1965. They had planned it in such a way that the Pakistanis and Ambassadors of Muslim countries would, on some excuse, come to meet the King and make a statement that they had the King's confidence. After all, out of 22 Missions, nine countries were the so-called Muslim countries. Pakistan always tried to cultivate Saudi Arabia, Turkey, Iran, Pakistan, Indonesia, and others into a substantial 'Muslim Bloc'. The Afghans did not like that. So, this was their trick to come out in support of Pakistan, the interpretation being that the Government of Afghanistan was supportive of Pakistan in the 1965 War against India.

I was able to meet Mansoor Shahab Ali, the King's uncle in the Royal Household. King Zahir Shah had nothing to do with the government and his engagements were made by the Royal Household. So, I told him about Pakistan's intentions. I said that I should also join the delegation as we had a very large Muslim population. In any case, I would exercise my right. And if I was not to join that group, then I would like to seek an interview with the King and explain my country's point of view. Immediately, Mansoor Shahab Ali advised the King to cancel the appointment.

The King cancelled that appointment and stated that whoever wanted to, could meet the Foreign Minister; not even the Prime Minister would meet them. So the whole strategy fizzled out and nothing came out in the Press. I must, with all due respect, acknowledge the Turkish position at that time. Turkey was a Muslim country. Kaya Toperi need not have told me anything. He must have had pro-India feelings. We became very good friends.

The Pakistanis were trying every bit to discredit India. For example, when the Government of Afghanistan asked for 16 teachers from India, *The Peshawar Times* carried the news that the Hindu blood was being pumped into Muslim veins. This was just to excite the people. But it did not have any effect. As I said earlier, the Afghans even invited our teachers to teach in schools, exclusively for girls in *purdah*. Except Saudi Arabia, nobody put any credence on that propaganda. Yusuf Al Fuzan, the representative of Saudi Arabia, was an ex-Consul General who was an Arab from Bombay. He was a complete lackey of Pakistan. He hardly knew any English and whatever the Pakistani First Secretary(my counterpart) advised, he would to do that. For example, when Jawaharlal Nehru died, all the embassies put the flag at half-mast. The Saudi Arabians did not do so. My counterpart from Saudi Arabia came to me and told me the same evening, "Please do not misunderstand Saudi Arabia. There is the *Ayat-e-Quran* in the Saudi Flag: *La Ilaha Illalah Muhammadur Rasurullah* [There is no God but Allah, Muhammad is His Messanger]. That is why our flag is never half-mast. We have a tradition, the flag never goes down because of the *Ayat.*" I said, "Fair enough." Everybody, all the Ambassadors, the Leader of Opposition, the ex-Prime Minister of Afghanistan – who was the first to come – and all members of the Royal family came to sign our Book of Condolence. That showed their regard for Nehru. Similarly, the Afghans showed great regard for Lal Bahadur Shastri. They flew more Indian flags than his status required during the preparation of his visit. These are the nuances of protocol in which a country expresses the depth of its friendship.

Then, at the end of my tour of duty, I was nominated to attend National Security and Strategy Course at the National Defence College, New Delhi.

CHAPTER 10

CIVIL SERVICE IN SIKKIM

The National Defence College

After my return from Afghanistan in 1967, I spent a year in the National Defence College. It is a prestigious institution where one learnt and discussed higher strategy. It was an inter-services course which included IAS and Indian Foreign Service (IFS). The major thrust was on the higher defence management. While 'Talibanisation' was nowhere on the scene at that time, there was a clear feeling that some kind of Islamic fundamentalism was building up. The Americans were encouraging it through defence pacts like South East Atlantic Treaty Organisation (SEATO) and Central Treaty Organisation (CENTO). It fact, Air Marshal Idris Hasan Latif who was the leader of our group, having been posted as an Air Attache to the USA, said that the Americans were supporting and encouraging those pacts. They did it to keep the Russians down. The Central Intelligence Agency (CIA) did all the funding, as they did in Tibet. The Tibetans are a peaceful people, a small nation. They could not have fought the Chinese. I stead of following the Gandhian method, they tried to do it in the CIA and Am rican way. It was the Americans who created the Islamic bloc, and today they ar-e ripping the world apart.

The course curriculum consisted of an interplay of Asian politics, political strategy and war-games when I acted as the Prime Minister of China, and thought about ways to defeat India. Another officer-student acted as the Prime Minister of Pakistan. China and Pakistan were the two major issues there. The role of the US was another major issue. During my tenure, we never allowed the Press to come in. It was an academic atmosphere, like that in University of Delhi; one expressed one's own views. One group had very much predicted that the Americans would make up with China faster than we thought. There was also a view that China was not our enemy. One feeling was that Pakistan was the enemy.

After the National Defence College course, my posting to the Ministry of Defence was announced. Sudhakar Ranade, who was the Joint Secretary in charge, had forwarded a list of officers who were to be posted to Delhi. My name was on that list. I got the letter of my posting one month before the termination of the course. The decision on postings was taken in the Ministry of Defence, at the level of the Deputy Secretary. But some officers from Central Civil Services represented that it was their turn to be posted in New Delhi. Then I was told that it was cancelled, and I was to report to the Home Ministry. That was how the inner wings of bureaucracy worked. I was not bothered. Knowing Jawaharlal Nehru and many others in power, I had all the opportunities; but my civil service ethics never allowed me to ask for any posting.

Back to Civil Service

So, I reported to the Home Ministry, which then posted me to the Department of Social Welfare. I was given a charge of Backward Classes Welfare and made a Director of the Central Zone, but posted in Shastri Bhawan. My job was to monitor the funds given for the welfare of the Backward Classes. The Scheduled Tribes had special attention, mainly for their educational progress. The Central Zone consisted of Uttar Pradesh (UP) and Madhya Pradesh (MP). At that time, it so happened that both the states were ruled by non-Congress governments. Sitting in Delhi, one really could not monitor the schemes, and although I was born there, I was not familiar with all of UP. So, I took a tour of MP and UP. Even South India was given to me because there were not enough officers. It was not a very glamourous post.

The weakness of our civil service today is that officers are always trying to seek their next posting. Once an officer comes to Delhi, he spends his spare time in trying to fix himself up to a cushy posting in the United Nations or some foreign country. I am being very frank because I am part of that tribe. The IAS officers also want to get out of the country on some excuse or the other. Of course, even earlier, bright officers who got Fulbright Scholarship or some such offer continued to go out. But at that time, the rat race was limited. Then, as everybody wanted to find prominence in their career, the race had started in a very gradual way. After all, how does one get posted to Delhi out of turn unless one knew somebody in the Secretariat or the Cabinet Secretary himself? Earlier, the ICS was a very small service, and everybody knew everybody. The sense of competition was minimal back then. At present, the Civil Service is very large, and specialisation is the order of the day. Thrust on specialisation started at the time of Jawaharlal Nehru, and while that has raised professionalism, it has also fuelled peer group race.

I was trained and experienced in administering the Frontier and the Tribal Areas. Because of that background, I was deputed to the welfare of the Backward Classes and the Scheduled Tribes. Finally, I told the Secretariat that my sitting in New Delhi would serve no good purpose, so I was moved to Bhopal. I used to take my orders from the non-Congress government in Bhopal, and it was a very good experience. I met Ronald P Noronha, the Chief Secretary of Madhya Pradesh (1963-68), who was the last ICS Chief Secretary. As a courtesy, I made a telephone call to him and said, "I have come on a posting in Bhopal. I would like to call you or meet you." He was not the one to keep distance and replied, "Yes, *sayankal ko char baje aap* Vidhan Sabha *mein tapak padiye!*" (Drop in at the Assembly at 4 o'clock, I will be there). I was a little taken aback by his very formal Hindi. The Chief Secretary had a cabin in the Vidhan Sabha where I had a cup of tea with him, and then he briefed me.

The attitude of the MP government was that fair. My being an officer of the Central government, they would not give me accommodation. There was no earmarked accommodation, and so, I stayed in the Circuit House paying 75 rupees a day as rent. When one is posted to a station, one does not get any daily allowance. Usually, when one went on a tour as a Ministry's officer, he would stay in the dak-bungalow at very reasonable rates; but one could not afford to stay in a hotel and pay high charges. After sometime, my boss Sundaram, who was in New Delhi, came to get his house made up and put it on rent. When I asked him, he told me: "You stay in my house. I know you cannot afford to pay me the local rent. So whatever House Rent Allowance you get, rather than giving it to me, spend it on the gardener and other maintenance. Live in my house, and when I come there, you would have to vacate it." It was a very simple and straightforward offer, which I accepted. That was the character of the man, Sundaram.

Political Officer in Sikkim

While I was touring the jungles and the tribal areas in MP, I got a message that I have been posted to Sikkim and I should return to New Delhi. The Home Ministry must have passed the order. I returned from the forests of MP to Bhopal and packing up, reached New Delhi on 7th or 9th August, leaving my wife who was in the seventh month of pregnancy. I stayed at the External Affairs Hostel. I was then briefed at the South Block, New Delhi, and asked to reach Gangtok on 15th August 1968. I left the External Affairs Hostel and reached Gangtok on 15th August at about 2:30 in the afternoon. The Maharaja of Sikkim was always invited for the Independence Day flag-hoisting ceremony. We used to have the flag hoisting at the India House, and the Political Officer, being a supervisory authority or link between India and local ruler, would stand under the flag.

This was my second visit to Sikkim, and I found the difference myself. There was nobody to brief me in New Delhi; nobody had the time. The Ministry officials just asked me to reach there. I asked, "Why was my reaching on 15th August so important? Anybody can organise the function, the First Secretary could do it." But they did not answer me. I wish they told me the reason as to why I was called back to the Foreign Office. I knew the Chogyal as a young *Maharajkumar*; when I was in Tibet, I had represented their interests there. As the Agent of India, I was also the Agent of Sikkim. It was just as if there was any issue in London that related to Punjab, it was India's High Commissioner in London, and not the Chief Minister of Punjab who would have to attend to that through his own links with the White Hall.

By the time I was sent, the Indian Mission in Tibet was closed in 1968, and all its files and documents were stored in Gangtok. Negotiations were also going on with Bhutan for opening an Indian Mission at Thimpu. Later, towards the end of my tenure at Gangtok, I had visited Bhutan twice and established our Mission there.

Situation in Sikkim

Sikkim was an Indian protectorate. There was difference between our relations with Tibet, Bhutan, and our presence in Gangtok. Economies of Sikkim and Bhutan were more linked with India than with Tibet. Before 1947, it was under absolute rule of the Maharaja who did not allow any democracy. He could have ordered anything and taken away any property that he wanted. Our presence in Gangtok was more or less like the British Resident's presence in Jaipur or Rajputana before Independence, when all Indian states were full-fledged members of the Chamber of Princes. Sir Tashi Namgyal, the Maharaja of Sikkim, was like any other Princes who had the British title of knighthood. In 1947, Sardar Vallabhbhai Patel did not go to Sikkim, the Maharaja himself came here and signed the Instrument of Succession. He always travelled on an Indian passport, and continued to use his British title all his life. Letters exchanged between the Government of India and the Maharaja of Sikkim were very clear about the status of Sikkim as a protectorate of India. That was the basic document on which the relations were built. A protectorate status meant that all external relations and defence would be the responsibility of the Government of India, while the Government of Sikkim would have all the powers like any other Indian state on all the internal concerns.

Let us consider the political situation in Sikkim before it evolved as a full member of the Union. There were no political parties, but Sir Tashi Namgyal, Maharaja of Sikkim, was a very fine, cultivated person, a great artist and a deeply religious person. There were good Maharajas and there were also indifferent Maharajas; there were the educated ones and the uneducated lot. Like most Maharajas of India, Sir Tashi Namgyal was a benevolent one, and there was no report of any atrocities. I had met Sir Tashi Namgyal several times while in transit to Tibet. I was not posted in Gangtok, but Gangtok was the headquarters of the entire Mission which was looking after India's relations with Bhutan, Sikkim and Tibet. Sir Tashi Namgyal was very friendly with his people, and always spoke in Nepali. He was bi-lingual. He was also a very fine artist. The two Princes of Sikkim were brought in the traditional way and used to wear the traditional dresses. The senior boy was being groomed as an heir-apparent and joined the Sikkim Guard, which, besides the existing Palace Guards, had been allowed to be raised as per the Maharaja's wish. He was probably trying to have some kind of an army. The Government of India sent him a Lieutenant Colonel to organise the Sikkim Guard and various other ceremonial guards.

The younger son, the Chogyal, was educated in a monastery but was called back because his elder brother, who was to be the Maharaja, died in an air crash. So, he was brought back and sent to Shimla to study. Then he came back and did his ICS training and his attachment to the Gorkha Rifles of Indian Army's Gorkha Brigade as a Lieutenant Colonel. Like the Nepali citizens, he served in the Indian Army too. Afterwards, he was made the Managing Director of the Transport Corporation. So, he was naturally being trained to be the Administrator of Sikkim. After Sir Tashi Namgyal's death (in 1963), this son, Palden Thondup Namgyal, took over as the Chogyal. After the death of his father Maharaja Sir Tashi Namgyal, Palden Thondup Namgyal had to perform a very sensitive balancing trick between the contending parties. He conducted himself with a display of nobility, and introduced some cosmetic changes in the system. His first wife was of Tibetan origin, a very traditional woman. But when he married Hope Cooke, an American, on 20th March 1963, the situation changed. Hope Cook used to dress like a Bhutia and talk softly like the royalty. Nobody could say with certainly at that time whether she was planted by the United States of America or not – Sikkim, afterall, was a strategically important outpost close to Tibet over which the Chinese ruled. John Kenneth Galbraith, the US Ambassador to India (1961-63) did attend the wedding, when he had demanded a higher precedence over the Indian Political Officer. The Bhutias themselves were not happy about that marriage. The alliance was more political than romantic.

Geographically, Gangtok was in one corner of Bhutan, Tibet and Sikkim. Whatever be the consideration, the Political Officer was virtually the Ambassador and the Head of the Mission, depending on the personality of the Political Officer. Political Officers like Charles Bell and others had done a lot of study and research on Tibet, and had written a number of books on Tibet. There was never any resentment against the setting up of the Indian Mission in Gangtok. In fact, the Maharaja of Sikkim gave the land on which stands what is today called the Raj Bhawan in Gangtok. Politically, Sikkim was stable; the political evolution came much later, when people got politically educated.

Although the majority of people in Sikkim were of Nepali origin, the ethnic Bhutias were the economically dominant elite. They were related to the Tibetan aristocracy as well as the Sikkim's ruling family. Among them there were the Tawang Buddhists and pre-Buddhists. There was very little difference between the two. All of them spoke the Tibetan language. Basically, all the tribes living in the frontier regions were pre-Buddhists who followed traditional practices of worship. There were also the indigenous tribes of Lepchas and the Gurungs. But the Nepali or Gorkhali-speaking people were all originally migrants from Kathmandu Valley. They observed similar religious practices, except in their higher society, they subscribed to Brahminical or Rajput traditions. Of course, there was no language problem. There was no discrimination against the Hindu temples, etc. But naturally, there was power politics.

Sikkim had much of autonomy, and had an elected Assembly. In the Assembly, the Constitution of Sikkim provided 50 percent seats to the Nepali-speaking people, and 50 per cent to the Tibetan-speaking Bhutias and Lepchas. I think one seat was also reserved for the 'sangha', meaning the monasteries. So, there was parity in the share of authority, with the Chogyal having the final say. There was also an appointed cabinet. As the population of Sikkim grew into Nepali majority, the Maharaja's (Chogyal) close relations and the ethnic Sikkimese subjects resented that. They were really worried about the demographic changes, like Tibet was worried about the Han settlers from mainland China. The Chogyal tried to introduce a Tibetan dress code; women were told not to wear saris. His own ministers set the example. The common people (mostly Nepali origin), however, did not like that kind of imposition. Then, the Administration was reorganised under the Lonchen, who was like a Prime Minister. The Sikkim police was also reorganised. A Commissioner of Police was appointed. More and more schools were set up. Sir Tashi Namgyal Academy – a residential public school – was set up by the Maharaja, and it was very successful. My wife taught in that school as an honourary teacher, because they did not have enough teachers; they had Ms Patterson, a foreign woman, who also taught at that school. Whatever the ruling class wanted to reorganise or build, they were allowed to do so gradually within the framework of the Constitution of India and the financial propriety, etc. But with his hold over the Administration, Chogyal gradually wanted to revise the treaty,and the relationship with India; though I have not seen in the archives any exchange of formal letters on this matter. So, Sikkim was gradually building up for a kind of a constitutional monarchy and elected government.

In the conventional sense, besides petty thefts and crimes, there were no serious law and order problems in Sikkim at that time. There was no communal tension in Sikkim at all. In 1954, when I first went to and travelled through Sikkim, I found that there was no social disability either – even though in certain other parts of India, there was social disability. For instance, in Jaunsar Bawar in the Garhwal hills, the bridegrooms of non-Brahmins and non-Rajputs could not ride *palki,* and a man of lower caste had to enter from a different gate and staircase. All these are over. Today, there are reservations among the Bhutias, Lepchas, Tamangs and Nepalis who are labelled as Scheduled Castes. Mostly, the claimants are bogus and unscrupulous persons who obtain bogus certificates. I can also say it with certainty that the same thing is happening elsewhere too.

In Sikkim, within the landlord-tenant relationship, the major produce was taken away by the landlords. That is true. All the cardamom trade was in the hands of a few families. But that did not cause any social disability because as in Tibet also, a certain percentage of the produce of the land was given to the monastery – but that was out of sheer offering. Here, the Nepalis were the cultivators. They had their own culture – music, songs, attire and drinks. Later on, it was only when the Palace official prescribed a dress and made the wife of a Nepalese minister wear the *chuba*that the Nepalis protested.

Developments in Sikkim

I travelled from Delhi by train, and then by bus to reach Gangtok. I had left my family behind in the External Affairs Hostel in New Delhi, because I knew there was some problem. As I drove into Gangtok from Siliguri Railway Station, I saw one or two signs on the roadside, as well as painted on the roads, stating "Go Back Indians". I was quite surprised to see this kind of resentment. I reached the India House late in the afternoon. By then, the function of 15th August was already over. All the guests had left after the flag-hoisting ceremony. The senior guest was the Commissioner of Jalpaiguri Division of West Bengal, adjoining the state of Sikkim. There was also the Maharaja of Cooch Behar, who was a friend of the Chogyal of Sikkim; both were members of the Chamber of Princes. N B Menon, who was the Political Officer at that time, and the Commissioner of Jalpaiguri were there. Menon told me that there had been some resentment... that some people were arrested, and the news must have reached Delhi.

When I reached Gangtok at 2:00 p.m. on 15th August, I told N B Menon, "I would not mind waiting. Tomorrow, I will put on my *achkan* and go to present my credentials." Menon said, "First, inform him." So, I told the Deputy Commissioner to inform the Chogyal about my arrival and find a convenient time for me to come to meet him. The reply came, asking me to come at 4:00 in the afternoon. I reached on time. I did not dress up in a formal *achkan* as it was a holiday. So, we had tea and after half-an-hour, I wanted to take leave. He said: "No, no, please sit down, Johorey Sahib." He talked of the old days. The Chogyal studied in the Bishop Cotton School in Simla. My wife had also studied in Simla. He had too many drinks, and kept on drinking. General I S Gill, the General Officer Commanding (Sikkim), also arrived. He knewthe Chogyal. It was sunset and he ordered some more drinks, and that continued till about 9 O'clock at night. I was there for five hours – from 4 to 9 p.m. The Chogyal was unburdening himself. He did not say that he wanted to join China. He wanted an equal status with India, but he did not say that in so many words. He wanted to have more dialogue with the Government of India.

I noticed that the Chogyal's first wife did not turn up. This was the first time I saw Hope Cooke, a white lady, there. She had started calling herself 'Gyalmo', meaning the Queen; the title of Maharani was also used. Gyalmo was a Tibetan word, which the Sikkimese elite started to adopt very subtly, so that they could claim that it was their indigenous language. The new Maharani of Sikkim was an American. She had been inviting her friends from the USA and foreign journalists to Sikkim, one of whom was Charles Harting Percy, the US Senator from Illinois (1967-85). I remember my discussions with Percy –who was a very high ranking Senator – very well. Many of the American visitors used to stay in the palace. There were no hotels, and so, Americans of some consequence would stay in the India House. The Maharani had her own links, and we in the Mission or the South Block (New Delhi) never objected to that. But it went on and on till it turned into a separatist issue. The Royalty and their minions must have resented the Indian behaviour in reining in what they considered their sovereign right. Actually however, it was not the Indian behaviour; popular demand which turned into a geo-political compulsion. The Indians did not behave the way the Chinese behaved in Tibet. The Chinese went on to occupy Tibet and make complete demographic changes. In Sikkim the Inner Line Regulations were still there so that the tribal people there were protected.

Earlier we had a series of visitors to Sikkim from the Planning Commission. The seeds of discord had been sown when the Chogyal and the Government of Sikkim told the Planning Commission that they would have a Seven-Year Plan, and not a Five-Year Plan. They also said that they would have a 'Lonchen', meaning

Prime Minister. It was like Sheikh Mohammad Abdullah who called himself a Prime Minister. In the beginning, New Delhi did not understand the political significance of the word 'Lonchen'. In the South Block (New Delhi), some of the officials were acting in an overbearing manner. Foreign intervention could also have contributed to separatism, apart from the insensitive personal conduct of the officers who were sent from Delhi, which was very important. They thought that they were like the political residents of the past, which was a mistake. An odd member of the central staff may also have been overbearing in his dealings with the public. At one time, S K Anand, the Police Commissioner of Sikkim, complained to me against Bajrang Lal, the first Police Commissioner who was very popular. Officials of Sikkim complained to me informally that some Indian officers parked their cars in the wrong locations in the palace, and thus violated the sanctity of the palace. One cannot go into the Rashtrapati Bhawan and park wherever one wants to. One must be polite and follow the rules. So I told S K Anand that he must have some respect for the Sikkim Police and allow them to perform their duties. Anand, an Indian officer who was loaned to Sikkim, was not strict in performing his duties. So that was one shortcoming. There was another example, Jitendra Daulat Singh, an Indian official who created a commotion at the airport in New Delhi. When the Maharaja of Sikkim got down – flying the flag of Sikkim, and he raised serious objections to that. The message could have been conveyed in a more dignified way if a more mature person had handled the situation.

There was definitely no clash of civilisation as such. The clash was that of personal interests. After all, nobody wants his chair or zamindari to go. The Chogyal of Sikkim was like a very big zamindar who would not have liked to give up his powers, privileges and lands. With a better understanding and deft dealing at the Foreign Office, integration of Sikkim could have been delayed a bit, and thus been made more dignified.

The Chogyal of Sikkim spoke of another tragic event. V V Giri, the President, was to come to Sikkim but at the last minute, the visit was cancelled because of bad weather. But the Chogyal thought that he was being discriminated against; this was not true. If it were true, then it was very stupid of South Block (Ministry of Foreign Affairs). It was just like when American President George W Bush was coming to India, and then went to Pakistan so as to have parity between India and Pakistan. If a helicopter was not there, V V Giri could have come to Sikkim in six hours by car. If he could not go in a helicopter, then what was there, after all? It was not a very big issue of protocol. Why was the visit clubbed together? V V Giri wanted to go only to Bhutan, and was treated like a King. The King of Bhutan was a blood relation, the first cousin of the Chogyal of

Sikkim. The Chogyal felt offended. He opened up to me to state that the cancellation of President Giri's visit meant a denial of Bhutan-status to him. I tried to pacify him saying that no pilot can be compelled to fly in bad weather – leave alone a VVIP like the President of India – to land in an improvised helipad in torrential rains and bad weather. It had no effect. That was a very wrong planning by South Block.

Officials of the Planning Commission visited Sikkim and gave approval to several projects. Loktok electricity generation was a major project which started off. The Central government was more than liberal on development of Sikkim. But the project on aerial ropeway to Tibet was stopped as something happened; it did not progress at all. One discordant element was that the Chogyal wanted to claim the entire sales tax collected from Sikkim. In fact, that was one issue for which I came along with the Chogyal when he was invited by the government, and when he had insisted on staying in the Rashtrapati Bhawan. He told me his case very clearly thus: "You are non-aligned, but I am aligned with you. Therefore, why do you treat me differently from Nepal?" It was a logical argument. I asked: "What do you want?" He replied: "The sales tax of three crore rupees should be refunded." We all knew that the sales tax figures were being fudged, as it is done everywhere in India. No accounts were kept by the shops which had permits. Which *paanwala*or*kirana* bloke would keep an account of sales tax? Today, they may have computers. In those days, it was all on faith. Sales tax was not paid by the Sikkimese, but by the non-Bhutia merchants from Rajasthan and Calcutta who made the majority of shopkeepers. All the bazaars and cinema halls were theirs. The Chogyals claim for refund amounted to several crores, and he made a very strong case.

In the beginning, the Planning Commission did not understand the political significance of Sikkim and considered it as an insignificant place. Even the junior level officials could not appreciate the ground situation. That was not the correct attitude. I have seen that attitude towards Goa, too. I can now say that whether it was the North Block or the South Block, our so-called planners had not ever been to Gangtok to see matters for themselves. Anybody who had been in the districts would understand the feelings of thevillage folks. Only the Foreign Secretary at that time, T N Kaul who had served as a District Magistrate in Dehradun and was from Kashmir, was very informal with the Chogyal and understood him well. They were on first name terms. The Maharaja used to call him 'Tikkila' and Kaul used to call him 'Thondupla; he did not address him as 'His Excellency'. He visited Gangtok during my tenure as a Political Officer after the departure of N B Menon, in whose tenure, the anti-India feelings engineered by the palace were out in the open and manifested on 15th August 1968. But

T N Kaul was a different man, but the attitude of some of the underlings in the negotiations in Delhi and Gangtok left much to be desired.

When we argued the case at North Block, the Finance Secretary asked me straightway, "Tell me, is this claim justified?" I replied, "Sir, you know that in sales tax returns, there is large-scale fudging – particularly in remote areas like Sikkim and Nepal. But the claim of three crore rupees by the Sikkim Durbar is certainly worth consideration." He asked, "What shall we do?" I replied, "That is for you to decide." Since Nepal was getting her refund, the political factor played up. So when we argued and failed, the Chogyal was very disappointed.

I had conducted various meetings with the Chogyal and finally, the day he was to leave, Morarji Desai invited him for breakfast. As a State guest, he accepted the special treatment. I accompanied him to the breakfast meeting with Morarji Desai; I was also invited. Morarji Desai had some *aloo-puri*, some *akhrot* and papaya, and a completely vegetarian diet. Then, he asked the Chogyal, "What is your proposal?" The Chogyal outlined his claim without citing the analogy with Nepal. Then, Desai asked: "What exactly is the claim?" I replied, "The figures may vary but in principle, the Chogyal wanted a refund of the sales tax to the Government of Sikkim because after the trade with Tibet was stopped, all the trade was being generated within Sikkim." Both agreed to the refund in principle. Desai asked the Maharaja: "Would the refund of three crore rupees be all right?" The Maharaja was very happy because three crore rupees was the real figure. Desai said: "Johorey, please issue a cheque. Will it be all right in two installments, Maharaja Sahib?" He did not call him Chogyal. Morarji Desai again said: "Maharaja Sahib, *theek hona chahiye.* Will it be all right? Johorey, please issue cheques in quarterly instalments. Put it in the Development Fund of Sikkim. Look at the state of finance straightway." It was not that the money went to the Maharaja's Durbar Account where he had absolute freedom. The money went to the Government of Sikkim. The Chief Minister and the Finance Secretary were present. The Maharaja formally accepted the offer at that moment. I must say that it was a great achievement and an act of administrative acumen, without berating any hostility. The Chogyal came back very happy. He thanked me saying, "Johorey sahib *aap ki wajeh se ho gaya, nahin to nahin hota"* (it was due to you, else we would not have got the funds).

The Chogyal invited me to all the functions of the palace. He sent me his son, who had come from abroad. The son was being groomed for becoming the Commandant of the Guard. An Indian Army Officer was also there to train him. I asked him to come and have breakfast with me. He did not turn up on time in the morning; he may have overslept. He was very fond of *aloo-puri,* so we had that. Then we went horse riding. I told him that he must be punctual. The next day, he woke up early and came on time. He was being groomed by foreigners to be more assertive. The Chogyal himself was very amiable, and had very great regard for Jawaharlal Nehru and B C Roy – the latter was the Chief Minister of West Bengal.

Political Tussle

Sikkim was a Frontier state where the foreign elements, the foreign commentators – even our own Indian media, was active. The Chogyal's point of view was that by the Indo-Sikkimese Treaty of 1950, Sikkim was only a 'protectorate' of India, not an integral part. Therefore, he wanted full independence to conduct Sikkim's external and security policies. He also wanted a review of the treaty whereas his cabinet did not want any such review. One example of th review he suggested was that Indians should need passports and visas to enter Sikkim – a rather impractical proposition which could make it hard for the people to survive. But he tried very hard and every time he did that, an anti-Indian f eling was whipped up. Apa Pant had extremely good relations with the Maharaja f Sikkim. The Chogyal was also very respectful of India. But after Apa Pant we t away in 1961, he started finding faults. There must have been some foreign i stigation and communal elements who were trying to excite the Chogyal. T e Chogyal then alleged that there was a Ganesh temple which disturbed his pra ers. That was bogus; the temple was started by somebody in his own family and isited by them and whole lot of lamas.

Obviously, the ruling family did not understand international politics. Tibet was fully occupied by China, and he could see the difference between the Chinese occupation of Tibet and the India's open relationship with his own Princely state. The treaty between Sikkim and India was not a China-Tibet kind of a treaty. Sikkim, in fact, was a member of the Indian Chamber of Princes. The major part of budgetary support to the Sikkim Durbar came from the Government of India. The Chogyal was given certain privileges like the flag, etc. On the other hand, for many years, the Chinese were openly claiming the whole of North-East Frontier Agency and Sikkim as theirs. In fact, they had been showing me in Lhasa, maps showing their claim lines. At that time the Chogyal took the title of 'Maharajakumar' because Chogyal was a Tibetan word, and that could strengthen China's claim.

There was no doubt legally that Sikkim's status was like that of any Indian Princely state prior to the merger. The only difference was that the title of the Indian Representative was Political Officer of India in Bhutan, Sikkim and Tibet, with residence at Gangtok. The Chogyal and his henchmen were actually planning to have the treaty revised, whereas the senior and sobre elements in South Block did not see any motives in demand of the Sikkim Durbar for a separate flag for Sikkim, raising of the Sikkim Guards, and re-designation of the post of Dewan to that of 'Lonchen'. However, in the context of the Chinese invasion of 1962, there was no room whatsoever for change in the relationship. Sikkim could not be left in a political vacuum. On the other hand, the majority of political parties had started to unequivocally demand for a democratic set-up. Then a series of incidents of political activism upset the calculations of the Sikkim Durbar.

The Chogyal was intent on repudiating India's control over external and political aspects of Sikkim's administration. When Jawaharlal Nehru visited, the Chogyal flew the Indian flag; but over a period of time, because of the foreign elements with whom he was directly in touch, the Chogyal kept on propagating a feeling of separateness. In 1967, an upsurge was triggered when the Government of India agreed to treat the boundary between India and Sikkim like an international boundary. That, however, was not workable because it would create barriers to free movement and the business, making life difficult in Sikkim. There was a feeling of discrimination among the common people. The Bhutias were the educated elite. About 10 per cent of the elite owned 90 per cent of the land. They were the upper class people who owned the cardamom and fruit gardens and other properties. The Nepalese, who comprised 60 per cent of the population, were not so educated. Thus, there was resentment among the vast majority of the deprived. The elite, on the other hand, resented Indians occupying most top jobs and the influence enjoyed by the Indian Political Officer. There was no IAS cadre in Sikkim, and the lot of the local convent-educated candidates – mostly from the families of big zamindars and the rich – wanted to be absorbed in the Sikkim government service. They did so without any difficulty at all, yet occasional resentment persisted. Of course, the Indian merchants were there, as they had bee present in Tibet. The merchants had their offices in Gangtok, Jalpaiguri, Calcutt and Delhi. So, the economy was not directly linked with Tibet. After all, the lin of communication from Gangtok to Peking (now Beijing) was non-existent, an movement to Lhasa was limited to cultural, spiritual and religious ties.

In sum, there was no reason for the Chogyal's resentment towards India – that was a false impression foisted by vested interests. In fact, there was a strong popular demand for Sikkim's integration with the rest of India. Besides the people's demand as they got educated, integration of Sikkim with India was also a geo-political compulsion. The usual charge against the Indian Political Officer of meddling into affairs of the state was not justified. After all, what was the work of the Indian Political Officer? India was the paramount power and he represented that power. But as education and awareness spread and people clamoured for democratic freedom, the Political Officer had to see in which direction the wind was blowing and shoulder his constitutional responsibility to take appropriate action.

Integration

From the late 1960s onwards, the Sikkim Durbar was gradually moving up its demand for, without saying so, independence. Behind the scene, moves were going on but whether it was a Chinese or an American move, one cannot say. But it was obvious that the whole picture started changing in Sikkim with the arrival of Hope Cooke. She used to dress like a local Bhutia and put on the *chuba* or *Baku* dresses, and observed all court manners to impress the Sikkimese elite. She also had a stream of visitors coming in. So, two forces were at work: the forces of the palace and the forces of democracy. During my second tenure in Shillong, the demand for changing the relations with India was being built up by the new Chogyal, who took over the mantle after Sir Tashi Namgyal's death. Assumption of the title of Chogyal was a very calculated move to do away with the title of Maharaja which had an Indian connotation. There were always Maharajas from ancient times, but the title he assumed was "Chogyal." 'Cho' means puja and'Gyal' means royal. The palace had started a newspaper of its own. In that, they were very critical of India, saying that the Indians had the biggest camp for the Tibetan refugees in Sikkim, and that these refugees were changing Sikkim's demographic structure. But the main political parties in Sikkim demanded democratic rights. They wanted to join the Indian Union. So, that was the cause of Sikkim turning from being a protectorate to becoming a member of the Indian Union over a period of time.

The political situation was heating up because there was the counter, and stronger, demand for democracy. The people of Sikkim consistently demanded a popular government with proportionate Bhutia-Lepcha-Gorkhali representation. All along the political party, the Sikkim State Congress, was also demanding democracy. But democracy also meant the rule of the majority, with the danger of the Nepali-speaking or Gorkhali-speaking people overtaking the original Lepcha and Bhutia inhabitants. So, they wanted to safeguard the Lepchas and the Bhutias from becoming minorities in their own land. They had the top jobs in the government because they were the more educated elite. A few Pradhan families were members of the Indian Forest Service. Then there were the Kazi families. The Kazis paid some tribute to the Chogyal for the upkeep of the monastery, palace, durbar and othersuch spaces. The Maharaja and the Kazis were the landowners who had an enormous stake in power.

In 1968, open demonstrations by the two sides started, and then the situation became very serious. By the end of 1970, there was a demand from Sikkim Durbar for the recall of the Political Officer who was actually a facilitator for the state; I had accompanied the Chogyal to New Delhi when he stayed for seven days and was put up in the Rashtrapati Bhawan. He was given all due respect, and according to protocol, Morarji Desai gave him whatever was reasonable. Gradually, the tussle between monarchy and democracy gained strength and the merger became inevitable in 1972 after the Bangladesh War. Palden Thondup Namgyal was the Chogyal of Sikkim from 1963 till April 1975, when he was deposed and Sikkim was formally integrated into India. N K Rustomji – the last Dewan of Sikkim and a great friend of the royalty in Bhutan – and Jigme Dorji, the Prime Minister of Bhutan, were a few personalities who were taking a leading part in the governance of Bhutan and Sikkim. The Bhutan King's wife, the Queen, was the daughter of the sister of Sir Tashi Namgyal. So, there was a very close family relationship between the leaders of Bhutan and Sikkim. Kazi Lhendhup Dorji was the first elected Chief Minister of Sikkim with a cabinet. The people of Sikkim wanted democratic rights, there was no question of secession. When the elections were held, popularly supported political parties brought about a peaceful change. Kazi Lhendup Dorji was the first elected Chief Minister (1975-79). His wife Elisa Maria, who was a foreigner, was a great friend of India. She had adopted a Nepali boy and brought him up. She was a very knowledgeable woman, and had some links with some Princes in Austria or Hungary. She was openly critical of the policies of the Chogyal.

By the mid 1970s, the political situation had turned real bad. The Chogyal wanted to have absolute power, his own cabinet and turn Sikkim into a constitutional monarchy. There were clashes between the majority of common Sikkimese who wanted democracy and a minority of Bhutia royalists and their henchmen who wanted monarchy. There were rumours of covert interference from neighbouring regions and fears of political turmoil, bloodshed and even Chinese intervention. Had India shown weakness in handling the situation, e would have been finished. We should know how to exercise power, not just bru e force but political and intellectual power to protect our interests. Later, the Chinese had to recognise the integration. However, the South Block failed to ha dle the situation in a more amicable manner after taking the Chogyal in confid nce. It was all a lack of personal equation which played the key role. It is surpri ing how sometimes personal equation comes into play. The Chogyal should have himself stepped down and gone as a Governor of some other state. But then, his ttitude had changed. Kashiraj Pradhan, a leader of the Congress, was a sobering influence. Pradhans were an elite group, and were also found in Maharashtra and

Nepal. They were Nepali-speaking Hindus, and were a very traditional people; the Pradhan women would not wear the Tibetan dress. The Chogyal, who did not lack in wisdom, should have appointed him to an important position. Kashiraj Pradhan's son Mohan Pradhan was an Indian Forest Officer, who later on became an IAS and a Chief Secretary. Finally, the Chogyal had to be divested of his monarchy by the cabinet, with the backing of the South Block. People welcomed the change. Reorganisation of Sikkim administration followed. In Sikkim today, except for a small number of people who are closely related to the Chogyal, nobody resents the integration of Sikkim with the Indian Union. The popular view was that the people should enjoy the same rights and privileges as elsewhere in India, and with full Indian citizenship, have access to the fruits of development.

So, this was the tragedy of Sikkim royalty as I would call it. The last Maharajkumar of Sikkim became a Chogyal, and from Chogyal to a non-entity. If he had contested for Chief Ministership, he would have won with cent per cent Bhutia as well as a large percentage of happy Nepalese votes. He could have also become a *Maharajpramukh*, like Jai Singh of Jaipur. His personal life was tragic. His first wife had died and his elder son left home and became a monk. I could not meet him during my last visit.

Sikkim has one of the finest nurseries in Asia, and its flora and fauna are unique in the world. Changu Lake is typical example of its natural history – botany, zoology, evolution of plants, animal life, chemistry and related subjects. Sikkim orchids have been documented with sketches. There were only three or four copies of Sir Joseph Dalton Hooker's *The Rhododendrons of Sikkim-Himalaya*. It was a very valuable book. Hooker was a botanist and Director of Royal Botanic Gardens (Kew, London) for many years. One copy of this book was in the Residency, another with the wife of the Chogyal, and a third copy was in the British Museum. A fourth copy was with the family of Mohan Pradhan.

The Bhutan Connection

Jigme Dorji Wangchuck, the King of Bhutan, was extremely careful in governing Bhutan. He favoured gradual reforms. He did not want to be swamped. He was a very simple person, and very down to the earth. He hardly spoke any English. He had two ministers, Home Minister and Finance Minister, and one Prime Minister. Jigme Palden Dorji, the Prime Minister who was assassinated on 5th April 1964, was educated in Kalimpong. His sister, Ashi Kesang Dorji, was married to the King of Bhutan. ('Ashi' means a Princess). Essentially, Bhutanese were all tribal people engaged in animal husbandry and cultivation, but the climate being very harsh, special methods were adopted.

The King was known as Druk Gyalpo or the Dragon King. The Maharani was Ashi Kesang Dorji, the present King's grandmother, a very fine lady. Their son was sent to the UK for studies at that time because they did not have public school teachers. The King had his own share of affairs; apart from the Queen, he had another woman. In their own social set-up, this was not considered abnormal. Ashi Kesang, who was Western or convent-educated woman, did not like this. Therefore, a personal cleavage developed between the King and the Queen. In public, they would present themselves as a couple but lived separately in reality. The Queen had a house in Paro, which was located about 5000-6000 feet above sea level, and was a very pretty place. So, there were two centres of political power, the *Paro Pellap* and the *Hap Pellap*, which was the King's side. Paro Pellap had its own land and properties. When I had to go and meet the King, I also had to call on the Queen separately so as to not upset the balance of power.

Democracy as we understand today was not there. It is a small country, and there could be direct rule. The whole country was governed by consensus, tradition, convention and tribal laws, and controlled by Paro Pellap and Hap Pellap. The Government of Bhutan kept a house in Kalimpong, which is a part of West Bengal and about two hours' drive from Gangtok. Unlike the Chogyal, the King of Bhutan was not educated in an English medium school. The King of Bhutan always compared himself with the Chogyal and, of course, they were very closely related to each other. But they never used to meet on official visits. Maybe, they met personally sometimes, but generally, first cousins kept apart. That was the scene in Bhutan.

When I was posted to Afghanistan, I read about an attempt on the life of Jigme Dorji Wangchuck, the then King of Bhutan, in July 1965. Some alleged that there was India's hand in it! Then there were certain elements who thought that the King was going too close to modernity, that the process of modernisation was too fast. Further, there were two discordant voices. One was the fear of the Nepalese immigrants coming and swamping their region, and another fear was that if Bhutan was exposed to the outside world, then the Bhutanese masses would not respect the local traditions, and the whole system may fail. There were assassination and counter-assassination attempts on the life of the King of Bhutan. There was a big enquiry. There was no police worth the name in Bhutan, and there was no intelligence system there. They asked the Government of India to investigate. Besides the King, another centre of power was Prime Minister Jigme Palden Dorji. There were also the opposing groups. One group was led by a Brigadier of Royal Bhutan Army. This was an internal tribal feud which may have been inspired by foreigners. Prime Minister Jigme Palden Dorji himself had been murdered on 5th April 1964, maybe because some people from the other group thought that he was too forward looking, with a scientific outlook and too pro-India. This could have been one reason. After all, as the Prime Minister it was he who invited Jawaharlal Nehru to Bhutan. There was also this feeling as to who was going to be at the centre of power, whether it was to be the absolute monarch or the Prime Minister. After Jigme Palden Dorji, I do not think Bhutan had a Prime Minister for many years – from 5th April 1964 to 25th July 1964, the post was vacant from 25th July 1964 to 27th Novmber 1964; Dasho Lhendup Dorji was the acting Prime Minister, and from 27th November 1964 to 20th July 1998, the post stood abolished. The King was at the top, then there was a Development Commissioner and then some ministers. Now, there is a new system in Bhutan.

King Jigme Dorji Wangchuck was a very simple person. He used to carry his own baggage. He told me that even in his father's time, it was royal custom that within the palace he would not wear shoes. He used to eat normal, simple food. Of course, the only weakness was that he was very fond of drinks and his personal relationship with a particular woman, Ashi Kesang Chhoeden Dorji, who became a centre of power and an embarrassment to him. Kesang, who was a very highly-educated and sophisticated woman, became his weakness. But his subjects were never bothered about these personal liaisons. Bhutan and Tibet were different societies altogether. They were both polyandrous and polygamous at that time. To the outside world, it may have appeared to be a different and strange situation. Although in his personal life the King was very indulgent he died of alcoholism and other excesses, in his political views, King Jigme Dorji Wangchuck was very clear. He had great regard for Jawaharlal Nehru, who was the only political leader to visit Bhutan in those times. His contact with India was through Apa Pant, the Political Officer, with whom he was very friendly and whom he respected. The King was very friendly with India. He invited Jawaharlal Nehru to visit Bhutan – who became the first foreigner to do so. In fact, he even invited a team from India to train the Royal Bhutan Army. After the visit of Prime Minister in September 1958, Bhutan opened its trade with India, but not with the outside world. But Bhutan also wanted to be politically equi-distant from China and India, and therefore, it did not want to be a party to the India-China differences. They never openly condemned the Chinese invasion of India, but were very much worried. The King of Bhutan was not interested in politics among nations. His whole focus was on building up his own country. Bhutan was way back in time; there was hardly any postal and other services... it was a completely different world. Whereas in 20 years, the Chinese completely changed the picture of Tibet; Bhutan had struck to their identity mainly because of the insistence of the King and his understandings with the neighbours. The Chinese kept away. India always had goodwill towards Bhutan. We never resisted their demands. Whatever was within our means, we did to help. We have a treaty with Bhutan that guides our bilateral relations. According to that treaty, Bhutan cooperates with India on their defence matters. They have their own small army but should any calamity descends on Bhutan, India would come to their aid.

The British did not involve themselves in the development of Bhutan. Development work was started by India in 1958, after Prime Minister Jawaharlal Nehru's visit to Bhutan. The initial meeting was held in Bomdi-La, and not in Bhutan. I remember Jigme Dorji, the Prime Minister of Bhutan, visited Bomdi-La via Arunachal Pradesh(AP adjoins Bhutan). General Jagjit Singh Arora was with him and took part in the discussions; they spent two nights there. Indian Political Officer Apa Pant also came to Bomdi-La. Once the developmental plans were finalised, Indian personnel were gradually deputed to Bhutan. The Government of Bhutan set up their office in Kalimpong in West Bengalas well.

As the Political Officer in Sikkim with residence in Gangtok, I was also the Representative of the Government of India in Bhutan. Therefore, I visited Bhutan's Capital Thimpu in January 1969 to maintain the relationship. A beginning was made with the setting up of a Special Office as a prelude to a full-fledged embassy. The journey from Gangtok to Thimpu took about 18 hours at that time. There already was a First Secretary in Gangtok. We now placed another First Secretary inThimpu. Earlier, the Bhutanese government had reservations with the post being referred to as 'Indian Political Officer'. It was only a question of nomenclature; the Indian presence was never resented. There was nothing personal about it, they just wanted an 'Indian Representative'. The Political Officer had the connotation of a superior power, overlordship or the imperial patronage through a pro-consul, whereas they wanted a relationship based on equality. Therefore, there was the need for a change of designation to 'Officer on Special Duty', and his office as the 'Special Office of India in Bhutan'. For the first time, a Special Office was set up, with B S Das as the Officer on Special Duty and two other diplomats. Then I took Amarnath Ram, who was designated as the First Secretary and stayed at the Bhutan Mission.

Reaching Bhutan was very difficult in those days. The easier way was through Tibet. Bhutan deliberately did not open its doors – not because of any hostility, but an abundant caution on their part. Maybe, had they opened up earlier, things would have been different. Even today, they are very cautious. They have trade, business and other interactions, but they try to preserve their innate chaculture and way of being; one finds their society, customs, architecture and lifestyle quite different. Only after the visit of Prime Minister Jawaharlal Nehru in 1958 did the Government of Bhutan formally open its door to cement Indo-Bhutan relations in totality, within the framework of the Indo-Bhutan Treaty of Friendship of 8th

August 1949. Subsequently, our constitutional experts helped the Bhutanese to write their Constitution, and to create certain representative institutions like the Tshogdu Chenmo or the National Assembly. We respected their dignity and internal autonomy.

Thimpu was bitterly cold. There was just a barrack to house the Indian Mission where the Secretariat was set up. Then the developmental plans for Bhutan started. The Government of India helped with funding, and whatever was wanted by Bhutanese officials to reorganise their police and district administration. We trained their officers and the police. We loaned our officers who indicated their solidarity and respect by dressing like the Bhutanese locals. The districts were given local Bhutanese, and in some cases, even Indian names. So, it was an open and transparent involvement. My role was to assist Bhutan in every way possible, prepare plans for development and give any assistance that they asked for. Twice, I went to establish the link between the developmental plans of the Governments of India and Bhutan. Personally, the King of Bhutan was very friendly with my predecessor N B Menon, and me. Our Mission in Bhutan is now called the India House, it is a full-fledged embassy. Bhutan, too, has an embassy in New Delhi; notably, it is not a member of the Commonwealth Nations. At that time, they wanted to be left alone till they caught up with the rest of the world. As Bhutan progressed, they naturally wanted to become a member of the United Nations. Gradually, as Bhutan progressed, in September 1971, the country took its place in the United Nations Organisation.

The palace was very particular about the dress code. Every single person, whether he was a clerk or the King, wore the same dress during the working hours. They wanted to retain their culture. The danger was that the illiterate population could be suddenly swamped by the outsiders, thus causing social upheaval. There were so many motivated offers of help coming from various other countries who could create trouble in the area, but the King resisted these moves. India was the only country invited to join in their development plans; even today, there is free movement between India and Bhutan, as it is with Nepal, though the treaty with the latter is on different lines. One school was set up with Indian help. The Indian Army's team of trainers trained the Royal Bhutan Army and helped organise the command-structure. We also trained their Foreign Service. There was never any political demand from their side. Of course, in the 1980s, some groups of Nepali migrant population did create some trouble, spilling over to armed violence – but King Jigme Singhe Wangchuk took charge himself, fought and defeated the insurgents.

Indigenous communities in Bhutan always behaved well with India. This was because under the leadership of Jawaharlal Nehru, India adopted a humane policy towards her own tribal people, and that example helped. All the administrative officers who went to the North-East were told to respect the tribal customs. The same respect was accorded in Bhutan and Sikkim. Their traditional festivals, holidays and native languages were/are respected and protected from being misused. The Bhutan budget was given full support and whatever was asked for, was given. I did not know the figures at that moment, but all assistance was given for the construction of infrastructure in Bhutan.

Bhutan had their own unique postage stamps which they got printed from Switzerland. Their coins and currency were different, whereas in Sikkim there was never any separate coins and currency. Tibet had its own coins and currency, even though Indian currency was in circulation everywhere. In its relations with India, Bhutan always wanted the status of Nepal. Leaders of the two countries used to occasionally meet elsewhere in this context. This was a natural evolution, and not an induced motive. At no point did the Government of India try to resist or stop that natural evolution. If Bhutan wanted to invite the Chinese or the Americans, they were free to do so. We had no say in that matter.

Some people now say that we should have taken control of Nepal when King Tribhuvan escaped to India in November 1950 to reclaim his authority, which had been usurped by the Ranas. Jawaharlal Nehru, in his wisdom, thought over it very clearly, because the treaty with Nepal was very clear on this aspect. The Nepali King was reinstated in February 1951. There was also a contention that Jawaharlal Nehru had made a mistake on Bhutan; that Bhutan should have been a part of India. It is a ridiculous opinion because if we had attempted any such move, there would have been much more trouble. Conversely, if we had not helped Bhutan, some other country would have come to fill the vacuum.

There was one similarity between Afghanistan, Nepal and Bhutan: all the three were landlocked countries. The royalty of Nepal did not play their card very well but royalty of Bhutan did, and that is why they are surviving. The royalty of Afghanistan, too, handled the internal situations well; but because of the continuous interference by the Russians, the Americans eventually came to intervene. I would be horrified if the Afghan King had otherwise permitted the Americans to interfere. The Bhutanese, too, have resisted the outsiders from settling, even Indians. They had their business links in Calcutta, but did not want the flood of Indian merchants to open shops there; in Bhutan, it was all Bhutanese. They very zealously protected their indigenous culture, and any intrusion into their privacy was deeply resented. So, the progress among the indigenous communities happened with fewer clashes between the various sects and communities. That was a more humane policy and a very scientific approach to governance.

India is a big country and we always suffer from the big brother-approach. Such an attitude could be easily misunderstood in Bhutan, as it happened in India-Pakistan relations. Another factor was the vast difference in size of the country, and that psyche was still there. But I must pay a tribute to the foreign po icy that avoided alienating the Bhutanese: a policy was followed under the guid nce of Jawaharlal Nehru, even though there were a few mistakes made here and th re. Indeed, we were very cautious in our approach to Bhutan and Sikkim. The criticism that they resented India's position was unfair. In the aftermath of India s independence, the question was not of resentment towards India; the distance kept was a calculated move by the King of Bhutan to make sure of the survival of his monarchy. Therefore, it took several years for the Indian Mission to be started in Thimpu.

From Sikkim, I was posted to the NEFA Secretariat in Shillong in 1972 as Home Secretary and Development Commissioner (NEFA), and then as the Deputy Commissioner, Along, Arunachal Pradesh. Within a few months, I was posted to Delhi.

CHAPTER 11

EXPERIENCES IN DELHI ADMINISTRATION

Exposure to Delhi Culture

Aditya Nath Jha was the first Lieutenant Governor of Delhi (1966-70). He was an ICS officer and a great scholar of Sanskrit. Jha also had his own style of functioning. Like the District Magistrate of the past, he would sit in the lawn of the Raj Bhawan and call the leaders of Sikh and Muslim communities. He would hear their complaints and give orders. A complaint came that the Central Secretariat 'babus' were going to Hanuman temple in Connaught Place (now Rajiv Chowk) on Tuesdays after lunch to offer pujas there, and then goingto see the matinee film show after that, thus neglecting office work. Also, at the temple, there were some reports of eve-teasing. Then came the issue of kiosks – filth from flower, sweets and shops – and congestion in the whole area. So, as an administrator, Jha said: "A temple is a place of worship and cleanliness is a must in such a space." He told Vijay Kumar Malhotra of the Bharatiya Jana Sangh, who was in power, that he should first talk to the owners of kiosks as their removal would hurt them. He added,"That is your work, you try. If you fail, we can give them a 15 days' notice to vacate." After 15 days, Vijay Malhotra told the Lieutenant Governor that it could not be done. Then Jha asked the ADM to hire 10 trucks and labourers, and remove all the kiosks on a Saturday (which was full working day) and on Sunday, so the offenders would not be able to approach the High Court. He ordered that there should be no use of force. So, this was practical administration. He said, "Nobody should be disturbed. All the kiosks should be put in trucks and taken outside the municipal area." That was the job of the municipality. So the operation was carried out. There was no resentment; everyone was very happy because the Hanuman temple area became clean; even Jawaharlal Nehru was very happy.

Then on Monday morning, the local leaders were called. There was initial resentment as the Hindu sentiments were hurt. A N Jha said, "You probably do not know, but I stood first in Sanskrit in the ICS Examination, and I am from the family of the Maithili Brahmins who are amongst the highest of Brahmins with a whole family tradition. Therefore, you must remember that I am also a Hindu." Local leaders understood that. What Jha desired was done. It is important for an administrator to get the feedback from his/her eyes and ears, the District Magistrates, and not the officials in the Secretariat. Of course, the Secretaries were always there, but even a brilliant physicist would not have the ground knowledge.

Civil Supplies in Delhi

There were four postings in Delhi within a period of three years, when I went out of Delhi on promotion or on routine transfer after short tenures. My first posting at Delhi in 1972 was as the Commissioner of Civil Supplies, when I was given the job as a special nominee. This job was to strengthen the public distribution system, which was already introduced and popularly called titled 'rationing'. During the World War II, there was rationing... and then came the Partition. When the British withdrew, there was no public distribution system. The whole economy was in such a condition that there was a need for control and public distribution for the Central government employees – who came from areas far and near to work in Delhi. At that time, one and a half lakh people used to visit Delhi, and one and a half lakh people of Delhi used to visit the peripheral areas every day as well. That was the ground reality.

I had mildly protested, "Sir, civil supplies is not my field. I am an engineer by training but was told that as an IAS officer, by one's intelligence and hard work, one can do any job." When I told my old friends that I was in 'rationing' department, they said, "Sahib, *phir to bahut badia hain, theek hai*" (that is great!). I started getting invitations to every wedding. I knew neither the bride nor the groom or the parents, or the tenth person, or cousin – no relationship at all, but people still expected me to attend these functions. The culture of Delhi was in proudly announcing that 'so and so visited'. That was part of old Delhi's tradition. The Deputy Collector sahib was invariably invited.

It was around India-China War that the government re-introduced the rationing system to control the prices of certain essential items like wheat flour, rice, sugar, kerosene oil, cement and coal. A certain quantity of food was allotted to rice-eaters and wheat flour-eaters. People in the North usually consumed *dal* (lentils) and *roti* (Indian bread). *Dals* and *maida* (refined flour) were not controlled because these were items of luxury. Indira Gandhi's idea was that everybody should get the basic minimum food. If a consumer got a certain minimum quantity of flourand sugar, he was quite happy. One could then buy varieties of *dals* which were always more expensive. This was the rationale behind it. Not only did the government employees, but also the other residents of Delhi had ration cards. It was a universal practice. There was no rule that a rich man could not get a ration card. But mostly, it was the government servants because they were the local residents with limited income and fixed salary. They could not afford to buy from the black market and, therefore, applied for ration cards. The quantity of food was same regardless of one's salary, but the 'units' of entitlement were fixed. If one had one child, one would get one unit. There was no half unit. If one had a maid-servant, they accepted one's word for that. The first problem was that the government officers who had to collect rations used to spend a half-day waiting in the queue, and thereby missing half a day's work. Therefore, I submitted to the government that the Civil Supplies Offices should open earlier at 9:00 a.m. That was not accepted, but 9:30 a.m. was, which still a concession. Some members of the staff were telling lies that they were standing in the queue for rations. Mostly, it was genuine, but it did give them an excuse to be late. So, that was one administrative change that I introduced.

Then, there was the question of fake ration cards. There was question in the Parliament that there were many bogus ration cards, and that was true. When the question was raised, I replied that it was correct. I gave that draft reply to the Executive Councillor, who was my political boss. The set-up in Delhi was that they had four Executive Councillors. That was a British legacy: the Viceroy and four Executive Councillors administered Delhi. One was in charge of the Civil Supplies, which was the most sought-after post. The population of Delhi was 40 lakhs at that time, and there were 24 Food and Supplies Officers (FSOs). So, I wondered as to how one FSO could organise food for more than one lakh of population. I suggested that instead of 24, we should have 40 FSOs because there were a lot of complaints and unmanageable queues outside my office on the Under Hill Road.

My office was located at an old luxury hotel behind the Chief Secretary's house on Rajpur Road. That was a hired building which is still there. It was an old British structure, but there was no space for visitors to sit. To my horror, I once found the Director of the Intelligence of Bureau, Mr Sen, standing in the queue. I saw him when I entered the office. I used to step out of my office at 9 O'clock to visit the shops in the field areas. I would return by 11:00 a.m., when the time for contact with the public began. From 11:00 a.m. to 12:00

p.m., anybody could come and see me. So I asked Sen, "Why are you in the queue?" He replied, "I have taken leave. I am building a house, and I want 10 bags of cement" (can one imagine a senior officer with long years of service standing in a queue?). I took him aside with me and sent for the number two man, but he was not at his seat. Anyway, I called the Inspector and I asked, "How do you issue cement?" He said that they would see whether the *naksha* or house-plan was passed, and then decide on the quantity. Sen had given a formal application with a copy of the house-plan, so I immediately issued him the quantity of cement he wanted. I asked the Inspector: "What will you check? Are you a qualified engineer or a qualified architect? When an architect had signed and the Municipal Commissioner had approved, it had already been through the filter-process." The visitors as well as the Inspectors were taken aback.

Cement was going into the black market. Instead of 18 rupees a bag, it was being sold for 28 rupees a bag, with 10 rupees being the margin in the black market. A two-bedroom house requires 1000 bags of cement. From foundation to upwards, one can imagine the cost to the builder or the owner. Another rule was that five bags of cement would be given without any *naksha*. If the roof of an old Delhi resident's house was leaking, then as a registered ration card holder, he would go to the shop outlet and get the cement. The cement stockist also did ot play a fair game. They collected hundreds of ration cards from the poor peop e, gave them 10 rupees each and thus, many bags of cement were siphoned off. E en the servants and the *jhuggiwalas* (slum-dwellers) who had ration cards star ed doing this business. They were all out to defeat the whole system. So, I asked my political boss. He said that there was nothing one could do about this systemati ed corruption. It was shocking! When I wrote that there were bogus cards, the - Executive Councillor was very upset and said, "How can we, as a government, say this?" That was true, but how could we deny that?

Mohan Kumaramangalam, the Union Minister for Steel and Mines (1971-73) who also looked after Civil Supplies, was a very enlightened person with Leftist leanings. He often called me from old Delhi to brief him at 9:00 a.m, before the Parliament opened at 10: 00 a.m. I always enjoyed the interaction; excellent coffee and aroma of the cigar was a perfect combination – he was an Oxonian and a cigar smoker; he also had an absolutely superb accent. I had given up smoking by then. He talked about the question in Parliament on bogus ration cards, and asked me for the truth. I replied, "It is true that there are bogus cards. How can an Inspector go to a woman in *purdah* in Chandni Chowk to ascertain the size of the family and the number of adults and children in the household?" Then I explained to him the system, and that it would be unpopular to be strict on ration cards – and so, we could not do that. Then the Prime Minister asked the Home Secretary about the matter. When called up, I replied that bogus ration cards were there. I was told that we must take strong measures to curb this. I agreed.

Practice of Hoarding

The commodities sold through the ration shop were rice, flour, kerosene oil, sugar, cement and coal. After the permit was issued by the Civil Supplies Commissioner, the supply was controlled by a Deputy Commissioner in-charge of food, and another Deputy Commissioner in-charge of coal and cement. Then, there were Food Supply Officers. Coal was issued through the ration card, and the quantity was not mentioned, but arrangement was made to issue a small quantity of coal at a fixed price. Even the MPs complained about shortage of cement and coal. Then, the Department of Weights and Measures was separate.

Coal was issued for heating in the winter and for the *bhattis* (industrial ovens) in the summer. Kerosene oil was issued to labourers. The storage facility was very poor and problems arose, especially during the monsoons.

One day, Inspector-General P V Rajgopal called me up. We met at the control room, which used to be below the Chief Secretary's office at 5, Alipur Road. He said, "There is hoarding going on. But the hoarders are so powerful that a junior officer would not be able to handle them. Therefore, though a Commissioner normally does not go for inspection, you should do so." It was the job of the Food Supply Officer, and the team was to be led by me as the Civil Supplies Commissioner. The police advised me that if we take a police van, then the hoarders would disappear. So, we went in our old Ambassador, and another staff car of the Civil Supplies Department. Seven Inspectors plus one Deputy Superintendent of Police and myself formed the raiding party. We found 40,000 unaccounted bags of wheat.

That company was of the Modi family in Okhla. I did not even know the name. The lights were switched off and the guard said that he had no keys with him. So, we said that we would wait for the key. For half an hour, he must have warned the others that a raid was on. Then we said that we would not wait any longer and would break open the lock. Then one Mr Goyal, the manager, gave up and handed the keys. There were about seven silos and a huge steel frame, which held an air-conditioner or refrigerator. Anyway, with the light from the torch, we could see the grains of wheat; one does not store wheat in air-conditioned potato or apple godown. Inside, we found 40,000 bags of wheat stocked. Then the electric light went off. We immediately came out. One Inspector was left inside when we came out. So, we quickly took him out. That was an attempt to bolt us inside and kill us so that we could not find as to who these people were, and nobody would know the next morning that we had come. Then the DSP sai ,"Sir, you come out now and we would proceed further." I asked, "Have one got ny force?" He replied, "We have not brought any force. But I have got a pis ol and six bullets: *Char lashien to main nikaal hee dunga yahan se, lekin aap mat jayiye."*(I will deal with these goons myself, you do not go there). Anyway, we came out and left without arresting the manager because we did not have a magistrate with us.

On the next working day, I informed the political boss. I thought that he would be very happy about the busting of the mafia who diverted wheat meant for distribution to the public into the black market. But he was absolutely quiet and did not have even a smile on his face. The body language said it all. I just told him, "Sir, it was a successful operation and I have informed the Chief Secretary on the telephone earlier." It was a Sunday morning and the office of the Lieutenant Governor was just across. So, I walked into his room in the morning and gave a full report. Next day, the Maintenance of Internal Security Act (MISA) was applied against the owner, who was perhaps one of the Modis. As soon as the MISA was invoked, the warrant of arrest was issued.

On Monday morning when I reached office, the news was carried by the newspapers. *The Hindustan Times* owned by the Birlas published the news with Modi's name. One Leftist newspaper, *The Patriot,*also carried it. The other newspapers did not report this because it was 'insignificant'. The Birlas and the Modis were business rivals, like one finds in most business houses. Then, people started pulling the strings. I started getting phone calls from all over – from people I had never known or met at all. One very senior person said that he wanted to come and meet me. A retired and very distinguished Chief Engineer, who was my brother's boss, and another person from the same family, came. They arrived by rail and landed up the next day. I said, "Sir, there is nothing that I can do about it. I am not the competent authority for the MISA. I am not even a Magistrate. I may be called the Commissioner but the law, the Criminal Procedure Code (Cr.PC), is different." When some of the Modis' name cropped up in the case, within two days I was asked by the Chief Secretary to hand over the charge f the Civil Supplies Department. He thought that because it was supposed to be very 'wet post', that is, the whole department was absolutely corrupt, I would - be unhappy. Bahadur Ram Tamta, who had started indulging in politics, was made the Civil Supplies Commissioner. I was very happy.

So, the story was that K N Modi's father, Rai Bahadur Gujarmal Modi – founder of the Modi Group of Industries and a Padma awardee – went to meet the then Prime Minister Indira Gandhi, and she refused to meet him. At the level of Personal Assistant, she informed him that she was not dealing with subjects relating to Delhi. He must have influenced somebody to have telephonic contact. They said, "Please go and meet the Home Minister." So, a phone call was sent from the PMO by somebody. This was the story that was in circulation. When a telephone call came from the PMO, that so and so, a very leading industrialist of the country wanted to meet the Home Minister, the Home Minister gave an appointment straightway, and some kind of an agreement was reached. The Home Secretary was in the background and orders were issued immediately. K N Modi was living across the Raj Niwas but apparently, he could not be arrested. Three or four years later, in a relaxed atmosphere, a Modi employee told me that he could not be arrested and the MISA was revoked. There were questions in Parliament and that was why Piloo Mody said, "MISA *lagao, paisa banao,* MISA *hatao*!" (Invoke MISA, make money, and revoke MISA!)

When the MISA was removed, questions were raised in the Parliament. *The Indian Express* carried a report that K C Johorey has been shifted. Questions were asked in the Legislative Assembly of Delhi and Parliament as to why K C Johorey was shifted. The government gave the reply that he was the senior-most officer, and one with the highest integrity. The moment an officer of the Civil Supplies Department was changed, it was assumed that he must be very corrupt! I was told later on that there was an attempt on my life. The powerful lobby sent me a message that up to the rank of Joint-Secretary to the Government of India, they could get anybody shifted. They had tried their very best to send temptations through a cousin and some others: "Bungalow *chahiye,* car *chahiye,* Joint-Secretary *ka* posting *kara denge*" (you want binglow, car, we will get you a Joint Secretary's post).

Cement Allotment

Here, I have an interesting anecdote. The Maruti car factory (later Maruti Udyog Ltd.) was being set up. One of my visitors was Wing Commander (retired) Ahluwalia, a young chap who came to me for 1000 bags or some very large quantity of cement for building of a Maruti car factory. I checked up from the Deputy Commissioner what the stock position was. The Deputy Commissioner came and said, "The quantity of cement released by the Central government is meant only for the people of Delhi. So we give cement only to the builders of small houses in Delhi. The Maruti car factory is not situated in Delhi. For the industries being set up in the neighbouring region of Delhi, the Central government gave cement directly. Such customers could procure it directly from a cement factory." The visitor was very unhappy with that blunt conversation. He went and complained to Om Prakash Behl, the Executive Councillor in-charge of Civil Supplies in Delhi, saying that K C Johorey did not want to issue cement.

Behl summoned me and I very politely stated the position. He said, "*Wo* Prime Minister *ka ladka hain isliye aap nahin kar rahen hain.* Tata, Birla *hota to aap kar dete*" (he is Prime Minister's son so you are not helping, had he been a businessman, you would have obliged). For any civil servant, any aspersion on his integrity or efficiency is a serious matter. I said, "I beg your pardon, Sir. I neither know a Birla nor a Tata. I am only telling one that I am bound by the rules." He then named Sanjay Gandhi as the beneficiary. I said: "Excuse me, Sir. It is in the national interest that the factory should be set up. So why don't you write to the Chief Minister of Haryana? I can retain one with 10,000 bags of cement to offload in Gurgaon, if that is desired. The Central government controlled the movement of cement. I would draft a Demi Official (DO) letter for you, or you please write to Mohan Kumaramangalam or to the Chief Minister of Haryana. Besides, you may issue an order on this application. Wing Commander Ahluwalia is waiting outside. We certainly want to help."

Then the Executive Councillor of Delhi cooled down. But he was much too clever. First, he said, "We have political power to rule."To which, I replied, "Sir, I will be very happy to send you all the applications. I will come exactly at 10 O'clock to the office and clear all 100 applications within 10 minutes, and forward to you for decision." Behl said that he didnot want to take my role and authority to issue permits as per rules." Frank and honest about his bias and support to his partymen in the constituency, he added in the same breath: "If I write in the application 'Please Examine', it means I am interested in the applicant. And for the rest, you may act as per rules without any undue favour." I was quite taken aback because I was not used to that kind of talk.

Ahluwalia went back and reported to Sanjay Gandhi and to the Lieutenant Governor, Baleshwar Prasad (1971-74): "Johorey Sahib is not issuing cement." The Lieutenant Governor summoned me. He asked the Prime Minister's Office if they had sent Ahluwalia. Back came the reply that the Prime Minister has not sent anybody, and that we should follow all the rules and regulations; that very morning, a question was asked in the Parliament about people talking of Vijaya Lakshmi Pandit wearing expensive clothes. The Lieutenant Governor was satisfied. Bureaucracy is a system, there was no alternative but to follow the system. Otherwise, we would have a dictatorship.

Financial Commissioner

So, my tenure in the Department of Civil Supplies gave an insight into the workings in Delhi, because I had no idea at all that money would pass through to the various political parties. I was told that Behl, my political boss, was a leader of the associations of owners of rickshaws and scooters. He knew my integrity but because of the political compulsions, he was made to go to T N Chaturvedi, the Chief Secretary, to complain about me. As a minister he could not humiliate himself, but he could not have ordered Chaturvedi to transfer me. Then they made me the Labour Commissioner of the Government of Delhi. When my posting was announced as the Labour Commissioner, O P Behl was facing problems in the Delhi Cloth Mills (DCM). If I became the Labour Commissioner,I would have been under Behl, the same minister. Look at the irony! I, therefore, decided to proceed on leave.

When I came back from leave in 1974, I joined as the Financial Commissioner, wherein I had the judicial functions and was number two in the hierarchy. I also moved to the bungalow of the Financial Commissioner, having given my charge. Then O P Behl sent me food. He and his wife came to my house because he was instrumental in my posting out.

When Indira Gandhi, for the first time, wanted the lighting of the Red Fort, it could not be done. The Junior Engineers' Association of Punjab had sabotaged the work because their demands were not met, citing lack of protective equipment. Therefore, the work had to be stopped. When I went for the inquiry, I went to each electricity maintenance centre and found that all the safety was there, but unused. Under the Electricity Act, one cannot get a licence to be an electrician unless he is qualified and uses gloves and gumboots to prevent shocks. Similar, labour laws are applied on the workers who clean roads. That rule has always been there. But electricians rarely bother to follow the rules. When I asked a worker as to why he did not wear the safety kits, I found that he had sold off his gloves. The administration was weak and did not implement the safety laws. It worked both ways. When applied properly, we see the workers in the Delhi Metro Rail Corporation wearing helmets.

Madan Lal Khurana had great regard for me. His opponent, the Chief Executive Councillor Radha Raman, also had great regard for me; my relations with them were good. I served three Chief Ministers of various states, including the most sophisticated state like Goa. When I rendered advice, sometimes it was palatable and sometimes it was not – but they understood my points of view.

The Emergency

The Emergency had its effect on officers in Delhi. The Law Secretary was a senior, sobre person with a judicial temperament. We used to walk into his room exactly at 1:30 p.m. and after lunch we dispersed at 2:00 p.m. There were four female IAS officers in the group. There, one officer said that he had been asked to arrest, and had disagreed to do so. They were very young officers with just two years of experience. I told them, "Look, you know the law. If I say that a certain person is a bad character under a particular section of the Criminal Procedure Code, you, the Magistrate of the area, should declare that person as a *goonda*(goon) under the Goonda Act and send him outside the territory of Delhi under your authority as a Magistrate. It is your judgment. If anything goes wrong, nobody is going to support you, neither the Chief Secretary nor the Chief Minister. If you think that a man was not to be harassed, say so on the file." Some officers did not do that. In fact, one woman officer named Aruna Roy resigned in protest. She was a brilliant officer and was married to a fellow IAS officer named Bunkar Roy, who earned name for his social service in Rajasthan. She had the courage.

Manipur

In mid-1975, I was nominated to attend the Advanced Professional Programme in Public Administration (APPA) Course for senior Civil Servants in Delhi. After that in 1976, I was posted to the Cabinet Secretariat located in Imphal, Manipur. In 1978, I was posted back to Delhi government at the post of Financial Commissioner.

CHAPTER 12

CHIEF SECRETARY, GOA

Posting to Goa

In 1981, as I was still with the Government of Delhi as the Financial Commissioner, a message went to Sunder Lal Khurana – the Lieutenant Governor of Delhi (1981 to 1982) – that K.C. Johorey was posted as the Chief Secretary, and that he should be relieved within two or three days. Khurana conveyed the message to me, and asked me to come over. He said, "I will not relieve you if do not want to go. I will tell the Home Ministry that I cannot spare you. Have a word with the Home Minister about the urgency to move out from Delhi to Goa. Remember that it is an accomplishment of a civil servant to be the Chief Secretary of a state, big or small. Every civil servant wants to retire as a Chief Secretary. So, think twice about it. If you do want to go, I will be very happy."

So, I came to the Ministry and was told later on by the Joint Secretary who was handling Goa that the government in Goa was about to fall, and that no work was going on there. It had been decided that the Chief Secretary's post was to be filled up soon, as a big conference was coming up there. The post of Chief Secretary had been vacant for six months. The former Chief Secretary, a local person, was from the Portuguese Imperial Service. He got his age reduced by 10 years after Goa joined the Union of India and nobody noticed that, though the Ministry might have come to know of this by word of mouth. He spoke Portuguese and was very prominent. Three or four MLAs were with him, and they could make a difference. So, the Chief Minister had to pacify these people. When I came to Goa, I had no house to live in. The designated house of Chief Secretary was to be given to the Law Minister. There was horse-trading because the government was falling and the politicians had pacified my predecessor to acquiesce to that. I put up in the Circuit House and I had my food at the army mess. The Circuit House was very expensive but food in the mess was not. Still, it was quite a lot of expenditure.

I asked the Under Secretary in charge of the Public Works Department (PWD) as to what the position regarding government quarters was. He said that some houses were coming up, and those would be allotted. The Under Secretary called the Chief Engineer and they decided to allot a house to the Chief Secretary. But that house, which was still incomplete, was going to be given to a Judge of the High Court. It took about a year for the Judge of the High Court to come. The Law Minister wanted me to have another minister's house which was vacant – that minister was his opponent Dayanand Ganesh Narwekar, a contender for the Chief Ministership. Had I taken that house, it would have created a major controversy. That was the inner dynamic. I told Chief Minister Rane that I was not going for that house. So, for a month I stayed here and there. Then I moved into a house even though it was incomplete, and there was no electricity. I asked my wife to come. She and the children arrived there.

There was one interesting development soon after. One day Rane, the Chief Minister, asked me: "Why don't you buy a house for yourself? I told my wife about the suggestion. My retirement was coming through in four to five years; she advised me against it. So, I told the Chief Minister that I did not want to do that. A civil servant is never restricted to one place, so why should I? The next day, Ramakant Dattaram Khalap, the Leader of the Opposition, came in the morning. He was a flourishing Barrister, very handsome, very fair with white and grey hair, a Saraswat Brahmin. Most of the high caste people, who could resist the Portuguese, had refused conversion; otherwise they became Brahmin-Christians, although the name remained the same – Sirimavo and David Bhandaranaike of Sri Lanka for example. David was a Buddhist. Some D'Souzas are Hindus. This is a very peculiar feature in Goa. So, Ramakant Khalap came and told me in his French accent: "Johorey Sahib, welcome to Goa. But I must say that you are the Chief Secretary of a Cabinet which is corrupt, and it is a Brahmin Cabinet." I said: "I beg your pardon! I do not follow your charge of corruption." He replied, "Your Chief Minister has taken seven houses from the Housing Board – houses meant for middle class people like you and me, preferably from Goa. I am going to give a Press Conference tomorrow and then raise this question in the State Assembly the day after, on the opening day." I was taken aback. That was my first contact with him. So I said,"You have the right to say so but since you have been so frank with me, may I request you to postpone your Press Conference and the question by a week? After all, the Assembly will go on. Since you have reported officially, I take cognizance and I will certainly inquire into it."

The next day, I rang up Gurdayal Singh Mandher, the Inspector General of Police, Goa. He was the Chief of the Indian Hockey Federation and a very upright officer. He said, "I cannot say. I, too, am new here. But give me at least two days." Sure enough, after two days, he came to me with a list and a copy of the complete file which showed the *benami* (fraudulent) transactions. The Chief Minister had usurped the corner plots, three on one side and three on the other. The only saving grace was that the allotment was not made public. I then met the Chief Minister and said, "Sir, the Leader of the Opposition had come to me the other day and complained that seven of these houses have been allotted *benami.* This will be a hell of a scandal, apart from being illegal, and there would be a reaction." What the Leader of the Opposition said was: "Opposition *walon ko bhi* one or two *deten, to wo chup ho jaten.* Politicians*aapas mein sauda karten hai. Wo kuch nahin hua, sabhi maar diyan unhone*" (illegal allotments could have also been made to the opposition leaders, they would have kept quiet!). S K Gandhi, the Commissioner for Housing, was a party to it.

The Chief Minister asked what should be done. I said, "The allotment of flats must be cancelled immediately, and Gandhi should be removed from his post." After seeing the Chief Minister, I called Gandhi and asked him. He replied that the Chief Minister asked for the file, and so he had given it to him. He must have been a party to it. He was a favourite of the Chief Minister. I asked Gandhi to hand over the charge, marked the note to the Chief Minister, and marked it to the Lieutenant Governor, so that even if the Chief Minister did not agree, the file would go to the Lieutenant Governor. I took that precaution.

The Kind of Job

The Chief Secretary was the chief among all the secretaries, and he manned the Secretariat. He was also the Cabinet Secretary, and the key advisor to the government. The relationship between the Chief Secretary, the Chief Minister and other ministers was also very intimate, and that was why the Central government took the state government's informal consent before his appointment. The practice was that the cabinet would approve two or three names for appointment as the Chief Secretary from among whoever was in the zone of promotion. The salary depended on an officer's own length of service and position in the cadre. The Chief Secretary may be drawing 4,000 rupees in those days or less, and it was not a fixed salary. The Cabinet Secretary and the other secretaries to the Government of India had fixed salaries. Similarly, the Additional Secretary's salary was fixed. It used to be 3,000 rupees. So, that was the hierarchy.

The role of the Chief Secretary was coordination among all the secretaries. He was not only primus inter-pares, but being the senior-most among the secretaries, he was the head of the civil services in the state. That does not mean that all the files went to the cabinet through the Chief Secretary. If that happened, then no work would get done. But he kept a record of all major policy matters decided by the cabinet, and then passed it on. The cabinet proceedings were recorded, and the Chief Secretary was privy to that. So, the Chief Secretary could not say that he did not know what was being decided in the cabinet. If he was asked, he gave advice also. The system was that there used to be weekly cabinet meeting on Wednesdays, unless the Chief Minister was out. It was the Chief Minister's prerogative to call a meeting on Mondays. The Chief Secretary's own meeting was on Tuesdays. The agenda was prepared and proposed by the Chief Secretary, who drew from the entire secretariat as to what it was that the ministers wanted to discuss – depending on the directives from the Central government, or the issues that were to be raised. Whatever items were on the agenda were discussed, and the decisions were recorded. Later on, the Chief Minister might or might not give a Press Conference.; that was his prerogative. If he asked the Chief Secretary to stay, he could. But by convention, the Chief Secretary did not stay for a Press Conference. The Chief Minister dealt with the Press. There was a government spokesman who could be a serving officer, or somebody else, for that purpose.

The agenda included the directives of the Central government to the Chief Ministers. One such directive was on the question of language, and another was on the Mandal Commission's Report submitted on 31st December 1980. The Mandal Commission or Backward Classes Commission was appointed by Janata government under Prime Minister Morarji Desai (1977-79). It had certain parameters or terms of reference, and the Report was submitted. For its implementation, the States' consent had to be obtained. That is how the federal system works. 'Reservation' was a matter regarding personnel, about the policy on recruitment and terms of service. Since the portfolios of the Personnel Department and Home Ministry were directly with the Chief Minister, I was also asked to give my comments. Other ministers discussed the issue and every time it came up, the cabinet did not agree to implement the Mandal Commission's recommendation that 27 per cent of the State government jobs should be reserved for Other Backward Classes (OBCs). But they did not say 'No' either. After a free discussion, they deferred the item.

The population of Goa had a certain number of people who were Christians(Roman Catholics) and because of the Portuguese influence, the Catholic church was predominating. At the best of times, the population of Catholics was 30 to 40 per cent, never more than that – even after the withdrawal of the Portuguese. Portuguese did not spare even Goan Christians – they were not given access to higher education. So, they used to escape to Bombay to work as cooks, bearers etc., and taking up all kinds of professions. Some of them, who got educated and had the minimum qualifications, got selected in the army, and many became army officers. I remember General S F Rodrigues, the Chief of the Army Staff, (1990-93), who was a Catholic from Goa. The Naval Chief Admiral Pareira was also a Catholic. Many Christians held senior positions in the Armed Forces, and in various other professions – including the Civil Services. Patric Fernandes, one of the senior-most IAS officers, was my predecessor in Goa.

The recommendations of the Mandal Commission were irrational. How can one reserve 27 per cent of the Central and State government's jobs for the Other Backward Classes when their population was much less? The problem did not arise in Goa. Goans were either Brahmin-Christians or Rajput-Christians. Their women still adhered to old traditions. They had made some kind of a compromise and stuck to their language, Konkani. They also learnt Portuguese and French. For some time, the gazette was published in Portuguese and French. But after Independence, it was changed to English. Their pattern of holidays and office timings were different. For example, the Portuguese would close the Secretariat from 1:00 to 3:00 p.m. for their afternoon siesta. It was a small place, and they would go home and have their lunch with children. One of the things which I revised was that two hours of siesta. It was ridiculous! I had to implement the rules of the Union Territory of the Government of India. Whatever be the timing, I said that so many hours of work per week was necessary and employees could have one hour break for lunch. It was observed by the staff, but very reluctantly. But gradually, they came round.

The Goans were an easy-going people. The shops were nearby and in the evening, they would go and sit down there. There were no clubs there. All the entertainment was within the homes. So, their social system was confined to strong family ties in a small island. There was the Roman Catholic Church, and their whole world was surrounded by the church and the family. Large groups dancing in the city square are a recent development. Sunday was observed and much celebrated. Everybody was God-fearing and went to the church. The Hindus were not like that. At one time, the crusaders inflicted extreme atrocities. In the whole eastern region from Macao onwards, people who did not convert to Christianity were banished and sent to the jail. Fort Aguada was the jail where people were put in for various crimes, and one of the crimes was refusal to convert. This was 400 to 500 years back. Unlike the British, the Portuguese mixed with the rural population. They had marital relations with the local people and learnt the local language. For example, the President of the Daman Congress, who was a Portuguese lady, stayed back in India. Her husband also stayed back, but some of her relatives returned to Portugal. Before Independence and merger with India, there were MPs – one was a Hindu, Count Deshprabhu and his family, and two others were Christian Counts. The District Judge did not go to Portugal. His brother went but his family stayed back. So, they came to terms with the ground reality.

The Chief Secretary's role was really one of coordination between various departments for development. Whatever subject the Chief Minister wanted, the Chief Secretary attended to it. The Chief Minister had the Forest and Finance portfolios with him. So, that was my portfolio also; although there was the Finance Secretary who did all the work, those files used to go through me. It was important for the Chief Secretary to ensure that there were no deviations from major policy matters. A good civil servant would definitely ensure that. If a minister said 'do this', and if a civil servant had a doubt, then he should record that and send the file again to the minister.

At one time, there was conflict on various issues with the Chief Minister and the MLAs because the relationship within the cabinet was very dicey. This was a Congress government, and the Congress had a simple majority in the 60-member Assembly. The party's strength was 34. Four or five persons were just horse-trading up and down. There was an atmosphere of uncertainty, and they were all in tenterhooks. The PWD minister, Dr Wilfred Anthony D'Souza, was a Congressman and a very cultivated person as well as a surgeon of eminence. He was also a Fellow of the Royal College of Surgeons. His practice in those days was 20,000 rupees a month. So, he did not need money from the party for his political work. The party needed his money! So, these were no corruption in that sense.

Similarly, Pratapsinh Rane, the Chief Minister of Goa, was a big land owner from the Ranes of Satara who had resisted the Portuguese rule. But he had some internal family problems. He had cousins. Sanyogita Rane, one of his sisters-in-law, had a large estate. She had great faith in the system, and personally used to come to me and complain against the Chief Minister. I dealt with the cases of revenue- related dispute that came to me. Peculiarly, the Chief Secretary in Goa was originally called as the 'Secretary General', who had some legal and appellate powers also. So, I said that since it was a revenue matter, I would certainly look into it very carefully. The records were all in Portuguese. My Personal Secretary, Angela Menezes, was a portly woman with four or five children. I asked her to bring all the records. She knew Portuguese, and so, I asked her to translate them for me to go through. In Delhi, all the records were in Urdu and Persian. When I was Financial Commissioner in Delhi, I could go back to the old records at the National Archives of India; because of my knowledge of Urdu, I found out about the trial of Mughal Emperor Bahadur Shah Zafar (1757-1862) by a Captain in the British Indian Army. Similarly, in the Goa Archives, I found that Pratapsinh

Rane's family's claim on the estate was totally wrong. The estate belonged to Major Z S Rane, who was in the British Indian Army. He was the husband of Sanyogita Rane. He came with Sanyogita Rane, who was also a Member of Lok Sabha (1980-84). She asked for help. At a certain time, people could come to me without any appointment. I kept up the old traditions. The Chief Minister also asked me and I agreed to look into it. It was a judicial matter; I went through every record and recorded my judgment.

Conference of the Commonwealth Heads, 1983

The relationship within the cabinet was difficult. One of the major events that took place during my tenure, the planning of it, was the Seventh Biennial Conference of the Commonwealth Heads of Governments (CHOGM). The conference was held in Delhi from 23rd to 29th November 1983. It is held once every two years. This was the first time when there was what is called 'bush shirt diplomacy' or diplomacy at the highest level – at a retreat in Goa, where the heads of governments interacted in a very informal way. They all stayed in the resort with no formal dresses or timings, and talked informally. They could talk politics or anything on the side-lines. The main conference was in Delhi. As the Chief Secretary, I had to coordinate. On Indira Gandhi's instruction, I took permission of the Chief Minister to leave the station and go to New Delhi with Subhash Tendon to meet her and work out the details of the arrangements in Goa. Many times, there were tussles between the Central government and the State government on simple issues like supply of water to the delegates. The Chief Engineer and I pointed out in writing that bridges over the rivers were failing, and that one bridge had already collapsed. Luckily, the main bridge was all right during the conference, but it collapsed after three years.

The PWD minister was Dr Wilfred D'Souza. The Finance Minister was the Chief Minister himself. The PWD had a major role to play. Accommodation for 44 Prime Ministers was not available in the Raj Bhawan. So, some other safe place of stay had to be arranged. We decided on Fort Aguada. It was a heritage village managed by the Tatas in the Private Sector. They did not have more than 24 cottages. So, the remaining number of cottages had to be added. Each cottage had to be identical; one cannot put Margaret Thatcher, the British Prime Minister, in a cottage with less facilities than those available to Indira Gandhi. Only the Prime Minister, or the Heads of the Governments of the countries where there were no Prime Ministers, were to stay in the venue. Even the Foreign Ministers were accommodated somewhere else.

There, a very tricky situation arose. One of the Prime Ministers of African countries sent his Security Officer, who said: "My Prime Minister will not stay in this cottage. There will be security problems. Some torpedo boat may come and shoot. He will stay in the palace of the Governor-General" (Raj Bhawan was called the Palace). I said: "I will convey this to the Government of India. Your point is well- taken, but we do not have 44 rooms in the Raj Bhawan and in any case, it is a matter for the Commonwealth Secretariat to decide. At that time, Shridath Surendranath 'Sonny' Ramphal, the Secretary-General of the Commonwealth, had also come. He was from the British Guyana. Now, it is called Guyana. Indira Gandhi made two visits to check every detail. She was absolutely meticulous. In one day, she went through the details of where every guest would stay, how he would move and so on.

Of course, the complete programme had yet to materialise. Here again, the conflict between the Prime Minister and the Chief Minister arose. Rane, the Chief Minister, spread the word around that Indira Gandhi would lay the foundation of a dam for which the government had to acquire some land. That land belonged to Rane, and it was his mind work. Suddenly, he shot off a letter to invite 25,000 villagers to attend a public meeting in which the Prime Minister would come to lay foundation stone of the dam. This was done without telling me or Air Marshal Idris Hassan Latif, the Governor, who was in Bombay. There was no separate Governor for Goa. The Governor of Maharashtra acted as the Governor of Goa, Daman and Diu. Governor Latif told me, "KC, I am in Bombay. Unless there is a war or such emergency, you please do the routine administration. I would sign any paper that you send to Bombay by courier. If you want me to come, I would." Naturally, when the Prime Minister came, he also came. I had made the Prime Minister's programme in complete details as per instructions in the Blue Book. Every minute was accounted for – arrival, departure, who would wait, what would happen, when and where, and the agenda for discussion. It was sent to the Governor and he approved it. It came back to Goa, and was sent back to the Prime Minister's Office under the signature of a Deputy Secretary.

Then, at 8 O'clock in the morning, I was woken up by R K Dhawan of the PM's Office. That was the only time that I talked to Dhawan, even though I knew that he was there. The Chief Minister used to go and wait on him. He asked me, "How has your Chief Minister issued invitations to lay the foundation stone for the construction of a dam?" I was taken aback, and replied, "As far as I know, there is no such programme because every programme that was suggested had been approved by the Governor and the Chief Minister, before being sent to the Prime Minister's Office." R K Dhawan said, "Please tell your Chief Minister that the Prime Minister will not lay the foundation stone." Now, I had to tell the Chief Minister the truth. Meanwhile,the villagers had been told that the Prime

Minister was coming, and much enthusiasm was generated. Then, the Chief Minister went to that faroff location and pacified them. They did not cause him any further embarrassment, but they were very disappointed. Apparently, an officer named S K Gandhi was sent by Pratapsingh Rane to meet Rao Birendra Singh, the Central Minister for Agriculture in Delhi, with a mission to get a project of several crores approved instantly. Obviously, the nebulous idea was rejected, the project and the Prime Minister's Office informed.

Petty Corruption

I was in Goa for two and a half years. Some of the MLAs were corrupt. One case of D F Desai came to me. He was allegedly a member of a liquor mafia. But the industrialists and the industries of Goa were different from the rest of the country. The Dempos and the Chowgules were highly educated people, who were in the shipping industry. They were not small, fly-by-night contractors. They lived in great style and used to travel abroad and in the rest of the country.

There was some distance between the Collector or the District Magistrate and the public. It was not so in Goa. Goa has iron ore and other raw materials. Small businesses, which lead to corruption and permit Raj, was not there. How can one cancel Chowgule's shipping licence which was approved by the Government of India? So, it did not work that way. The police, for example, was not corrupt. The kind of police atrocities that we have here, were never heard of such things in Goa, where they had a completely different and open society. But there were some cases of theft of timber, which used to pass through the forest. So, the forests were one area of corruption where smuggling of timber took place.

Then some Goans started a business in the issuing of passports. There was no Regional Passport Office in Goa, and official of the rank of Deputy Secretary or Magistrate could also certify the genuineness of a passport applicant. The MPs could also do so, but he charged 500 rupees for signing each form of the passport paperwork. That was his fixed rate. There was no corruption in the bureaucracy and the police in Goa. But yes, smuggling was going on. The two major items smuggled out were alcohol and timber.

Bombay to Goa was a beautiful overnight journey by ship. People could board on the upper deck or a cabin, depending on their capacity to pay and early next morning, the ship would arrive opposite the Secretariat Building in Panjim (now Panaji). After a gap of a few hours, the ship would leave Panjim in the evening and reach Bombay the next morning. Bombay was a dry area. About 40 to 50 boxes of alcohol used to be smuggled in collaboration between the Captain of the ship and, maybe, the police. In this case, D F Desai, the owner of the consignment, was an MLA. When the Superintendent of Police got the information that so many boxes of liquor bottles were being loaded into the ship, he seized them. Then he summoned not the Captain of the ship himself, but the number two person. The police station was located in a very fineold Portuguese building with lovely carved furniture and Belgian glass windows. This was quite unlike some of the aesthetically poor district offices of Superintendents of Police in Delhi. The ship's number two man came in when the Superintendent of Police asked him if he had done this. He replied, "No, I do not know what the consignment is." The Superintendent of Police got upset. He just took out a ruler and said, "*Tumko hum abhi theek karega, tumko abhi band karega. Humko pukka khabar hain. Abhi pakad ke laa raha hai chalis baksa*" (I will sort you out and arrest you, I have information about your 40 boxes). The man got scared and blindly ran out towards the door and hit it. There was some small cut and bleeding from his nose. He noisily ran out and reported to the MLA, who was the owner of the illicit bottles ofliquor. The MLA complained to the Chief Minister.

Pratapsingh Rane, the Chief Minister, called me and complained: "Your Superintendent of Police has beaten up this person and one must suspend him immediately." I said,"Let me seeto this matter. Who is the complainant? I will find out and let you know."The Chief Minister said, "I am going to issue an order straightway," to which, I replied, "Sir, you cannot issue a suspension order. An order can be issued only by the Ministry of Home Affairs, and that too, after an inquiry. You can make a complaint." The Chief Minister said, "No, you do it. I am telling you to do it." I said, "Alright, I will do it. But give me a chance to see to the issue."

I rang up the Superintendent of Police and said that a complaint was being forwarded to him. He was S S Deol, who had earlier served as a young Superintendent of Police with the National Security Guards in Delhi. He said, "I have not beaten him. I did shout at him and threaten him. He ran out in fear and injured his nose. There was no other injury. Have him examined." I told the Chief Minister, "I have taken the statement of the officer. We cannot punish him." The Chief Minister said, "Suspend him." I said, "I am sorry, this cannot be done. Even if you give me in writing, I shall not do it. I have to protect this officer because he is truthful."

Then, as the Home Secretary, I asked the Superintendent of Police to file an FIR and arrest the suspected MLA. He replied, "Sahib, one cannot do so because he is an MLA." I went to the speaker who said, "Please do not arrest him within the Legislative Assembly; when he is outside, you can do so." He was hiding in the Assembly building to evade getting arrested. Then he went across to Bombay and asked for return of the confiscated goods, and threatened to give call for a strike. This was how the politicians worked. Then he returned to Goa. I stood my ground and did not recommend a transfer of the Superintendent of Police.

Eventually, the same MLA and his mafia became active in smuggling timber. There was a simple forest barrier, with one forest guard who had no telephone. One night, the forest guard stopped the mafia's truck loaded with timber, and unloaded the contraband. The MLA, who was driving, was drunk. In the scuffle, the forest guard got injured but survived, and was picked up by another forest guard who got him admitted in a hospital. This report came to P P Malhotra, the Chief Conservator of Forest, on the third day. The MLA managed to escape before he could be arrested. The police kept up their search for him. I told the IGP and the Forest Department that they must acquire wireless sets to check smuggling. I recommended that the Forest Department must have their weapons, and should be given magisterial power. There should be better liaison between police and all the others. Later on, I believe, in some fracas in Madhya Pradesh, that MLA was killed.

In 1983, I was posted back to Delhi for my last tenure, which ended in 1985.

Delhi State Industrial Development Corporation

I was posted as the Chairman of the Delhi State Industrial Development Corporation (DSIDC), which was a Public Sector Undertaking. For the first time, they put up a full-time Chairman because the activities of the Corporation were extending. As the Commissioner for Civil Supplies, I was the ex-officio Director of the Company. One of the major aims of the corporation was to shift the industries from non-conforming areas to conforming areas. That was the starting point of the corporation. It was not put in place with a view to industrialise Delhi. The existing industries were to be reorganised. In the earlier phases subsequent to the Partition, they set up Okhla Phase-I and Phase-II. The main aim was to regularise the haphazard growth of the industries which were coming up all over Delhi, apart from the fact that the corporation also worked on exporting and mobilising the entrepreneurs.

The concept that was developed was that the first generation entrepreneurs, that is people who had not done any trading or manufacturing earlier, were to be given what was called the 'sheds'. A shed meant a piece of land with infrastructure like electricity and water supply, and then they were to start their own industries. Laudable as it was, it ran into hopelessly bad weather, in the sense that all the vested interests began to exploit those people who had no experience of industry or trade. What they did was that they started giving these sheds to other people. Within a few months those people resold them by some underhand methods, with the result that we found somebody else was working in the sheds. So, the objective of building up the first generation entrepreneurs was defeated. Sheds which came up in various parts of the city with a view to provide employment were bought, for example, by somebody who managed to influence the Corporation and after a few months, resold them to somebody else. Not only that, they did not even pay the rent which was agreed. It was some ridiculous amount like 800 rupees a month; where would one get a shed for 800 rupees? Anyway, this charade went on and on. There was a trouble between the entrepreneurs and one could not find out who was the in-charge. Similarly, there was a tussle between the Ministry and the Corporation.

Industries allowed in Delhi at that time were of 'non-nuisance' making industries. Garment-making industries was there, but most of them was misused. Mining was another industry which was a concern of the corporation being open-cast mines. Right from the time of Shamsuddin Iltutmish (1211-1236) and Ghiysuddin Balban (1266-1285), one would find all buildings made of the red sand, *bajri,* which was popularly called *badarpur.* It was a very good binding material. It was mixed with cement, sand and water, and used in plastering. It was extracted from certain villages which were in the Indira Gandhi International Airport and the Chhatarpur areas, where deep craters were formed. The Bhatti mines which were more famous did not have any water. *Badarpur* extracted from the Bhatti mines used to be sold for about 100 rupees a truck in the bazaar. The Municipal Corporation of Delhi made some money out of it. There was also death of labourers, over which there was a fight between the Governments of Haryana and Delhi. When a labourer died on Haryana side, they would put his dead body on the Delhi side.

When I came on the scene, the mines were already nationalized, and an order was passed to take them over. Then the local people and President of the Delhi Congress, Chaudhry Dalip Singh – a very tall, handsome man – came to me and said, "Johorey Sahib,*aapka chadar saaf hai abhi tak. Aap isme kyo padh rahen hain?"* (you are clean so far, why are you getting into this job?). I told him that I didn't follow what he meant. He said, "The mines are our only bread and butter...." I replied, "This is an order of the Government of India, which has already nationalised the mines." Many of the local leaders like Heth Ram Sharma owned the mines. They were all ruined by nationalisation.

What happened was that the government did not get revenue because the labour used to work at night and carry the stuff on their donkeys. Most of the labours were refugees from Multan and Sind. They were very poor, but were expert in that mine area, which had no water. Nobody could survive in that. But being from the desert area and a migratory people, they knew the art of extracting sand by scooping out with hand implements at night in lantern light. Suddenly one day, a deep crater would cave in and labourers would die, buried alive. Others would not even know that. There was no telephone facility. So, having nationalised the mines, we needed to apply the labour laws. We placed some nurses and two doctors there. We also put up a school.

The opposition against nationalisation was building up. People kept on complaining. They had sent a deputation to Indira Gandhi, the Prime Minister.

So, Indira Gandhi asked Jagmohan, the Lieutenant Governor of Delhi (1982-84), to enquire. One fine morning Jagmohan, accompanied by H K L Bhagat and Rajiv Gandhi – both Members of Parliament – came to the site of mining. Arun Singh, who was one of the key advisors to the Prime Minister, also came. I was told that the Lieutenant Governor was visiting, and so I was there. I explained to them that I passed orders that we would not allow male and female labourers to work in unsafe mines, and sent a doctor for their medical check-up. I had decided to pay wages to the labourers, men and women, but would not allow them to go to the mines even if we would suffer a loss. There was a great opposition from vested interests. Many feared they would be out of jobs. So, I told the visiting team that nobody would be out of job. We had put up notices. The agitators were pacified.

A decision was taken to appoint a committee to go into the issue deeply, seal the unsafe pits and stop mining in that area. Arun Singh asked me, "How will you ensure safety?" I replied: "I will not allow the labours to do unsafe work but in safe pits, scientific mining with machinery would be permitted. We will hire the machines to do the scooping and stacking. Then we would grade the *badarpur* and sell it in retail. The whole thing would be reorganized." The dispute was about the ownership of unsafe and abandoned pits. Nobody knew who owned them. From those pits, a labour got hardly two rupees a day. There was corruption at every level. The *Choudhri* (headman) at the village put his own chowkidar and took two rupees from every truck. So, if about 1,000 trucks went daily, then he earned 2,000 rupees. The government officers knew all this but what could a Manager do, he had no police with him. The Central Industrial Security Force (CISF) was not yet born, and the Central Reserve Police Force (CRPF) was not trained to do this work. The mine area was spread out over several square kilometres, and there were no gates of entry or exit. People could enter from all sides. The trucks were coming from all over Haryana, and there was no boundary fixed between Haryana and Delhi. There were no roads. A few personnel of the Delhi Police were posted there, but they also got mixed up with the local people.

A Committee was appointed and I was made the Chairman of the Committee, with Lalit Maken and Sajjan Kumar as members. The question of protocol arose.

Sajjan Kumar, a Member of Parliament, was a thorough gentleman. He was the leader of that whole area which was inhabited by the Gujjars. Officially, the mines were owned by the state. Gujjars were doing the grazing. They had the traditional rights. Normally as a Member of the Parliament, Sajjan Kumar should have been the Chairman of the Committee. But Jagmohan said, "Johorey is a senior Additional Secretary, and he will be the Chairman." Lalit Maken represented labour interest. He was a leader of labour union and was also a member of the Assembly of Delhi. The Director of the Mine Safety was the technical member. So, a five-member team was formed. We had to give our report within three months.

I immediately arranged one meeting and visited all the mines. I must admire Jagmohan's efficiency; the order was issued by the next evening. A charter was given and the work started off. We contacted the Bharat Heavy Electricals and Bharat Heavy Machinery. It was one Public Sector Undertaking approaching another one. So, there was no need of quotations. That saved time. We took Sajjan Kumar and Lalit Maken to Nagpur on a study tour of the Indian Bureau of Mines. The Chief Engineer of DSIDC was a trained mining Engineer, who had trained the junior technical staff on the ground. So they did not need to go there, but the local people had to be trained. We showed them how to do open-cast mines work and what the safety measures to be adopted were. They came back quite happy. Within a month, we submitted the report. The report had many facets. One was the protection of village. All the identified pits would not be used. There were pits to be put under 'green cover' and in the deep pits, water bodies would be created for ground water recharging. Later, as population expanded, I believe some of those pits have been filled up by the people from the real estate!

Later on, during my last appointment when there was some agitation, I was called by the Lieutenant Governor. I drew his attention to that Johorey Committee Report. The government had appointed another Committee headed by Lovraj Kumar, who was a Secretary to the Government of India. His report was on protection of the 'Ridge', and identified all the encroachments on the Ridge. I said, "There are reports of Lovraj and Johorey Committees, and you take cognizance of that."

In the DSIDC, some managers the Raw Materials Division may have wrongly channelised certain items like steel balls and certain other quota-items like steel sheets, rods, iron, steel, copper, etc. The Raw Materials Division was full of corruption. I believe one Engineer who was in-charge of the Raw Materials Division had constructed a big house in Vasant Vihar. By the time I was posted, he had resigned and was released from the service. So, he was out of the control. At that time, we tried to curb the corrupt practices as much as we could within limitations.

The nationalisation of mines was done in haste and in a very unprofessional way. The Public Sector is not, and should not, be an employment-generating agency. We had two regular officers on deputation. A post was created just because an MP or somebody pressed for it, and the management simply buckled. They were government servants, and so, nothing could have happened to them. A huge staff was placed in the Connaught Place office complex, for which we paid a nominal rent of four rupees per square feet. A huge land was taken over in the manner of a business house. I must say that there is nothing wrong with the concept of the Public Sector being well-endowed, but there should be limits to allow that. Those were the pre-reform days, and nobody questioned unprofitability. My job was not to question the concept itself, but to manage it as best as I could.

When I was in the DSIDC, an agitation was going on and there was a blockade. Bhattacharya, the Managing Director, was held hostage. So I had to call the police to remove them, but they said that they had no power to do that. The Commissioner of Police was helpful. The police announced that obstruction of the traffic would not be allowed. The agitators removed the tents and other obstruction without any force. If the Administration is firm, one cannot obstruct a lawful citizen from going to his work. So, that is why the debate is going on in West Bengal on the right to strike. Ours was a government company and so nobody was bothered about the losses. '*Aaiye, chale jaiye, tankha to milni hain*' (come, go, whatever, pay you will keep getting!) was the attitude of the staff, who were ill-trained and laxly recruited.

Apart from *badarpur* and mining, there were other industries to manage directly, but we were not in the manufacturing field. We were also facilitating and helping people to export – like the export of 'Janta Shirts'. My predecessor had sent about a thousand bicycles to the Middle East, but they did not take delivery for reasons of poor quality. The DSIDC could not ensure any quality control. They just helped entrepreneurs to fill up the forms for supply of raw materials for a manufacturing unit to produce goods for export and local consumption. So, quality control was introduced.

The aim of setting up of Public Sector Undertakings in certain fields of the economy was quite different. Every State has its own Industrial Development Corporation and Delhi is treated like any other State. But Delhi's urban problem is different. Delhi had been a centre of distribution of goods right from the pre-British and British days. Merchants came and exchanged their goods in Delhi. There was hardly any local production, except consumable items like halwa and sweets. Delhi was a distribution centre for carpets from Central Asia. Cloth came to Delhi but it was not a production centre. This character of Delhi could not be challenged. Delhi had been the seat of the government in the pre-British, the British and post-Independence days.

Anyway, urban development of Delhi was not planned. Industrialisation of Delhi started later, and then came the scheme of shifting the industries. But there was no urban planning because it is the human nature to work where he lives. So the slums came up. One could upgrade those slums but one could not demolish these. We then took up the Narela Industrial Area which was unoccupied open land at that time. So, by nature of things, as it happens in bureaucratic and slothful organisations, activities of the Industrial Development Corporation, which had a very small beginning, kept on expanding rapidly irrespective of its effectiveness. They got the mines and they got liquor. But when they went in loss, one-third of the Corporation was separated into a Tourism Corporation. Also, a Khadi Commission was set up. Where was the need to expand just to perpetuate a losing venture?

Location of the Supreme Court could have been 20 to 30 miles outside Delhi. Why has it got to be right near the Central Secretariat? Nagpur, which had a very old High Court, would have been a very nice place to house the Supreme Court of India. It is the geographical centre and has good connectivity. The scheme of sending mail by air from the state capitals to Nagpur and exchange of mail-bags was started by Rafi Ahmed Kidwai when he was the Minister of Communications. With rapid urbanization, everything went out of control. All the green areas right up to Haryana and beyond are now coping with haphazard patterns of urbanisation. Huge malls are coming up, all the vegetable-plots are gone and urban pressure continues.

So, the DSIDC has a new role now. What they could do is to find, with the help of the Department of Labour, whether the industries are running safely or not, and then promote exports and reorganise the entire industry; like they conceived the idea of flattened factories in small double-storeyed buildings for manufacturing in crowded areas – which they learnt from Hong Kong and Singapore. So, this planning goes on. But we cannot change the occupation of the people. After all, even for production of food items for the *halwai* (sweetmeat makers), the home or residence – both are same. His wife works at the back side of the residence and the sale is done on the front side. Such practices have to be taken into account in planning.

Tihar Jail

One evening, a message came to me that I should take over as an ex-officio of IG of Prisons in addition to my basic post, the Financial Commissioner. So,

I made two to three visits to the Tihar Central Jail. They made me IG, Prisons, because it was not a post by itself, even though it should have been. I found the prison very crowded, with very primitive staff and everything in very primitive condition. I visited the 'deaths row', where I saw one terrorist who was hung later on. I remember that I visited the famous murder convict Dr Jain and Charles Shobhraj because they were famous, and a prisoner named Malik who was responsible for several murders. The prison was over-crowded and there was hardly any awareness of modern methods of reform. There were female prisoners; they did not have many complaints but over-crowding was certainly a problem. Even now, it is overcrowded; there is no doubt about that. Now, much more modern facilities are there. In those days, there were no cases of prisoners trying to escape. There must have been some inquiry into bad food or leakage of funds. I had nothing to do with that inquiry. After sometime, I was transferred.

My visits to the Tihar Central Jail were in addition to my other duties. I did report to the government that the makeshift arrangements in a prison like Tihar Jail should not go on. They did not have a full-time IG or a DIG. There was only a Jail Superintendent who was a very junior officer, without any training in modern methods of reform. He must be a jail official. A Jailor is not a policeman, he is a 'keeper'. He has to have some knowledge of psychology, social science, public administration and management. The entire staff was relic of the British times.

The prisoners were isolated from each other, but they came out and ate food together. Tihar Jail was not bad when compared to other jails, but with so many prisoners coming in, there was a huge shortage of staff. The accounting was bad and superfluous; nobody paid any attention to that. In the scheme of priority, it was not there. It was neither a cushy nor a glamourous job. A person, who is appointed to the job, had no heart or soul in it. He was there just because he had to earn his bread. He was just posted there without any kind of training – which everybody requires and is a must.

I did bring Tihar Jail to the notice of the authorities. But reforms were a tremendous task. Leading public men were appointed as Jail Visitors. I do not think many of the leaders at that time ever visited the jail. The Press was also not much concerned about the jail. They were only worried about sensational news. Only when a prisoner escapes then there is much noise. I talked to Charles Shobhraj. I asked him the usual question of how he was. What surprised me was that he had an air-conditioner! This was totally illegal. He was being treated differently. Other prisoners who were on trial for murder did not have it. There was a legacy of A-Class prisoners. The political leaders were considered as A-Class prisoners. In my view, all prisoners should be the same. The political prisoners need not go to jail. They can be detained in their own homes. But persons with criminal record or criminal offence should be treated alike. Dr N K Jain was charged with murder but he was such a good doctor that in his spare time, he could be allowed to come out to help others, so long as he did not escape. Dr Jain did not complain about lack of facilities.

Indira Gandhi's Assassination

One morning, when I reached my office, I found that some members of the staff were late. All India Radio had made some announcements which I heard when I reached the office at about 11:00 a.m. My wife was expected to come from Lucknow. So, I went to receive her at the New Delhi railway station. Then I went and signed the Book of Condolence. But the effect of announcement of the death of Indira Gandhi was that the crowds started gathering. So, one of the first things I did was to close the liquor shops. I did it when I heard that the situation was getting hot. I informed the Administration that it was being done. Some reply came, saying that the Excise Commissioner's permission was required. I said: "What do you mean? I am responsible for the sale of liquor and it is my responsibility to ensure the safety of my staff. If they open the shops then the mob would break open, get drunk and then start looting. I closed the liquor shops and advised the Excise Department to do the same".

When Mrs Gandhi's body was taken to the All India Institute of Medical Sciences (AIIMS), there was a large crowd. I did not go to the hospital. I was in my office. Tension had started to build up immediately after the news came. People were converging all over the place and there was utter confusion. From the AIIMS, the body of Indira Gandhi was sent to Teen Murti House (New Delhi) where military officers were put on duty. The TV was there. I did not go to Teen Murti House to pay homage. I remained in my post and alerted my staff to stop the sale of liquor. My Assistant Manager brought the news that there were some dead bodies in the railway station. I informed P G Gavai, the Lieutenant Governor, who asked me to proceed to Raj Niwas. I complied though I was not in the direct line of action of the Delhi Administration; I was neither the Deputy Commissioner of a District nor the IG, Police, I was the Chairman of the DSIDC. Looting was going on and there was a riotous situation. So he took a decision to send me to Police Headquarters. He knew that I was the senior most member of the IAS. The post of the Chief Secretary was not filled; and Suresh Bajpai was acting Chief Secretary.

When I rang up Bajpai, he was not there to respond. After all, he was a brother-officer; I must tell him what was happening. But I did not know where he was. I felt that it would be quite incorrect for me to go to Police Headquarters and sit over Subhash Tandon, the Police Commissioner. He was a very good friend and I had a good rapport with him. But basically the Police Commissioner's system was wrong in the sense that the Lieutenant Governor was responsible for law and order. So I said: "I will certainly go, if it helps in any way. Kindly send a message to Subhash Tandon". I reached there and told Subhash Tandon whatever information I had. I sat next to him and was given a telephone to pass messages to pass on. I was there the whole day and night. At nightfall Subhash Tandon said: "Let us go and talk to the Lieutenant Governor". I reported to the Lieutenant Governor whatever was going on. That whole night I was shuttling between Police Headquarters and Raj Niwas. I did not go home for 48 hours. The atmosphere in the Delhi Administration was one of absolute confusion. P G Gavai did not get full information. I remember very clearly that Jagdish Tytler came to me at Raj Niwas late at night and told me: "I am totally with you in restoring the law and order. I have not taken any part in this." To my mind, Tytler was not involved at all. I remember, he also came to attend a meeting of the different local communities at Raj Niwas.

I was at Police Headquarters where they had set up a Control Room. Charanjit Singh of the Coca Cola Company telephoned me to say that miscreants had come to his area nine times, and I informed the police authorities. During a discussion in Raj Niwas on the riots there was no proposal from any quarter to hand over any area to the Army but the troops were called in for patrolling. There was no request from the acting Chief Secretary, Bajpai, to the Army authorities for assistance at that time. The Police never said that they could not control the situation. I told Subhash Tandon that we must have Magistrates to order firing when necessary. I rang up the acting Chief Secretary Bajpai and asked him to the send me a list of Magistrates. The whole night we could not get a list of 14 Magistrates who were to go with the riot control teams.

The basic principle is that when the Army is called in aid of a civil administration, they are guided by certain rules. The order for the Army, that being the ultimate resort of the state, is to use minimum but 'telling' force, whereas the police have instruction to uses the least force and resort to firing first to scare the mob and then to inflict least injury. The Army units had to be accompanied by a Magistrate who could give his consent to firing when there was violence and looting. An Army Captain came and asked me for Magistrates to accompany the army columns so that they could open fire if there was any violence. The Army units were sent to protect the India Gate area (New Delhi); they were not sent to the far-off localities. But when looting and violence was going on in West Delhi and East Delhi areas, they were not given any clear instructions.

I had a similar situation in Goa once. There were fights between Lombadis and others. Fortunately, the Inspector General of Police who was there, was on the same wavelength and agreed that a show of force was necessary to avoid communal riots. I called out the Navy. Back came a telephone from the Ministry of Home Affairs, saying that the Chief Minister complained that his image had been spoiled. I said: "What would the image be if four people die in rioting? Who would suffer?" The preventive action of flag march by the Navy had the desired effect. Tackling such problems was the responsibility of the man on the spot, the Deputy Commissioner or the District Magistrate.

Similarly, Magistrates should have been present and the acting Chief Secretary Bajpai should have been be sitting in the Police Headquarters Control Room rather than going to Teen Murti House to pay homage to the late Prime Minister's body. The TV was covering the event and everybody wanted to notice: even the Municipal Commissioner, Police Commissioner and other senior civil servants were there. Take the Army's example. When there was an attack, the top commanders would not go on running here and there but act at his level. He would stay in his post, do the planning and thinking, and delegate powers. So, the Chief Secretary should be sitting in his Secretariat, not lobby with the MPs and feel important.

At the Teen Murti House, the Army, in ceremonial uniform, was in ceremonial guard, as laid down in the rules. They were on the vigil. They ensured the orderly control of the traffic and movement of people. I remember, on the first day nothing happened. On the second day, more people started came to pay homage. At night looting in various localities had started. The next day, a number of white Americans Sikhs with white kurta, pyjamas and turban were filing past. Then somebody started pelting stones at the band of American Sikhs. They took shelter in the MPs' quarters in the South Avenue. At that time I and my wife had gone there to pay our homage.

I went back to my office and then to Raj Niwas where I remained for the whole of night, shuttling between Raj Niwas and Police Headquarters. The next morning Jagdish Tytler came. I told him to call some leaders for them to report regarding their areas. They said: "Sahib, *hamara moholley mein to kuch nahin hua. Hamne sabko rok liya*" (we did not permit any mischief in our locality). Then, I told the Lieutenant Governor that I must go home, change and shave.

Earlier, my wife used to teach English and piano in Guru Harkishan Public School in Vasant Vihar (New Delhi), where the majority of students were Sikhs. When she came back to Delhi, the Principal of the School said: Sudha, you should rejoin our school. There is nobody to teach piano. Take the piano classes." Vasant

Vihar, being a posh area, the parents wanted the children to learn the piano. So my wife agreed to teach once or twice a week. The car was with her and she used to take the children to the school and back home, all by herself. On the second day, by the time my wife reached the school in Vasant Vihar, the piano was set on fire but the children were not harmed; much rescue work was undertaken by the Hindus and other people.

During the riots, I travelled only between Police Headquarters and Raj Niwas. I went with Subhash Tandon, the Commissioner of Police to Raj Niwas because the Lieutenant Governor wanted the latest report. Once, on the road outside the Char Diwari, there was a small non-Sikh mob, shouting: "Sardar *aa gaye,* Sardar *aa gaye, bachaiye"* (save us from Sikhs!). Tandon got down and asked: "Where are the Sardars? Why are you creating panic? He ordered them: "Go back. Otherwise face police action." The miscreants had seen the jeep and came to loot the vehicle but when they realised it had policemen, they gave up their intentions and disappeared. I did not find any act of violence on that route.

In reacting to the situation, there was a definite delay on the part of the Delhi Administration. Why could the acting Chief Secretary not produce 14 Magistrates? He should have been working day and night when there was a public crisis. Later on, I found that when there was a rally and he was on the dais! A Chief Secretary was not supposed to attend rallies. This was after Rajiv Gandhi was inducted as the Prime Minister. All the civil servants were very unhappy with that kind of the behaviour. But at that time, the Prime Minister's Office (PMO) was interfering and administration had become more of a *tamasha* (farce). It was deliberate act of neglect in the sense that after all, we were paid to govern, to exercise our power and ensure good governance. The Delhi Administration officers of the IAS cadre were devoting more time for their next posting and to please the bosses in North and South Blocks (seat of Government at New Delhi), rather than planning for development and maintenance of law and order which were their primary function. It was their failure and fall from the high professional and ethical standards of service.

How do you control a mob? You send a police force with a Magistrate. Announcement is made through loudspeaker that curfew was in force and gatherings were illegal, thus asking the crowd to disperse. Firing is the last resort and that too, with minimum use of force. The Army is trained to shoot, to kill an enemy. But in a civil situation, the Army is called out only when the police have failed. Here, the police resisted calling the Army. The very presence of the Army, when they march through sensitive areas, could have been enough to normalise Delhi. There was no instance of any pitched battle between the Army and the rioters. Even with the police, there were no pitched battles. The police had just used the *danda* (stick) to quell the mob. I know of no instance when a single policeman was attacked.

I do not know whether Sajjan Kumar excited any mob. I never heard of that. But I know for certain that some of the people who were close to Indira Gandhi, had rushed to the All India Institute of Medical Sciences and were bitterly crying and making a public scene, instead of letting the doctors do their work. One of them, M L Fotedar, burst into tears, and started howling. For a political leader to howl publicly and make one odd remark could have sparked violent reactions. At the All India Institute of Medical Sciences, the scene was emotional as was here at Teen Murti House. Around Teen Murti House, there was the Army vigil by men in ceremonial dress as per protocol and so the scene was dignified; there was no shouting of slogans allowed. But outside the Teen Murti House, mobs were building up, and the first incident was when the white Sikhs came out. There was hardly any police outside, but they may have been controlling the traffic etc.

My later assessment was that a meeting of the rioters was held after the gurudwara adjoining to the houses of Sir Shobha Singh and Khushwant Singh in the Ambassador Hotel area was damaged. What could have happened was that owners of scooters, kiosks and some others were targeted and some scooters were burnt. Rioters then set fire at the gurdwara. It was more of a class war, not so much communal, besides the lumpen attitude: '*Loot mar ho rahi hain, chalo ham bhi jayen*' (let us join the loot).It so happened that they targeted the Sikhs because with their turban they were an open, identifiable target. It was announced that a Sikh policeman had killed Indira Gandhi. So, the anger was directed against the Sikh community. Where was the need to announce that the killer was a Sikh? When Mahatma Gandhi died, Lord Mountbatten told very clearly: "Please go on announcing in All-India Radio that it was the Hindu who killed the Mahatma. God forbid, if some rumour has gone that a Muslim had killed, then, one would have seen a massacre." So, that was deliberately announced by Lord Mountbatten at that time. That is called an administrator's vision. What was the need for the top officials of Delhi Administration to leave their seats and make a beeline at Teen Murti House? There must have been some Deputy Commissioner or District Magistrate, or Additional District Magistrate who should have advised them. What was the job of Bajpai, the acting Chief Secretary at that time? Had anybody questioned him? I do not know whether they were called to question. If the political leaders had incited the rioters there must be some proof of it.

I advised the Lieutenant Governor to invite some community leaders. So, some Sikh leaders came and among them was Harcharan Singh Josh, who was in the Indian Council for World Affairs. He came along with Jagdish Tytler. I cannot remember whether Sajjan Kumar came. P.G. Gavai was made Lieutenant Governor only the next day. Mohan M K Wali was the Home Secretary when Gavai was sacked in November 1984. Wali signed his own order to become the Lieutenant Governor (3rd November 1984). Gavai was from the Maharashtra cadre and must have been in the ministry. So, it was Gavai who was the Head of the Administration and the next responsible person was the Chief Secretary. Gavai had been indicted for his lapse but I do not know what happened. I have not read the report. But my impression is that it was a total failure of the Administration, and if any political leader had asked them to misbehave, he should have been arrested straightway, at that point of time, instead of sacking Gavai later.

After three or four days, Rajiv Gandhi became the Prime Minister there was a big rally and instead of reorganising the Administration, he congratulated it. The officials of the Delhi Administration had made all the arrangements. As for his meeting with the Police Commissioner and other high officials, I was not invited to any such meeting. But when P G Gavai held a meeting the next day, I remember Hukam Chand Jatav (Additional Commissioner of Police) coming and saying: "*Sahib, inke* gurdwaras *ke andar bhi kuch* agents*the.*" At that time, some brickbats were exchanged and there were firings from inside the gurdwaras. This was the main issue in one conference which I attended. Then, they did not fill up the post of the Chief Secretary because again there was the 'ring' in the bureaucracy. They could have filled up the post but did not do so.

Compensation was given to the victims of the riots by the Government of India. The DSIDC was asked to do some rehabilitation programme like homes for widows and their training. So, I visited camps and gave whatever help the DSIDC could by giving permits and in many other ways. I could not give them jobs. The DSIDC was only able to set up rehabilitation homes and train the victims in setting up some business, industry and so on. We got seven officers from the Central Government as the task was so enormous that it could not be coped with on our own staff. The Municipal Corporation of Delhi gave those licences for shops, etc. As for the alleged police atrocities on the Sikhs, during the two to three days when I was a witness and a spectator at the Raj Niwas, streams of people were coming in and going out, but I do not think anybody complained of the police atrocities. Three or four Sikh leaders who came never complained. Among them was Harcharan Singh Josh who was a very devout Sikh. He never complained. When violence was taking place, the police asked me very clearly to give them Magistrates to guide them to open fire on rioters, if needed. A police Inspector cannot open fire on his own. There has to be a Magistrate.

There were allegations that the Administration did not even try to stop the looting and plundering of the Sikhs. The policemen just stood by and did not try to stop that. I did not witness any incident like these because I was in the Control Room of the Commissioner of Police. The complaint of the Lieutenant Governor was that he was not getting the information. So, my role was limited to attend to that problem. But there was a failure of the government machinery and that was why one went there. Magistrates were not there when they were needed. Any educated person could be made a Magistrate. In 1947 when the partition took place, I was in a very secluded area of the Indian Military Academy. The Headmaster of The Doon School who was an Englishman was made a Magistrate to help in controlling the situation. So, the government could vest the power on a Magistrate or on a Special Police Officer. In the old days, there was a rank called the Honourary Magistrate. My uncle was an Honourary Magistrate in Badaun. It was just an honour. Anybody, even a tonga-walla who violated the rules of the road, would be called to the court and just given a warning. In Delhi, Lala Ram Pershad, Mehraban Singh Dhupia and Lala Shri Ram were Honourary Magistrates. They were leaders of the community who were not merely Hindus or Muslims or Sikhs, but were the educated and respected leaders and, therefore, they were made Honourary Magistrates.

So why did the Administration fail to respond and give the 14 Magistrates? The policemen did nothing because they were ready but waiting for the Magistrates to be attached to them. When the Army Captain was called, he asked, "Where the Army columns should be deployed to quell violence? "So, it was the Army Captain who asked for Magistrates. Suresh Bajpai, the acting Chief Secretary of Delhi, would not meet anybody and even if he did, he was so arrogant that he would not respond. It was fantastic: He was either visiting Teen Murti House or was manipulating his next posting or whatever else. It was also true that the public was very shocked and their angry reaction was valid. The announcement that the killer was a Sikh policeman was basically very wrong. They should have never announced that. I am quite convinced that the riots were the failure of the Administration but I do not think any political leader would have told people of one religion to kill those of others. It was wrong for anybody to accuse a man like H K L Bhagat to have led a mob. In fact, his supporters were protecting the Sikhs; even Harcharan Singh Josh was present there.

But whatever be, that was violence and murder at the national level.

Chapter 13

Experiences of Service Life

Attributes of Bureaucracy

Before we talk of the role of bureaucracy, we must understand: What is the bureaucratic system? What are the attributes of bureaucracy? What are the functions of bureaucracy? What is the meaning of bureaucracy? Most of the observers, critics and admirers when they think of bureaucracy, they think of the upper echelons of the government and straightaway they say that it is the civil service. Bureaucracy is a very old system. The selection, even in the Indian system was based on a certain amount of knowledge of the Rajas. I am talking theoretically. Who were their advisors? They were the bureaucrats. How did the Raja select them? Maybe, he selected his own relations. The candidate was trained to acquire a certain amount of knowledge and capability before he was made an Advisor or a Raj guru or a member of the Council of Ministers in those days.

Similarly, in China the Mandarins were the most learned people. The system started there by virtue of selection. The selection process could be an interview, a written examination or a combination of both. It could be just hearsay, by various advisors whereby one finds a candidate suggested by word of mouth. The British did introduce bureaucracy. Bureaucracy is not only civil service, it can be a political bureaucracy; it can be a military bureaucracy. The purest form of bureaucracy was the Prussian Army in our modern times. They had perfect discipline and the selection was on merit. It was impersonal in the sense that one selected the most deserving person among the applicants. It was also bound by the rules and procedures according to which it worked, otherwise there would be chaos. If a decision was to be taken, what would be its affect and on whom? I might like a particular project which might not be feasible. So, the bureaucracy can only function well in a democratic set-up. That is something which is not to be missed.

Much has been claimed about the good the British rule did to India. They gave us the railway system. They introduced the rule of law. But all their thinking was directed towards their imperial end, whether it was in setting up of factories or in getting raw materials. Originally, they came as traders who worked in the Writers' Building in Calcutta. The British business interest was also a form of bureaucracy. The East India Company had a Court of Directors who took the major decisions. Whether the decision was right or wrong, it gave results. The Company's bureaucrats who worked in India produced results. The system spread gradually and then the British Crown took over the task of governance in 1858. Thereafter began the system of civil service. One of the earlier people were the ICS. So, bureaucracy was a system Bureaucracy and it had to be result-oriented. But in British Raj, civil servants were not servants of the people, they were the rajas. Their notion of a public servant is illustrated by the manner of their address. When a Collector wrote a letter to the Chief Secretary, he addressed the Chief Secretary, 'Sir, I have the honour to be your most obedient servant' and the last line was, 'the Compliments, Sir'. Towards the end he would again say, 'I have the honour to be your most obedient servant.' A public servant whether a member of the ICS or not, wrote in this format. The other was the demi-official format, 'Dear Mr Gandhi' or 'Dear Mr Nehru' and so on. The whole format of writing letters in English in the Secretariat had those two types.

The ICS contributed to two streams. One could choose the Executive or the Judiciary. They were selected by an open competition, and purely on merit. Although earlier when they started the civil service in England, they had an unorthodox approach, like selection was done by British Commissioners. That was continued but they did start giving some representation to the Parsees and the Muslims. Even at the time of Independence, a departure was made for the princes because they were the educated. They were not subjected to the same rigorous tests like the others were when they opted for government jobs, but this was done according to the set procedure. Thus for the majority, there was no reservation and selection was purely on merit through the public examination. There was a time when about 7,000 candidates used to appear in civil services examinations as against one and a half lakh today. Only seven or eight people were selected for the upper services and the rest for the junior services depending on the number of vacancies. So, the system continued by and large in the same manner that we inherited and we had a strong, dedicated civil service which adapted itself to the changing times.

Of the two streams in the ICS, those who were of the intellectual temperament, chose the judiciary. Those who were empire builders, continued in the administration and their aim was to become Chief Secretary, and further on, the Governor. The blue blooded, even if they were offered governorship, preferred to go to the Frontier, that is, to Razmak and Peshawar where the 'Great Game' was being played between British India, USSR and Turkey with Kashgar as the observation post.

About corruption, there were instances when the Viceroy visited a Princely State for *shikar* and his wife admired the necklace of Her Highness only to gift with it the next day. This was an indirect way of demanding. A Maharaja did that so that his throne, prestige and honour were safeguarded. When a Collector of a district visited a village, the next day he got a basket of mangoes free of charge. At the same time, there was a tradition that if one went to a village and if tea was offered, he accepted it. So corruption had its shades.

Some of the empire builders were very cruel. I remember Nethersole who was a District Magistrate of Badaun earlier, was posted in Ballia district during the 1942 movement. After suppressing the 1942 movement, Nethersole declared: "Ballia Re-conquered". He was known to be ruthless. People of Ballia say that every morning he used to go with the Superintendent of Police on a round of Ballia and treat the common Indian people very harshly. There was no public lavatory and if anyone was found with a *lota* (mug) easing himself in the open fields, he would whip them, chalan them or put them in jail. The truth is that even now we find people who ease themselves along the railway lines early in the morning. Tara Ali Baig describes this as Asia's biggest free lavatory and one have a *lota* parade every morning – the first thing we see when we enter Delhi.

My first contact with the bureaucracy was as a young student in high school from 1930 to 1940 in a small district which was a microcosm and an illustration of the British system of administration. The district had always been very important because it was in a district where the impact of the rulers was felt in every way, especially in the spheres of law and order, and development. After the take-over by the proclamation of 1858 of Queen Victoria, the real civil services started. The pre-Independence civil servants, the ICS, were mostly people of British origin. With the gradual Indianisation of the ICS, the British were replaced by Indians. They were naturally loyal to their own sovereign, and they had a clear goal. Then, the whole situation changed during the Second World War.

As the freedom movement gained momentum, the attitude of the British Government stiffened. But by and large in the princely India, the administration was that of the rulers, the Maharajas. In British India, the most important man was the ICS Collector of the district and he contained the freedom movement. Some of them were ruthless imperialists and some were dedicated and development-oriented. In Badaun they made the Victoria Park, a huge garden with a lot of new species of plants. They were so attached to the Park that they brought some plants from England. When they went on furlough they used to bring them along. Of course, they kept their distances. They did create a second line leadership and named them Rai Bahadurs, Khan Bahadurs, Nawabs and so on. Some others were scholars who did a lot of readings and writings, and kept away from the city. The Collector lived in his small colony where the District Judge, Superintendent of Police, and in some places the Forest Officer and Executive Engineer, lived.

In the post-Independence period there was a debate on whether to abolish the Indian Civil Service. Eventually, the Cabinet decided to keep the civil service with a different name. The procedure was the same. The Federal Public Service Commission became the Union Public Service Commission. People of the highest integrity were appointed its members and they continued that tradition. It is to the credit of the succeeding civil servants, the Indian members of the ICS, the IP and others that they adapted themselves extremely well. Those who did not want to stay in India took pension and went home. Those, who wanted to go to Pakistan, went there. But many others stayed on in India, including the British officers like Justice William Broome of Allahabad, who was an ICS and a District Judge as he took to the Judiciary.

Immediately after Independence, we made changes in the Secretariat. If one's name-plate was there, he would not write ICS. Then, the format of writing letters was changed. We began with, 'Sir' and ended with 'Yours sincerely'. So, the idea of a 'most obedient servant' was dispensed with and the servants became the rulers. The ICS was like a club of very few people who personally knew the Governor. In Uttar Pradesh, there used to be an ICS-Week every year. For three days all the Collectors came and they were addressed by the Chief Secretary and the Governor who entertained them and exchanged views. So, when the Ministries came in 1937, the Chief Minister of Uttar Pradesh continued that tradition. It was a very intensive administration. Gradually, over a period of time, in the post-Independence period the civil servants gave their best and some of them like T J C Acton and Edward Penderal Moon became very good authors.

As the freedom movement progressed it became a people's movement. The original demand of the Congress was to get the Indians into the ICS. The emphasis shifted from constitutional to agitational protests. The fight came really to a head during the Second World War when Mahatma Gandhi declared: "We cannot be part of a war without our own participation in government". That is how things moved very fast and the final battle of the Quit India Movement of 1942 began.

In 1947-48 the Indian Administrative Service was born and the ICS was merged into that. Some of the civil service traditions continued. We were fortunate to have Jawaharlal Nehru who never interfered with that. I do not remember an occasion when Jawaharlal Nehru ever asked for an officer by name. For example, if a person with the history background was to be taken, whosoever the Cabinet Secretary selected, he would accept. He had a list of officers to give his preference but he never did so.

The civil service had maintained its neutrality. Our critics alleged: "Look, you have become turncoats." We refuted; the relationship between a politician and a civil servant is like that of a husband and a wife. One cannot do without the other. The political master is the rider and the civil servant is the horse that carries him to the goal post. There was a joke that if the political master did not know how to ride, the horse could overthrow him. It depends on the political leaders how they use the civil servant. If they use him for their personal needs and other narrow objectives and he was a weak character, he succumbs. So, it is the weakness of character that leads to corruption and its growth. During the Nehru era there were very few cases of corruption. But then came the gradual erosion in the value system.

The Prime Ministership of Lal Bahadur Shastri was short-lived but he gave a new dimension. For example, he wrote down that the security and intelligence services was not a one-man-job, nor only a police-job. The door to these services should be kept open to all. The most important issue was how to analyse and organise our foreign policy. Everywhere it is built up through the interaction of lawyers and academics. So, a system of training was evolved. From Metcalfe House in Delhi the training centre was moved to what is now the Jawaharlal Nehru University (JNU). That estate was acquired and it was made into a University when the training centre was shifted to Mussoorie from New Delhi. The idea was better because Mussoorie is a small town and eventually the trainee Collectors would have to go back to the districts and villages to serve the first 10 to 15 years in the States they opt for. That was the concept in the Nehru era and it continued in the time of Lal Bahadur Shastri.

The number of persons in the civil service went up in the 1970s, with the result that control became difficult. The political leadership also mattered. Corruption started at the top. I give one the example of Haridas Mundhra scandal. Feroze Gandhi (Member, Lok Sabha, 1952-62), son-in-law of the Prime Minister Jawaharlal Nehru, raised this question in the Lok Sabha and K Santhanam did so in the Rajya Sabha (1960-64). But only a powerful manlike Feroze Gandhi could do so straight away. Corruption also started when some of the District Magistrates became tools in the hands of the politicians. They lost their élan. I would call this a weakness of both sides, the politicians and the civil servants who give in. If they cannot stand up to their ideals it is their weakness. And what does a politician want? He wants to fight an election. It is as simple as that. He wants money through the supporters. He might also take some advantages like getting a land allotment in his or his brother's name. These small minions who came from the districts, started being rude to the civil servants, as if they were private servants. Some of the civil servants stood firm by the principle and for some the punishment was a transfer. Transfer is no punishment but some people thought it so and, therefore, to avoid transfer they give in. When a civil servant gives in, I would call it his weakness of character.

At the time of Emergency, some people started writing notes in pencil. Special Assistants to the Ministers were appointed. They were also IAS officers. They just did what a Minister wanted them to do. They told their subordinates also to do the same thing. There is a case where Kishan Chand, the Lieutenant Governor, who committed suicide after the Emergency. Why was Indira Gandhi led to the imposition of the state of Emergency is a separate question, but the truth is that the Emergency was not in the interest of the country. There is a body of thought which says that it was her security advisors who said that a big mob would come with Jayaprakash Narayan who would lead it from the old city to the Prime Minister's house and capture the house and kill the children. Indira Gandhi gave in at that time, and may be it was her weakness that let her down. She chose her advisers and her advisors let her down. Jawaharlal Nehru did not choose his advisors. After all how would Jawaharlal Nehru know which person was better? It was the Cabinet Secretary who chose the right person. He would pick up people and empanel them. Earlier it was easy because the number was small. He knew the weakness and the strength of the personnel.

Intellectually the civil servants were better during the Nehru period. They came through a very tough competition and integrity was also built into the system. They were dedicated and sincere in their work even if they had their natural personal ambitions. People today say that the 'cream' among the young persons go away to other professions, but then there are three lakhs people still competing for this service. The erosion in standard was actually started by various political developments. Take, for example, caste-reservations. I am totally against reservations based on caste. I am all for giving help to the people below the poverty line. Give them facilities. It is true that before Independence or in the last 100 years, things were bad for the poor and deprived. But today who is socially disabled? You go in a bus, nobody knows the castes of fellow-passengers. We all wear the same type of clothes. Untouchability has been abolished by law. I would say that reservations are totally bogus.

Some of the Foreign Secretaries like Y D Gundevia, a Parsi, and M J Desai were extremely alert. They were all members of the old ICS. Subimal Dutt and M J Desai were there at the time when the Indian Frontier Administrative Service (IFAS) was formed and the whole frontier policy was given a shape. I am talking of the 1950s. From the 1950s up to first ten years members of the ICS also continued even after the IAS was formed in 1948-49. Badri Dutt Pande was absolutely of sterling quality among the ICS. There are two or three members of the ICS who were from Almora town in the Kumaon. That small town produced them. They were all from ordinary families. Vishnu Sahay and Bhagwan Sahay were both from Chandausi which was not even a tehsil of Moradabad district. They were from one ordinary college but were very dedicated and versatile. Bhagwan Sahay, who was the Chairman of the Delhi Urban Arts Commission and Governor of Kashmir, was extremely successful. Then, there were T N Kaul and K M Panikkar. Kaul was the First Secretary in Beijing and Panikkar was the Ambassador. Panikkar was an intellectual who has written a number of books. And they read History.

According to Max Weber there are five attributes of bureaucracy. One is the selection on merit. In China from the earliest times, the Mandarin was a cultured and educated man. In the Indian system also, Rajguru was an educated man. He may have been a Brahmin by caste. Even the King used to worship Rajguru, the Advisor and Minister, who had tremendous powers. They were all educated people.

The second attribute of bureaucracy is that it is rule-bound. There has to be some rule when making choices. I would give one a very concrete example. The Delhi Transport Corporation, which is a government undertaking, could nationalize any route but in the law, in the Motor Vehicles Act, it was written that all applicants would be treated as equals before the law. The first criterion was whether a vehicle had the capacity to run; second, whether it was clean enough and third, whether the vehicle was safe. Those were the criteria. But the Government of Delhi, in their wisdom, nationalized one route after another at random. So, the local people ganged together and went to court of law. In the law courts they argued their case and won it. The sovernment had a right to nationalize, but the rules had to be followed.

The third attribute of bureaucracy is that the rules have to be applied impersonally and in public interest. It should also not be inhuman. The fourth attribute of bureaucracy is that it is hierarchical. There is an appeal. There is somebody above me, above the Chief Secretary, or the Cabinet Secretary. The fifth attribute of bureaucracy is that it is democratic. One must have a totally dedicated bureaucracy which has to give very clear advice. If a proposal comes, they have to examine the pros and cons and then take a decision the way a High Court Judge does before giving a judgement.

If I have to describe bureaucracy the nit is a system which has four attributes: (i) Selection is by merit; (ii) Bound by rules; (iii) Hierarchical; and (iv) Impersonal. A wrong decision is acceptable; but a dishonest decision is not; there has to be personal and professional integrity. Professional integrity is when one does not give a wrong advice. As a Secretary to the Government of India or an Under Secretary or any other functionary, who are a part of the system, one has to give correct advice to the government. If he feels that something is not the right, he should say so and not say 'yes' because the Minister wants it.

Reforms in Administrative Services can be of many kinds. The new goal of transparency through the Right to Information Act 2005 is welcome. One step is having transparency as a part of the bureaucratic process. There cannot be any hidden agenda. Let there be an open debate, everything should be openly debated. Secondly, the process of selection should ensure that the best people are selected. People have devalued Dr K R Narayanan, the President, by saying, as did The Times of India; that he was the first 'Dalit' President. Then again, it was used by the Dalitlobby. What is the need of saying that so and so is a Brahmin President or a non-Brahmin President? That attitude to selection has to change. The second need is continuous vigilance. There is a saying: "Eternal vigilance is the price of liberty". One must have eternal vigilance, vigilance not only by the Vigilance Officer, but also by the community. The community leaders who had retired should visit the nearest village school. I have seen the village schools in my present mission where I go and see the poorest of schools and meet the youngest worker. There were all kinds of mal-practices which can only be controlled by the public and the Press. The Press also has been relentlessly exposing corrupt practices. For example, during the elections in Bihar, they tried to browbeat the Election Commission of India, but did not succeed due to the press. But stronger manipulators may have succeeded and got away with it. So, eternal vigilance is the price of liberty.

Finally, I support B K Nehru's thesis. We must have a District Magistrate or a Collector of not 10 years' service, but of twenty years' service. Give him more salary and he becomes the head of a team in a district where there is a Medical College and a University. He has to interact, and he would be the leader of the team and would be co-ordinating with senior experts and technocrats. The political authority would always be there in any case. If the Parliament is willing to give the power to the state, or the state is willing to give the power to the districts, then a lot more could be achieved. The fear was that the people in the panchayats, who were illiterate, would fight on the caste-lines. That is also true. It could happen in the beginning, but then it would settle down. I strongly believe that our strength lies in the districts. Today there are 600 or 700 districts. Having empowered District Panchayats and Deputy Commissioners, a Chairman or a Secretary is the only practical solution.

Often there is a controversy over the IAS. Many think that the civil servants are not doing their best and act as hurdles to progress. This is an extremely cynical view. The IAS represents a system of bureaucracy. There is no other system to administer. There is no alternative to bureaucracy. People who are disillusioned come up with all kinds of accusations and ideas. Those are the people who fail to succeed. If the civil service did not meet India's purposes, then why is it that three lakh people were coming every year for the civil services examination? The candidates selected in IAS examination go through a certain process of training and come up the ladder. Similarly, a political master is not supposed to be a specialist, he has to be advised by the specialist. So, the relationship between the political leadership and the bureaucracy must be seen as a supplement and complement to each other. One cannot treat them like one's private servants.

There are faults in the system. One fault is frequent transfers. Actually, nowhere is the rule for transfer laid down. But the convention was that unless one is allowed to serve for three to five years in a district, what development can he bring about? This matter is one measure of reform. Every time I went to Hardwar, I found a new District Magistrate. This was absolutely disgusting. A District Magistrate gets transferred because some MLA did not get a timely dip in the Ganga. A Chief Minister would order the District Magistrate to give a man a gun-licence. He could be a *badmash* (crook), he could go and kill. Similarly, the police would not be allowed to do their work without any political or other interference. The issue has to be decided by the political leaders, by the Parliament.

For democracy to be fully functional it would take another ten years. Even today the Panchayats are not functioning because they do not have power. Education must also spread to the lower levels. Years ago Dr Rajendra Prasad very clearly warned that the persons who executed the law had to face the most stringent competition, whereas the MLAs and the MPs who frame the laws lacked the educational qualifications for doing their job well. The makers of the laws are themselves fighting, shouting and creating lawlessness. But the situation has not gone out of control. I am very optimistic that we would pass through this phase also. There are Chief Ministers, who are making peace with the investors because growth and development is important and bureaucracy is rising to the demands of the day.

Indira Gandhi's style of work was different from others. She had taken a major decision in imposing Emergency. I do not think she consulted any of her bureaucrats, though I am not sure. But I heard that her key advisors were neither the Cabinet Secretary nor the Law Secretary. Maybe the Union Law Minister was consulted. Later on Rajiv Gandhi followed the same style. He was very imperious and young. One day when something went wrong, out of enthusiasm he said: "You will have a new Foreign Secretary", with the result that the Foreign Secretary, a perfectly competent person, resigned the next day. A Foreign Secretary is a part of the system. So when a civil servant or bureaucrat has been there in the department for 30 years, one should respect his views.

Morarji Desai was a good administrator. He was very dedicated to his responsibilities. I remember, he came to Manipur which was in trouble those days. His management of time was perfect. He never deviated from his food habits. He would clean his own chappals. He followed a perfect discipline like in the Army where every soldier did all his own work even during a war. He was for prohibition and vegetarianism but he would not force these on the unwilling others. So having been a civil servant himself, he had his views but would not force them on the others. People in business accused him of giving a free hand to the bureaucrats. In Bombay, his son Kanti Desai represented the industrialists. Morarji Desai was an out and out rightist. He had no time for Socialism, attraction of which was coming back. But I do not think he interfered with bureaucracy. For example, when he was the Prime Minister he did not change his Secretary. I do not think he changed N F Suntook, Chief of the Research and Analysis Wing (RAW) (1977-83) and who served three Prime Ministers. He had risen from the State Civil Service to serve the country in the high offices of Chief Minister, Governor and Prime Minister.

Today the Governor is a constitutional appointee who is basically supposed to overview the State administration. He is the head of a State, and unless a Chief Minister runs amok, he will not go to find out what happened. The Governor is also a political appointee who is totally subservient to the Centre or the political party in power. He therefore cannot always take judicial view of matters. That again is a part of the system. So, the political leaders in power have a role in not only the appointment of the IAS officers, but also of the Governors. The appointment of the Chief Justice of the Supreme Court, of course, is totally separate. There the political leaders do not have a role. The Supreme Court of India, the Union Public Service Commission and the Election Commission of India are constitutional bodies. So there are the checks and balances in a democracy.

Whenever we made a mistake in appointing a Governor who was subservient, the result was there for everyone to see. But many Governors have stood the test and have been very successful. Some of the very successful Governors were Dharma Vira, S Fazl Ali and Jairamdas Doulatram. Although Doulatram was not a civil servant, he was at one time the Mayor of Karachi. Fazl Ali was a lawyer and not a party-man. Conversely, some of the persons appointed as Governors were absolutely third rate fellows. I would not name them but they are known to the people.

In sum, bureaucracy is but a cog in the larger democratic system with all its goods and bads.

Indian Frontier Administrative Service (IFAS)

The Indian Frontier Administrative Service (IFAS) started when after the partition there was a sudden movement of the civil servants back to the UK. Some went to Pakistan. Some had to move to the Secretariat because many persons of the Secretariat, including the Secretaries had left. So there was a shortage of personnel. The Planning Commission was established and the focus was on development, law and order, the movement of population, pre-partition and post-partition riots, refugees and their rehabilitation. So the country was facing enormous problems. The tribal people in the NEFA did not know much of administration. The area itself was called 'Partially Excluded Area' or 'Excluded Area' or the 'Inner Line'. There was no bridge on the Brahmaputra River and it took four days to go there.

The British would always consult the Political Officers who were the best people to be consulted on the Frontier affairs. They were also the Empire builders. If one asked a British ICS officer, "Where do you want your posting?" The reply would be: "Send me as a Political Officer in the NEFA. But it is not only in the IAS or the IFS that one may look for the right man, although they may have the expertise. The right man for the right job should be the motto, not the cadre. If the Nehru Memorial Library needs an official who is concerned with the Library, then one would not put an Army or an IAS officer there, though he could manage. So a circular was sent to all the Departments and Services for service on the Frontier. It was very clearly mentioned that conditions of living there were very hard. My first place of posting was six days journey from the nearest airfield. There was no electricity. I walked for six days to reach the headquarters of the District Collector. Out of about 2000 volunteers, 14 were selected to the IFAS through a process. And before the selection was made, the Prime Minister asked: "Have we tapped the universities?" His idea was that service in the Frontier was not the exclusive privilege of any particular group or profession. To be an able administrator one must have background knowledge of the area he was to administer. This is a basic requirement. He could not wait for the IAS to develop that experience.

The people outside the IAS were equally patriotic and intelligent. And if some of them volunteered for it, they could not complain over hard postings. The rationale behind the move was that we have to spread to the frontiers, otherwise the Chinese would move in. People criticized the Forward Policy but there was no other way. If the NEFA is a part of India then civil servants have to go and work there. If Jammu and Kashmir is a part of India, one has to go and work there. Not many people wanted to go to the North-East or Nagaland. But earlier some civil servants of British India went there. Charles Pawsey lived there for 14 years as the Collector. They were quite happy to serve the Empire. They had a very clear goal and pursued that goal with determination. After Independence that spirit was not forthcoming. Whatever be the reasons, we were not finding enough personnel.

Unless we stayed there we could not govern, we could not just go from Dibrugarh once a year, have a party and come back. That was the pattern which the British Political Officers followed. My predecessor Peter James managed to go to the forward areas during the Christmas. Of course, it was difficult but he did go there – one winter here, the next winter to some other place and the third winter to yet another place. After Independence it was not possible to do that. While touring one was then expected to live in a village for 15 days. That was possibly the reason why the IFAS was formed. The first selection to the IFAS was in 1953 and the second was in 1955-56. There were three selections and the total strength of the personnel was 75.

The IFAS officers had specialised training in the Metcalfe House and the South Block (New Delhi) and the faculty was drawn from various departments. They were given special courses by Dr B S Guha, Director, Anthropological Survey of India and Dr Verrier Elwin, Consultant and Advisor on Tribal Affairs, Government of India. The emphasis of training was on respect for the tribal people, their traditions and practices. We were told to respect the tribal traditions. I remember having read Dr Verrier Elwin who has recorded that one of the officers laughed at a tribal funeral in the British days. At this the tribal people got very angry and there was a lot of violence. So, respect for the tribal traditions and beliefs were to be kept in mind. We had to introduce the changes very gradually. In 1954 there was nothing in that area but today many roads are coming up. Even now, it is very difficult because of the geography, the difficult terrain. There is hardly any railway line. That was in the nature of things. The India-China War of 1962 speeded up the process of change.

On the North-Eastern side, Assam, Meghalaya and Arunachal Pradesh are the states that comprised the frontier belt in which the members of the IFAS worked. The Union Territory overseas is the Andaman and Nicobar Islands. So, the UT Cadre was formed. The initial UT Cadre was formed out of the IFAS. They were again subjected to the various procedures of the Union Public Service Commission. Contribution of the IFAS before and after the War in 1962 has been remarkable. It is a tribute to the band of volunteers of the IFAS that Arunachal Pradesh which was carved out of that area, is an island of peace. Even in Nagaland which was formed in 1963, members of the IFAS handled the situation very well despite provocations from the across the border and foreign machinations.

From the sixteenth century one cannot suddenly leap into the twentieth century. Some of the tribes were living in the Stone Age. They had no idea of currency and coinage. Literacy was a very different thing altogether. They were next to the 'cave' period. I remember, in one village where I went, my wife was the only woman who was wearing something above the waist. They were totally naked. Their way of living was different. They lived on hunting and fishing. The economy was a pastoral or hunting economy. Those people had to be brought into the national mainstream. One cannot do it overnight. So the officers were told to respect their traditions and beliefs. We were given lectures on that. Jawaharlal Nehru himself briefed us. Further we were guided by the ideas embodied in 'A Philosophy for NEFA' by Verrier Elwin.For example, when as ICS man was posted in the Madras State, he learnt Tamil. When somebody went to the Punjab he learnt Punjabi. Every Collector had to learn the local language. In the same way we were made to pass language tests. I was told that within six months I must learn the local language so that I could conduct the court cases. I did that. I did not need a *dwi-bhashi* or an interpreter. My wife also quickly learnt to speak to the tribals. We learnt to take what is called the path of the golden mean between the two extremes. That did not mean that we allowed a murder although we respect the tribal laws and tradition. I had to deal some very difficult cases of divorce where the people of two villages were about to fight over a teacher who was an Assamese from the plains and who had married a tribal girl. We could not allow the torture of that girl. But it took a tremendous effort for seven/eight days of listening to them and I could succeed only as it was in a small area.

In the NEFA, the entitlement was 45 days of earned leave in a year, but our entitlement was 30 days. We were also told that we would get free and furnished accommodation. But the Ministry of Finance rejected the demand for a free and simply furnished accommodation. Actually, the accommodation was a bamboo *chatai* (mat) walledroom of 15x15 feet or so, a roof of palm leaves, a bamboo table, a typewriter and a flag flying outside. That was all that was the house of the DC. The first sheet of tin was dropped when the Governor visited for the first time. We were told that if we were married, we should take our wives with us, otherwise we would be running all the time to our wives back home. It was a hard life. It was not easy. When my first child was born there was no doctor and that was just too bad, that's all. From Dibrugarh the flight was once a week and that too, if the weather was all right. So these were the conditions of extreme hardship and only the really dedicated signed for it and went there. None o-f us complained. IAFS officers were no doubt most suited, by aptitude and experience, for the administration of frontier areas.

As was the tradition in the IFAS, in the first month I used to be out for 20 days, moving from village to village, camping, spending a night or two at one village, meeting the people, and taking decisions over their cases and disputes. I learnt much more about the traditional law by being on the spot. There were no lawyers, but I knew exactly the laws of divorce and land settlement. Land was demarcated with stones placed on one end to the other. All would accept that marking. There was no corruption at that time. I could ask the PWD to give contract to one village which would complete the work on a time-bound basis by mobilising labour locally. A Junior Engineer, or Overseer as they were called, would make the designs, which was not very complicated. Many of the Political Officers in the British days were also town planners. You read 10 books on town planning and if you are dedicated, you can become an amateur town planner.

One may ask as to why the IFAS was disbanded. The service consisted of men from the ICS, IAS, IPS, Universities and Army, Navy and Air Force, who already had five years of experience. They have been through the process of selection in their own field and were all dedicated people. Then, the question arose that in the tribal areas only the tribal people should be posted and there was the kind of murmuring about quota which was the hidden agenda. At diplomatic level people started questioning that if the NEFA was a part of India then why should the Ministry of External Affairs administer it and not the Ministry of Home Affairs. The Government of India rightly thought that an area which was a part of India should not be administered by the MEA which had different ethos and practices. Besides, as the first batch of 14 officers increased to 75 after two years, inter-service jealousies started. The Foreign Service thought that their jobs were lost. The IAS thought that it was their job. Therefore, the decision was taken that there was no need for a separate Service.

The IFAS was disbanded after 1965. It was wound up because of two more factors. First, how would one keep officers in that confined employment for years?

A civil servant also looks for what is called cadre management. If he joins a particular Service he aspires to climb higher up the pyramid. If he starts life in the Secretariat as an Assistant, he wants to be an Under-Secretary. Similarly, in the field of education he wants to become a Dean or a Professor. So, management of a small cadre became difficult. Then there is a new specialisation needed to - administer the tribal areas. The approach to planning had to be based on local surveys and experiences. That was the specialisation necessary.

So, to sum up, the IFAS was created to meet a situation and it had served its purpose. But, tribute is due to the yeomen work done by the 75 men of that Service and their families. Many of them were killed in accidents and had health and other problems. Even now, I feel that the personnel who were specially trained for the Indian Frontier Administrative Service (IFAS) were the pioneers.

Advanced Professional Programme in Public Administration

The day the Emergency was imposed I was working in Delhi as the Financial Commissioner. Politically, it was very hot. I was sent on a course called, Advanced Professional Programme in Public Administration (APPPA). This was the first course for the mid-career senior officers who were taken off the executive responsibility and sent to participate in what may be called a sabbatical. Earlier, they used to be sent to Oxford and Cambridge Universities on Queen Elizabeth Scholarships. So, it is very important from the Human Resource Development (HRD) point of view to take time off in-between and interact with experienced people and learn.

The Indian Army always had refresher courses and then the civilians have also started that. This was a prestigious course meant for personnel of the level of the Deputy Secretary and above, which means officers with 12 to 15 years of service, who were sweating to be the Joint Secretary in the Audit and Accounts Service, Indian Forest Service, IPS, IAS and other services. Now, even personnel from the Army go for this training in Delhi. Even a Professor from Allahabad University which is a Central University can attend the course so long as the university pays. For that one year, one stays in the hostel, interact with others and follow a course-syllabus which included the Constitution of India, economic studies and followed by field-visits. One can choose to visit states all over India and write his thesis and to get a Master of Philosophy (M.Phil.) degree or a diploma in Public Administration. They designed the course for the first time on the basis of the experiences of other countries. This course was conducted at the Indian Institute of Public Administration (IIPA), New Delhi, which was inaugurated by the Prime Minister Jawaharlal Nehru on 29 March 1954.

After Jawaharlal Nehru came to power, he invited Paul H. Appleby, a very senior expert from the USA, to advice the Government of India on management and administration. There is the Appleby Report in which he pays compliments to the bureaucratic system; it was very interesting to read it. Therefore, this course was approved by the Government of India, and they found it useful. The Home Ministry wrote to the other Ministries to send one or two officers to join the course as trainees when they would be required to stay in the Institute while continuing to be on the rolls of his office and draw the salary of their old post. In my case, that was done and I went for the course.

Impressions of the North-East Frontier States

In Arunachal Pradesh, Meghalaya and Manipur, the urge for development naturally led to an urge for representation and decentralisation of power. The Manipuris were culturally far more advanced. One may call them tribals but they have very rich culture, good music etc. Similarly, Tawang, Bomdi-La and all the Buddhist areas have a very rich culture. There were also the totally primitive areas where nobody had ever seen even a coin. When I first went to one Naga area in Neusa Sub-Division, I discovered that my wife was the only woman with anything above the waist and that astounded the locals. The headmen had twenty-two wives, all living in one place without any inhibition, all having their own roles in running the family. Whatever it was, they were not immoral. The trend of societal exclusivity continued till 1956, when troubles in the Nagaland and Manipur started. They wanted to have a separate state at the cost of the State of Assam, but even if there was no justification, that turned out to be inevitable. As to how small the States could be is a matter of administrative, social and political compulsion. Naturally, small is beautiful. But howsoever small was a district, cultural boundaries would always be overflowing the geographical entity. Some languages would overflow. Some Jats would be in the Brahmin area, some Muslims would be in Hindu area; the State of Haryana is an example. But if it was taken to absurd lengths then that would be silly. That was the view which B K Nehru had taken.

Finally, it was the demand for political representation, and later, for reorganisation into a separate statehood that grew among the tribals. But one cannot club all the States into any one category. Arunachal Pradesh is an island of peace because of 20 years of intensive administration by the dedicated members of the IFAS, who were also the Political Officers. The District Magistrate of today is not a political official, he cannot be, the MLA tells him what to do and he has to do it. That is why his authority has diminished and he would be courageous to say: "Yes, certainly, this road should come, but that village needs roads more than the others." Maybe the Political Officers would have controlled the situation better.

In the North East, the idea of interlinking of rivers was a good thing. The railways were based on the lines of the needs of the economy. The history of the Indian Railways shows that raw materials were sent to Bombay and finished products came back to us. This story of cutting the weaver's thumb may be just a tale, but that meant that the British were ruining the cottage and handloom industries. So, we were told very clearly that we would not interfere with the local crafts but encourage that. Encouragement of the local crafts did not mean that we were creating separatism. It was to give them a feeling of the dignity of man.

The plantation labour of tea-leaf pickers mostly came from the neighbouring areas. Hardly any tribal people got management jobs in the tea plantations. Technically, nobody was qualified. The population of the tribal people was very small. The problem of unemployment is coming up now; it was not there at that time. Some young tribal graduates would opt for Government jobs and some were willing to work as our porters, but many of them were not willing to do so. They did not need money as food was given as wages. The girls would be paid some money in coins, which they would make into necklaces. All the Gandhi-coins were made into ornaments. The girls would go to the nearest shops in the bazaar, and our merchants would send the coins to the silver smith to prepare ornaments. The girls also got cloth, oil, tea and salt.

Intelligence Bureau (IB) had an important role in the North-East Frontier States. Some of their people were brilliant analysts. The role of the IB was to provide all shades of intelligence including military intelligence. But I do not think any IB functionary was there at the district level from 1947 to 1954; I met no IB official in the field till 1962. The IB was there in the war of 1962, but for the early years, there was little application of political control in the governance of the NEFA. The Governor was an agent of the President, and so, my reports were sent to the Governor. The Governor was advised by an Advisor who was the rank of a Joint-Secretary to the Central Government at that time. The first Advisor visited the NEFA only in 1954. Today, the IB has expanded. At that time there may have been only one or two Indian Police Service (IPS) officers with the IB.

Nagaland

The word 'Naga' was not really derived from 'Nag', the snake. Perhaps it was because of their scant clothing to cover their bodies that the plainsmen started referring to them as *nagnamanus* or the naked people. I have seen myself the

Naga priests in the villages. They had fringe of hair like the Tamil Brahmins and they tied a knot exactly in the same manner. If one sees old photographs, one would find them sitting down and recite their *mool* (basic) mantras. They worshipped Lord Vishnu and Lord Ganesh, but *Donyi-Polo* or the worship of Nature was predominant. That was the major religion: Worship of Sun, Moon and Grass. There was also the belief in the male-female concept – Sun as the male is on one side and Moon as the female on the other side. Bhupen Hazarika, the great singer philosopher, has also recorded some of these concepts when he visited as my guest after the Bangladesh War of 1971.

In Nagaland, the insurgency started as a separatist movement. Then, the Government of India took to emergency measures because foreign collaborators had instigated it. Their motivator, Z A Phizo, fled to London and enjoyed the privileges of foreign support. Nagaland, of course, had always been socially distinct. But the Nagas started claiming parts of Burma too. That was a ludicrously impractical demand.

Onnaming of the State of Nagaland we were not consulted. I do not know who, how and why the name Nagaland was suggested. Initially it was called the 'Naga Hills District'. During my tenure of four years I interacted with many leaders of the seven North-Eastern States including the Chief Ministers and the rebel leaders and explained my role. I told the rebels: "We would not use the police, the Assam Rifles or the Army. If you think that you are not Indians, you can leave, we cannot stop you. But if you come back again, then we shall have no option but to take action". This is what happened. Laldenga and his group went out to secure foreign support and as he was coming back with the first batch with 75 rifles and other weapons he was intercepted by the villagers. Being a Mizo, he could not enter Manipur. Later on, when he was elected the Chief Minister of Nagaland, we deferred to him. That is the beauty of democracy. The tribal people understand that. We gave in to much of their demands. B K Nehru was the Governor of the seven states, and he was very clear about our objectives. A Raj Bhawan costs money and so at that time we could not have a Raj Bhawan in every State. Now, we have separate Raj Bhawans and separate Governors as per the local requirements.

Manipur

The Emergency was already been declared in June 1975. At the end of the course, the choice was to go back to the Government of Delhi or on another posting. I was already drawing the salary of a Joint-Secretary. The Financial Commissioner is a full Commissioner's rank. I had a lovely, old-fashioned bungalow of the Commissioner, which had four lawns, one garage in the Rouse Avenue which is now called the Deen Dayal Upadhyay Marg. Then the Cabinet Secretariat called me up and explained that there were problems in Manipur, and asked whether I would like to go there.

The Cabinet Secretariat of the Government of India picked me up because I had been in the North-East Frontiers and I knew the local leaders. Manipur had become a State by that time. Therefore, the Chief Commissioner, who was posted under the Cabinet Secretariat, was withdrawn and S.M. Krishnatry became the Chief Secretary of Manipur State (1966-68). Braj Kumar Nehru was the Governor of Manipur (1972-73) when I arrived there. B K Nehru, who had been the Governor of the seven states – Assam (1968-73); Nagaland (1968-73); Meghalaya (1970-73); Manipur (1972-73); Tripura (1972-73); Jammu and Kashmir (1981-84) and Gujarat (1984-86) – made it clear to the Government of India that he would be holding a Cabinet rank. I have found his monographs on this issue, which can be used for further research. Then came L P Singh as Governor of Manipur from (1973-81). When I arrived there, Indira Gandhi had lost the election. In my time, Morarji Desai became the Prime Minister (1977-79).

The main job given to me was the counter-insurgency. Manipuris have a long time grievance of being neglected. They thought that their traditional lifestyle would be adversely affected by being a part of India, and so and there was a rebellion. When Indira Gandhi visited Manipur, there was an agitation and then the government decided to delegate more power to them. It took a long time for the Centre to do so because of uncertainty regarding of the locals being able or willing to manage their affairs according to constitutional provisions. I was under the Cabinet Secretariat of the Government of India at that time and not under the Government of Manipur state. So, I did not report to the Chief Minister or the Chief Secretary. I reported to the Governor. When L PSingh came, Manipur was a full state. Rishang Keishing, the former Chief Minister (1981-88 and 1994-97), was very good friend of mine, and so were the other ministers. I used to interact with them.

History states that Manipur was once conquered by the Burmese, but repulsed them later. Manipuris are very strong, tall and handsome people ofTibeto-Burman stock. In the caste system of Manipur, there were only two castes, the Brahmins and the Rajputs. Their language is Meitei. The Manipuris had suffered attacks from Burma. While the Burmese were expelled, the British finally conquered Manipur. Then, the British Resident was invited to the King's programme of dance and was pounced upon and killed. So, to the British the Manipuris were traitors and unreliable. This kind of a feeling continued. After the massacre of a

British Political Officer, the British captured the Manipuri fort. The hill tribes of Manipur were under the influence of the British administration. Two appointed Ministers and a British Political Officer used to look after the administration of the hill areas. Occasionally, the Government of British India used to send columns of armymen to go in winter, in good times, stay there, keep the British flag flying and come back. So, till 1947 there was no stress on development. The Maharaja ruled over the Valley areas though the British did interfere now and then.

The Indian National Army (INA) came to the outskirts of Imphal where Subhas Chandra Bose had hoisted the flag. That spot has become a place of pilgrimage and tourist attraction. The INA first attacked Imphal and then Kohima in the Nagaland, which were contiguous to Burma. Manipuris never saw eye to eye with the Burmese. There were two villages just across the Burmese border where fourth generation Sikhs lived. During the War, they settled down there, married Burmese women. The men wear pugri, but they hardly retain any feature. They speak Burmese. The Indian border between Burma and Manipur was a loose border and people used to come and go, like they do in the border between Tibet and Sikkim. When the popular Ministry came in Manipur the Congress was in power, but there has always been tussles within the Ministry and between the two or three political parties.

The Manipuris are highly individualistic. They felt that they had a unique civilization and a King of their own. Manipur Valley has a very strong Vaishnavite following because of the influence of Chaitanya Mahaprabhu. The British however kept the Kings and their subjects confined to the Valley and never allowed them to rule in the hill areas. But they themselves started interfering with the tribals. They introduced the missionaries and converted the tribals to Christianity, introduced Roman script in tribal areas and gradually bought pieces of land. So, there were two parallel centres of power. Even during the Maharaja's time, the British Resident looked after four to five districts, the so-called 'Hill Districts'. When the new Ministry was formed under a Chief Minister, Maharaj Kumar Priyobroto Singh, and two other Ministers, were in charge of those Hill Districts.

Manipur Valley has a very rich soil. Rice grows there and in particular, black rice. The lotus flower was the main symbol of Manipur. They have some unique wildlife. The bazaars were controlled by women. In the evening there was a unique bazaar where the women would sit down with the lamps, and sell their small wares. The 'R K' prefix to the Manipuri names means 'Raj Kumar'. There were hundreds of R Ks. All the royal progeny were Raj Kumars, and they were very proud of their aristocratic background and their level of knowledge. Of course, dress-wise, they wore dhoti-kurta in Bengali style. Their dress, *phanek,* is quite different from the Burmese and other dresses. Manipuris had their own belief in the manner Lord Krishna's image was to be made.

In the Manipuri dance there is no communication between the dancer and the audience. A dancer has a veil and would never look up to the audience. They are supposed to perform in very slow movements like they have in Thailand and Burma, somewhat like the Kathakali but quite unlike the Punjabi *Bhangra*, *Bharatanatyam* or *Kathak*. The elders wanted purism in their culture, they did not want any interference. Dr V K Narayana Menon, Secretary of Sangeet Natak Akademi (1963-65) and a great music critic came to Manipur during my time and we had a good talk. I was a regular visitor to the Manipur Academy and Binodini Devi also was very active at that time. Priyobroto Singh had retired. He was like an elder stateman who tried to guide the people, but then the insurgency broke out.

Priyobroto Singh was the King's son and a very educated man. His sister, Binodini Devi was a Padma Shri Awardee (2009). She was educated at the *Shantiniketan*, and was a very good dancer. Traditionally, in the temple of *Govindji*, the King's daughter always used to play the role of *Radha*. The King used to sit there as a *bhakt* (follower), not as a God reincarnation, like in Nepal. Like any other Maharaja, he was the repository of both faith and culture. Manipuris say that their mother-tongue 'Meitei' had no similarity with Sanskrit. So, they had that feeling that they were a distinct ethnic group with a distinct language.

After Sardar Vallabhbhai Patel advised Bodh Chandra Singh, the then Maharaja of Manipur (1942-47), to accede to India, he not only acceded to India but also gave the reigns of administration to his people though he was an absolute ruler. On the advice of Sardar Patel he appointed Bob Kathing who was the only graduate in the state, as a Minister. Kathing was a very highly decorated army officer, a winner of the Military Cross and later on, a Padma awardee. He is a Tangkhul Naga and his wife was a Khasi woman from Shillong. Along with Maharajkumar Priyambada Singh, Kathing formed a cabinet. Some members of the royal family joined the Army and Maharaj Kumar Priyobroto Singh was also in the IFAS. Then, there was Salam Jaishankar of the powerful Salam family.

Merger of Manipur took place in 1949. At the time of Independence, Manipur was a small, Part-C State, and was certainly isolated. It used to take five to six days by rail to reach Imphal. There was only one airport. Today also, there are no railway lines in Manipur. Imphal, the capital was in geographical isolation. Then following the report of the States Reorganisation Commission, the States were reorganised. Later, when Indira Gandhi visited Manipur in September 1969 as the Prime Minister, there were some protest demonstrations against the status of

Manipur, stone-throwing and some firing by the police. After that the Government of India woke up to the aspirations of the Manipuris and a change became inevitable. So, from a Part-C State, it became a Union Territory, and a Chief Commissioner's province. Rameshwar Prasad Bhargava was the Chief Commissioner of Manipur (1952-55) and after him came P.C. Mathew (1955-58). Earlier, Sir Akbar Hydery had been the Governor when it was a part of Assam and the Governor of Assam. The Manipuris were very suspicious of the Governors of Assam and West Bengal and also of the intentions of the Government of India itself, which was seen to be not giving them their due.

The Union Territory was controlled by the Central Government in Delhi because of the budget. Naturally, nobody wanted to part with that power. It had advantages also; being a Union Territory, the Central Government paid for all their expenses and send officers to serve there because Manipur did not have enough of state cadre. Even today Manipur-Tripura Cadre of the IAS, by itself, would be a very small cadre to manage. Imagine a person who went there and kept rotating within the three districts. So, professional growth suffered where the districts were few and the population was small. There was also a question of administrative viability. Manipur was a one district state; today it has nine districts. It had a Chief Commissioner and one Deputy Commissioner. A distinct advantage was that it was an intensive administration. A Deputy Commissioner was available and had direct contact with the villagers, whereas to create a State or carving new districts needed crores of rupees to build the infrastructure. Finally, out of one district, many more were carved out as they did in Haryana also. The status of Union Territory was a logical step for Manipur before the Statehood was accorded in 1972. The Congress Party was like any other party there and many people were loyal to the Congress. Today, Manipur has a 60-member Assembly. When a Ministry came to power, Rishang Keishing, who was earlier in the Socialist Party, became a Minister. The Chief Minister was R K Dorendra Singh (1974-77).

Insurgency in Manipur was partly because of economic reasons and partly inspired by the Chinese and the Pakistanis who came to fish in the troubled waters. The insurgents also found sanctuary in the Shan State of Burma where there was hardly any law and order. In my earlier assignment in Khonsa-Taminlang of the Tirap Frontier Division on the Burma border, we used to go and have meetings with the District Magistrate of Michiana district in Burma. There was the old Stilwell Road to go over the hump into Burma. It was very difficult road which the troops patrolled.

The Manipuris are culturally very rich. Their fear was that the outsiders would come and destroy their culture. Manipuris have a distinct culture, quite different from the Bengali. The script is Bengali but there was demand that the Meitei script should be adopted. The discontent among the Manipuris was that they thought that their language would be swamped out and the Bengalis, who were more educated, would come and acquire the big jobs. So, there was great suspicion of the Bengalis and Assamese. When I arrived there, this demand was coming up. There was no university in Manipur for over two decades. One of the grievances of Manipuris was that they had to send their children either to West Bengal or Assam for higher education. Then, a campus of the Jawaharlal Nehru University was put up there. So, as the demands were growing the Government of India was also responding. In the federal structure Manipur was also entitled to a hospital. When I was there, the Regional Medical College had gradually come up. About 50 doctors who passed every year from that college but they could not be absorbed in the nine districts. They would have to go outside. So, that was one of the causes of discontent because they did not want to go out.

The Assam Rifles which was a para-military force, comprised partly of Nepali-speaking Gurkhas and there were hardly any Manipuris in it. So, another force, the Manipur Rifles was created out of the old levies and others. The Assam Rifles was given the Kangleipak area which had the fort of the King, and which had been taken over when the British Resident was murdered. Possession of that fort had become a bone of contention between the State and the Central Governments, although the Assam Rifles and the Manipur Rifles maintained that area very well. But year after year, the Government of Manipur renewed that demand and I used to faithfully convey it to the Government of India. The Army was resisting, not wanting to move out of the fort.

There was some influence of the Nagas and the Mizos on the Manipuri insurgents. Manipur borders the Nagaland, the dividing line was the *Tangkhul* tribes. Tangkhul was one Sub-Division by itself, while Ukhrul is a district now. Then, there were the *Paithes*, the *Gamthes* and the *Mizo* tribes. For every thing, the insurgents depended on external help; they did not plan or act by themselves. They used to go out and collect arms and come back, and then loot and harass, collect taxes from the innocent fellow tribals. That was the problem. Local Mizos never wanted political independence. The Nagas did. The Nagas claimed that they were not Indians and wanted a separate state. But the Mizos were quite satisfied with the autonomy through the District Councils.

Manipur was another peculiar case. The Hill Districts were still not with the Government of Manipur. The insurgency was in the Hill Districts of Manipur and not in the Valley. Now, the Valley is also on fire. In the Hill Districts of Manipur there was influence of Nagaland. Manipuris are not Nagas. They are Tangkhuls. There is nothing common between the Nagas and the Tangkhuls.

Some Mizo influence was also there. These were small village republics where the chief had a say. It took many years for democracy to take deep roots in Manipur. Government of India's reason for delaying the statehood was the paraphernalia needed and its financial implications. The financial burden was tremendous and it had to be subsidized in the beginning. Today, there is a direct flight from Delhi to Imphal via Dimapur. The nearest railway station is Dimapur. Roads were constructed keeping in view mainly the climatic and the geographical factors. But even today, I do not think Manipur has the finances for railway and roadways.

To tackle insurgency in Manipur, I told the Government that I did not wish to have any police force with me. Even my personal guards were from the local people. We had set up a Village Volunteer Force (VVF) which was development-oriented. They used to live in the village, cultivate the land and see that the village was protected. The VVF was given some rifles to maintain law and order. Of course, there was the usual police, the SP and other ranks. So, they had the feeling of association with the administration. The traditional leadership was encouraged to help set up the institutions. That was how we had at that time, one of the first surrenders by 75 insurgents with Chinese weapons. They came across from Burma and surrendered.

There was one leader of the insurgents, Laldenga, who later on became the Chief Minister of Mizoram (1986-88). Laldenga was very clearly told that he had to be an Indian citizen, and only then would he get all the rights and privileges. We told him: "You can fight the elections and become a part of the political process. If you want to leave India, you can go, but if you come back with arms, then you will be dealt with accordingly. If you give up your nationality, go to London like Z A Phizo did to enjoy the Scotch whisky". For years together, the British Intelligence or the CIA looked after persons like him. Laldenga had went, despite our warning, to collect arms. When he was returning to India he was intercepted and arrested. Then the negotiations started. A lot of surrenders took place during the time when L P Singh was the Governor of Manipur. In fact, many of them surrendered through the VVF and other government agencies. They came and gave the weapons to the Chief Minister but they remained politically demotivated. The Kangleipak Army – 'Kangleipak' means the fort – broke into several small splinter groups of insurgents, which were encouraged by outsiders in Burma. It was an indigenous movement in which R K Madhuryajit Singh's son also got embroiled.

Madhuryajit was my very good friend and an IFAS. A Major in the army, he joined the service in response to the call of Jawaharlal Nehru. He was a very senior man. I called on his son and met him. Madhuryajit was crying, not knowing what to do. I said: "You call him, let me talk to him." After some time, he came to see me and gave his part of the story. He was very nice. The next day, he disappeared again and joined the underground. I do not know whether he come out later. Madhuryajit's second son was more sensible. The first Chief Minister Dwijamani Dev Sharma's younger son, Bobby Sharma too, may have joined the terrorists. No privileges were given to the Scheduled Castes and Scheduled Tribes in Manipur and that was also a reason why they got angry. Manipuris who joined government service were very much against violence so they became targets of insurgents. The police and other supporters also became targets. Terrorists would come, open the door and shoot government employees or supporters and loot the weapons.

The Manipuris are trying to progress. Today, the discontent is because of unemployment. How many Manipuris would get a government jobs in Delhi or anywhere else for that matter? So, this problem had very deep roots. As long as they were not educated they were quite happy in backwardness, 'noble savages' as defined by Thomas Hobbes. They were quite happy in their own little sphere, in their own shells. But as the communications opened and ideas spread, they came out of their shells. I feel that if more responsibilities were given to the young Manipuris, they would be able to return to the path of peace. It needed a lot of patience to bring changes among the tribals. If one hasten the process of change and development, it could be very dangerous.

It could be partly that the people who were sent out from Delhi to govern them, did not live up to the expectations. It was mandatory for an IAS officer to learn the local language and pass the examinations in that language. I do not know how successful it has been even today. How many IAS officers know the Manipuri language? They go very reluctantly to such postings. Then it was for the Chief Secretary to see that there were officers at the district level, and they remained in contact with the maximum number of villagers. There was extreme corruption in the delivery system for public goods and the direct benefits of development would not reach the villages in time. There was a lack of political will among the central leadership in solving the problems of Manipur.

After Morarji Desai became the Prime Minister he visited Manipur. I was there at that time. One of the ministers of Manipur told him very clearly: "Sir, no ministers or officers come from Delhi to Manipur." Morarji Desai replied: "I will send one Central minister every month to Manipur." Within a week of Morarji Desai's arrival, Surjit Singh Barnala, who was the Minister of Agriculture, came in a three-piece suit. He was a tall person with a beard. Now, of course, he wears the kurta and pyjamas. He spent two days and being a Minister for Agriculture he was shown all the farms, etc. That had some effect. After that, some other

Ministers came. It was only after a visit that Indira Gandhi realised the problems and announced the Statehood.

The Meitei youth wanted the Manipuri language to be made the language of administration; they wanted Statehood; they wanted more reservation and jobs. But where can one set up factories in those Valleys? Of course, they wanted a University too. I was asked to be on the panel of selectors for the Jawaharlal Nehru University Centre and campus in Imphal. They constructed some buildings and started functioning. When they demanded so, I agreed that they should first try to produce Meitei books for Classes VII and VIII and focus on university level education later. I gave them six months' time and that satisfied them. Two very bright persons were selected for that work. The teachers and doctors who came from outside as volunteers were treated very well in Manipur as they were in Nagaland also. One day a Manipuri student leader came and asked: "Sir, what is the works budget of our State?" I asked him: "Why are you asking this? "Works budget means budget for buildings and roads. Nearly 30 to 40 per cent of the government expenditure was on works which was carried out by the CPWD or the Central Government. It was a very sizeable budget. In a State, it was even more. The student leader said: "Suppose 10 crores rupees was the grant for the PWD, the PWD minister takes away half". This minister was very unpopular and thoroughly corrupt because from 10 per cent cut at every level, up to the 30 to 40 per cent of the grant was taken away by politicians down to the junior most accountant. The students came and openly expressed their views to the Selection Committee of the Jawaharlal Nehru University (JNU). Moonis Raza, Rector of the JNU was the Chairman of the Committee at that time. He came and stayed with me. That was at the height of insurgency. Moonis Raza addressed the students and said that India was like a garden where every flower blooms, and so the Manipuris should have nothing to fear. His speech went off very well and was well received. Corruption at the political level was the main issue. If there was corruption at the political level, then there would be corruption at all other levels too.

Some of the government officials were very arrogant with the local people, but not all of them. That was also one of the grievances. What was the use of sending officials who were not willing to go to Manipur? The IFAS officers was more successful because it was very clear that accommodation and conditions of living were very hard they were all volunteers. But by 1965 that Cadre had disintegrated. The States had their own agenda so the officers also became frustrated rotating within a State all one's life.

To build up confidence among the people, all the money was spent through the Government of Manipur. My job was more of advisory and I was a link between the Central and State government. The Chief Minister was there as the head of the administration. I would give him advice only when he asked for it. The press also kept on doing their work. The government was changing now and then; every time the MLAs were bought. There was no political stability. Although maintenance of the law and order was a State-Subject, the Central Reserve Police Force and the Border Security Force were utilized to fight the insurgency along with the local police and all the paraphernalia of the State. Our job was mainly to organise a VVF in every village. They all lived in the villages and informed the State government when a particular village had any difficulty, like water shortage etc. They maintained law and order and provided intelligence to the government agencies. That experiment was sometimes successful but some of these volunteers were also killed. Many of their camps were attacked by the insurgents. The outsiders and smugglers also joined the local insurgents. Timber was smuggled into India from Burma. If one did not allow that to come, then they would work against the government.

The Army's role in such places was not much appreciated by the local people. A jawan was trained in the army to shoot to kill the external enemies. The army should never be used for internal disturbances. That is the job of the police. If the police want any help, give them the weapons, training and other resources. Insurgency can be stopped only by rapid, all round development. That is my view. I wrote a ten-page letter on insurgency and sent it to the Union Home Se retary. We learned from the way Malcolm J MacDonald tackled insurgency in alaysia after the Second World War.

There was a visit of the National Police Commission to Manipur. Dharma Vira was the Chairman of the Police Commission and K F Rustomji, N Krishnaswamy Reddy, N S Saksena, M S Gore and C V Narashimhan were members. The Commission's report (31 January 1980) is a valuable document. I gave evidence before the Commission which brought out that political interfer nce in the law and order agencies should be reduced to the minimum to let the police carry out their job, but that did not happen in practice. The moment a Chief Minister was changed, the first thing he did was to change the IG of Police, and the Deputy Commissioner of the seven districts. There was a demand that the local officers were sent and one Meitei IAS officer was posted there. He was killed by the tribal insurgents. Khudanpur Narsimha Raghavendra Rao, Assistant Commissioner, Tamenglong Sub-Division was also shot and killed while he was on duty there.

Insurgency cannot be curbed by violence. It can be curbed by planned development, better education, greater awareness and contact between the public, leaders and administration. At the cutting edge, one should try and avoid delay in the delivery system and healthcare. There was only one hospital in Manipur. Even now, the resources are limited. That again was the grievance of the Manipuris. They would ask as to why not build a railway line to connect Manipur with Burma? The proposed Asian International Highway from Bangkok to Istanbul was to pass through Manipur. But this was a disturbed area and there was no easy solution. One can put an IAS officer, but what would he do the next day? It requires tremendous patience, education and awareness. One may sanction 100 crores today, but over a period of time, unfortunately, because of corruption, especially in the PWD, not much progress would be made. There was no doubt that the PWD Minister of Manipur, Govindas Konthoujam, was corrupt but not the other Ministers. Later on he was beaten up and I do not know whether he survived. There was an attack on him. The Maharaja of Manipur had in any case become totally defunct.

Meghalaya

Meghalaya had a different culture and a distinct language. So, based on the policy of formation of linguistic states it was a logical conclusion that the Khasi Hills District was created. For a deeper understanding of the people of Meghalaya one must read, *Khasis and Garos* by Williamson. A. Sangma was the first Chief Minister of Meghalaya (1970-72). There was only one centre of the Ramakrishna Mission in Cherrapunji; all other missions were British. Khasi dresses have chequered patterns like the Scottish Highlanders. In those days, some or more of the British Political Officers, Deputy Commissioner and Missionaries might have been of Scottish origin and they might have influenced the Khasis to adopt Scottish songs, music, bagpipes and dress. Otherwise traditionally, the Khasi dress is quite different, their men and women wear pugri. The Khasis have a matriarchal society like in Kerala, where the daughters in the family inherit property from their mother. Then there were the *Khasirajas* who had just nominal power. The real power was vested with woman. She was the center of power.

I wish to narrate a very humorous incident about one of my colleagues, a Khasi Political Officer, and a fine gentleman. In those days, gazetted officers signed their pay bills which were presented to the Government Treasury. But there was no Treasury in the NEFA. So for six months or so after an officer got promoted and by the time the office order was received, he could not draw salary. This officer's wife being head of the family and the owner of all the property, she was also the owner of whatever the husband earned. She sent a notice to the Governor thus: "I will file a case against the Accountant-General that I have been deprived of my money-property. If he does not respond then I am going to file a case". This created a furore and the officer felt very embarrassed. The issue was sorted out soon.

Arunachal Pradesh

I served in the Kameng Frontier Division, the Siang Frontier Division and the Tirap Frontier Division. Each Division had four districts which was all-right, because that was the area that a District Magistrate or a Deputy Commissioner could practically tour.

First, take the Kameng Frontier Division which is named after the Kameng River. The British had given it the name of 'Abor Hills', after a bird. The name Arunachal Pradesh was given because it is the eastern-most part of the country where the Sun's rays reach first. All the local leaders agreed on the name Arunachal Pradesh. The local people said: "Please do not call us 'Dafla' or 'Abor'. We are 'Apatanis', call us 'Adis', the original people. Adi is our language. We do not call it Abor language. We do not call ourselves by our sub-tribal names like Pasi or Miniong or Padam, we are all Adis." I learnt the Adi language.

Hindi and Assamese are commonly understood languages now. Another policy decision taken by Jawaharlal Nehru was that the language or the dialect which had no script, would use the Devanagari script. That decision was reversed under the political pressure, by whom, I do not know. Dr Verrier Elwin suggested that we should appoint research personnel to be called as Assistant Research Officers (AROs) in each district, so that they could start compiling the statistics of the tribal customs and the languages and so save these from dying out. Dr B S Guha also agreed, and AROs were appointed in every district.

The AROs were permitted to take photographs. The first direction was that there was to be extensive photographic records, but if it was a taboo to the tribals, then they were not to take photographs. We were warned by our interpreters to respect the local beliefs. The more direct contact we had with the people at the level of the Assistant Political Officer and the Political Officer, the easier it was. The AROs had to prepare a lot of monographs. There was some delay in implementation of these policies because of the lack of decentralisation in the hierarchy. But it was a blessing in disguise because if a man was suddenly transplanted into a new environment he could have even died. We hastened slowly. For example, we gradually started to put prematurely born babies in incubation. But some eccentric Political Officers, in the name of preservation of tribal culture, went to the extent of stopping the sale of blouses in the bazaar. That was silly and made no sense. The tribals asked: "Do you think that our girls would remain bare-breasted for all times to come? What is this nonsense?"

The Kameng Frontier Division has five or six tribes and as many tribal languages. In the Buddhist areas there was the Tibetan script. But you have to have some meeting ground, a lingua franca. Therefore, Hindi was introduced as one of the languages in the High School. When that was done, the Press in Assam was very critical, because all the teachers were from Assam and there was no question of sending them away. Then, there was the Bengali-Assamese controversy because many of the doctors in Assam were from Bengal. So, in Arunachal Pradesh, the doctors were very keen to see that the Assamese-Bengali controversy did not overflow. We also had people from the Punjab and South India.

People of Arunachal Pradesh never asked for the Scheduled Tribe status. This demand is now coming up. In those days, there were no untouchables there. A tribal chief and his people were equal. After a shikar, everybody would sit outside where the chief would distribute food to all. It was more like a commune and a best form of social order. The chief would probably get an extra piece of liver, but nobody was deprived. It is also necessary to clear the misunderstanding about the practice of 'slavery' there. To a tribal chief a slave meant manpower, his labour. The patriarch who had the so-called slaves for generations, himself worked on the fields. He was a feudal chief even now, but there was what we call a benevolent despotism. The practice was stopped with the abolition of slavery.

Tribal leaders did not ask for statehood. But they wanted more say in the administration and more of their own tribesmen as officers. For example, the moment Dying Ering passed the matriculation, he became a senior Tehsildar. The Governor had asked my wife to help him and so I put him up in my own house. I brought him up like my own son. He used to write letters to the Prime Minister. As a government servant one had to go through the proper channel. There was a hierarchy but he would not understand that. So, I told Dying Ering that his letter would in any case come back to me from the Prime Minister's Office. Jawaharlal Nehru was very considerate and did not consider it as my failure. But second time, when his letter came back, I told him: "Now that one are a Gazetted Officer, I am going to lock you up and beat you if you do it again". He replied: "*Baba, ab nahin karega*" (Father, I will not do it again). Later on, Ering resigned from the government service and was appointed as a Parliamentary Secretary in the Government of India. Someone told him to take the house at 25, Ashoka Road in Lyuten's Delhi, because the previous occupant had been a minister. He took the house and was made a minister. After he came to Delhi, he began to put on white churidar pyjamas and achkan, like Jawaharlal Nehru, and looked elegant with his round face and small, stretchy eyes. When I came back from Afghanistan, I did not have any accommodation. But such was his regard that he gave me the keys of his official quarters for us to stay inuntil we arranged our own.

1971 War

I was in Shillong at the time of the war and creation of Bangladesh in 1971. After Bangladesh was born, the Bengali people of East Pakistan got their freedom on the basis of the language, not religion. Creation of Bangladesh had to come someday even if the Punjabi soldiers of the Pakistan Army did not perpetrate atrocities on the Bengalis. But the freedom struggle became violent because the Punjabis wanted to rule over them and behaved as an Army of occupation. A Secretariat was set up in Calcutta for the refugees coming from Bangladesh. It was an enormous burden on the Government of India. The problem of influx of Bangladeshi refugees' migration was tackled well.

Migration from East Bengal was actually going on from the British days, for the last 50 to 80 years. If one refers to the decennial census, the people from the Mymensingh and the adjourning area migrated because of the economic reasons. They were clearing jungles for agriculture on forest land. The ecological approach was not there in the Government at that time and the Forest Department had not become active. That deforestation would affect rainfall and the whole ecology would be disturbed, has dawned on us now. Ecology has not only economic implications but also security and political implications. For example, people from Meghalaya would not go to Bangladesh because they were the Khasi people whereas the Chittagong Hills District which was a Buddhist area. It should actually have been in India, but the Radcliffe Award did the damage; the British Deputy Commissioner of that time and even the Indian officials acted in completely bogus manner.

Post-liberation, border trade between Bangladesh and India started very afresh. It was seven or ten days old when I went about 60 to 70 kilometres to see some of the areas though I could not go to Dhaka.

Union Territory and Statehood

Creation of Bangladesh hastened the process of formation of new states because Indira Gandhi and the Cabinet realised that they could not stop it because matters had gone too far. For the North-Eastern region, new Union Territory status and then the statehood was inevitable. A Union Territory serves a particular purpose. For instance, Delhi would remain a Union Territory for all times to come because it is cosmopolitan. I would even advocate that Mumbai becomes a Union Territory for the same reasons. If there is a referendum, the people of

Mumbai would opt for the status of a Union Territory and so would Bangalore (now Bengaluru) and Hyderabad. Nagpur too is centrally located. The Congress held its session there and there used to be a High Court in Nagpur. It is not that the Central Government should have absolute control. In funding and most administrative matters, a Union Territory is autonomous. But in Delhi, which is part of a National Capital Territory, there is demand for full statehood. So, a new theory of reorganisation may evolve. One does not know what would happen in future. But the logic is that the sooner we decentralise and empower the panchayats, the better it would be for democracy in India.

Systemic Wrongs

In the North-Eastern states, particularly what is now Arunachal Pradesh, there was no corruption in the bureaucracy or the local political leaders. The contracts were given openly to the villagers for roads and buildings. The design and architecture was based on the local climatic conditions and the materials available, that is, bamboo, cane, timber, etc. and in the inaccessible areas the CGI sheets were air-dropped and carried by the tribal porters.

But in Goa and other places, corruption was of the political kind. During the Emergency, professional integrity was lacking. There were two aspects. First, personal integrity: 'This spoon belongs to the government and I do not steal it', or if a contract is given 'I will not take kickback'. Second, the professional integrity: 'I do not consider that person is a goonda and yet act against him because he belongs to the Jana Sangh or the Muslim League'; and that is lack of professional integrity. Professional integrity of some bureaucrats were so low during the Emergency that Kishan Chand, the Lieutenant Governor of Delhi, had to pass orders right and left through his own Special Assistant. He was appointed through the courtesy of a friend and his work during the Emergency was totally devoid of any justification. He committed suicide after the Shah Commission was appointed. That was all because of the bad advice given to him. He left out his own judgment, and worked through his Special Assistant and others who were in the Administration at that time. Uncomfortable people were removed and sent out on various petty assignments. That, I would say, was lack of professional integrity.

I did not know about corruption in money matters. That was the CBI's job. In those days, I never heard of officials having crores of rupees. Today I hear that so and so has got 'crores'. My driver Chandan Singh told me one day: "Sahib *dekhiye, abhi sab kar rahen hain*" (all are corrupt). I am still not reconciled to a situation where an IAS officer can possess 20 crores of rupees. My father left a

24-room house and we, five brothers, all with good education, could not maintain that house; with the result that strangers occupied it and even sold it away. The story of diverting quota of cement to Maruti Udyog Ltd. has already been narrated. Iron ore is exported from Goa to Japan was in private hands. In the shipping dockyard there was political corruption. They wanted to have dry docking facilities in Goa. The nearest dry dock was in Singapore. On that issue there was a fight over profit and control between the two Ministers in Goa. Hassan Haroon Shaikh, the Law Minister would say something different from the other Ministers. Political leaders of Goa could never reach an agreement on that issue.

Corruption was there in the British days also. A Chaprasi used be tipped with a rupee or eight annas from the District Magistrate sahib for lifting the curtains. When a Rai Bahadur, Khan Bahadur or *Zamindar* sahib came, there was 'salam huzur' and '*ek rupya bakshish*' (one rupee tip). A *Patwari* who was well to do in a village, used his position to get preferences and advantages. I remember the case of one ICS District Judge of Badaun district who overspent his salary of 400 rupees. He was not corrupt. He could not meet his requirements with that money in the 1930s. The District Judge was an Indian and his wife was French. He borrowed some money from my father and gave a promissory note that he would return it when his remittance came from the UK. When he got transferred, he also left some bills unpaid with a local shopkeeper who got panicky thinking that he had lost his money. The shopkeeper thought the Judge had left for good. So, he filed a complaint against the Judge. Somehow, the complaint reached the Governor. The Secretary of the State, an ICS, immediately appointed an inquiry. When the authorities asked my father who had a high reputation in the Bar, he told them that the Judge was not corrupt. He was from a very reputed family and never mixed with anybody. But it was indiscreet of him to borrow. So, overnight they changed him from the Judiciary to the Executive. For a Judge such indiscretion was not permitted.

Up to the first ten years of Independence, if one sees the press reports, he cannot find many cases of corruption. The bureaucracy was somewhat insulated in the first ten years. They were not eating out of the hands of the politicians. An error of judgment was different, and omission and commission was also there. Corruption started in the upper class environment. In the post-Independence era the slide came gradually. But as and when public opinion got stronger, more cases came out in the open as, for example, the Tehelka case. But I do not think that in the first 20 years of my service, anybody approached me with what to do or what not to do. Maybe, it was my reputation that worked. There was no political pressure but when in one or two cases political pressure came, I resisted.

It is unfortunate that the decline started a decade after the departure of Jawaharlal Nehru and Lal Bahadur Shastri. There are two reasons for this. The power politics in the States and the weakness of senior civil servants starting from district officers (Collectors, Deputy Commissioners and District Magistrates) who could not withstand the local pressures, caused them to seek transfers to Secretariats in the State capitals. Similarly, the move from States to the Central Secretariat in Delhi became a one-way traffic. Having served a posting in Delhi as a Deputy Secretary (for three to four years), most officers utilised their time to lobby for retention in Delhi in some form or the other even if it meant a deputation to the public sector or to a different Ministry. Even when the Department of Personnel tried to enforce the 5-year rule, the minister-in-charge would intervene on his behalf. Then, I would point out to the weakness of the bureaucracy that they could not withstand the pressure. A young official, with a wife and two children, what would he do but to just succumb? Transfer was a punishment to some; under the rules, one cannot protest transfer. So, these were the various methods of arm-twisting of the bureaucrats. They would get the pliable officers and started to ask as to who wanted to be posted as the Chief Secretary of a State.

I remember an issue which came up when I was the Chairman of the Industrial Development Corporation of Delhi, which was purely a Government company. I proposed to supply the Electronic Voting Machines (EVMs). The Additional Secretary in charge of that in the Ministry and the Chief Election Commissioner himself suggested that I could do so. But the Government of India did not allow us to buy the EVMs. When one is counting the ballot papers physically, one know what happens – booth capturing – and that was the reason! There are loopholes which the corrupt officials utilize to further their self-interest. It starts from small manipulations. When an officer is transferred, he yearns to return to Delhi because the situation in the States is bad. For instance, in the North-East, housing was neglected and an official had to leave behind a young wife. Officials also often gave the excuses of sickness.

In the Army, if one was out in action, the wife would be looked after in the Cantonment, the child would go to school and there would be security. But members of cultural teams in the North-East and employees of All India Radio in Shillong had problems in getting accommodation. One day, one person came to my house and I had to ask the Army to take care of his children's education. So I requested the Ministry of Home Affairs that officials going to the North-East be allowed to retain their accommodation in Delhi. Later, the Home Ministry made a Cabinet note and approved some extra leave to those posted to the North-East. We were expending towards the Frontier bordering Tibet and Burma and not bothering about the welfare of the staff whose families lived in the foothills or the plains of Assam or in Delhi. For some, transfer was a punishment, so they went out of the way to compromise, and sought favour. If one asks for a favour then one has to return the favour. Then the nexus between the politicians and bureaucrats begins. Mostly, corruption started with postings and nothing more than that. Salary of an IAS officer started with 350 rupees per month. He could live only if he did not compete with the affluent and rich. Corrupt persons keep on sending cakes, pastries and gifts to subvert the system but when one lives beyond his means then corruption starts. Then, a stage came in Gurgaon when the post of the Deputy Commissioner was sold, like in the old days when the position of the Captain of the Port of Goa was sold to select families by the Portuguese.

Politicians in the States started saying that for the Governor's post, they should be consulted. The Central government conceded that, rightly or wrongly. But that does not mean that one puts his favourite man in the seat of the Governor and the Raj Bhawan becomes another centre for doing the party-work. That is highest form of corruption. The highest form of corruption was also to have kickbacks. Foreign investors encouraged kickbacks to get contracts. Therefore, they did not mind giving a lavish party in Ashok Hotel (New Delhi). In my time, I remember very clearly that anybody below the rank of Deputy Secretary could not accept invitation to any foreign embassy. Now, when the people go with high level delegations and stores worth millions of dollars are bought, what does the Defence Secretary do? He says: "I do not want to get involved. You form a committee, go there, come back and submit a report." Who is in the committee? It is the same people, up and down. So, it is the question of environment. The international environment is corrupt.

Little has changed over the years. Ministers are like those in the Laloo Prasad Yadav's Raj. A stage has come when the High Court has started guiding the Executive. But when executives do not work, then where else the can the citizen go? The Legislature's job is to make laws, but how much time does the Parliament spend in making laws? Corruption started because of such the weaknesses within – the human, not the systemic weakness. So, making of new laws would not help, honest conventions would. That is why the British Parliamentary system evolved more by conventions; there is no British Constitution as such, yet it functions well.

Reservation Policy

Wrong reservation policy of the government has brought about social tensions everywhere. Our Manipuri driver was one Thongjum Sharma. His son passed

Class XII with honours, and wanted a seat in the School of Planning and Architecture in New Delhi for a five-year programme. There was only one reserved seat for Manipur. Thongjum's son's marks were higher than that of the any other candidate from Manipur, and he was also a Central government employee. Lal Biac Thanga, the Chief Secretary, was a Mizo IAS officer and a good friend of mine. His son, too, passed from the same English medium school but with lower marks. But since Thongjum's son's name bore the surname 'Sharma', so Lal Biac Thanga, the Chief Secretary's son, got admission as a Scheduled Tribe candidate. Thongjum felt very sad that his son did not get admission. My daughter, who was a topper, had also applied. There was no chance for her, but she got admission because I was an officer of the Central Government in Manipur. She, however, changed her mind and decided against joining, and being a topper in Mathematics, opted for admission in an Honours Course in Mathematics. That youngman joined the underground movement later on, after I left. Lal Biac Thanga was from a chiefs' family and was affluent, educated and a Chief Secretary, and yet his son got the advantage of reservation. Then his son started taking narcotic drugs. When the second year's report upset his mother, I met the boy. He was becoming weak. He could not pass the third year. He was failing and they were about to expel him. He died in Delhi. That was a sad fallout of wrong reservation policy.

When I was the Chief Secretary of Goa, Daman and Diu, the Mandal Commission Report had come up for discussion. As the Chief Secretary, I was also the Cabinet Secretary. My duty was to advise the government and include it in the agenda at the meetings of the cabinet. The Central government would routinely send advisories and circulars to State governments. Being a policy-matter, the Chief Minister would put it in the agenda to secure a consensus. In Goa, Daman and Diu, there was not even one per cent of Scheduled Castes. They were either Christians or Brahmins or Rajputs. There were a few *Lombadis*, the nomadic people, very few of them. Where was the need for any reservation then? We ascertained the views of the church, the student leaders and others. The item was on the agenda and all the secretaries gave their fresh views. We were all completely against reservations. Notes were consistently prepared and as the Home Secretary, the final note was mine. Although I put the item on the agenda for discussion, it was deferred because the cabinet itself did not want to implement the reservation policy. But they did not have the courage to openly say 'no' to reservation. The Chief Minister should have advised the Prime Minister at that time. I do not know how many Chief Ministers did so. So, I informed the Chief Minister that if he approved the policy, then we would send it to the Cabinet Secretary who would put it up to the Central government. Then, it would go to the Parliament and Mandal Bill would be passed. But for several years, the matter was deferred.

My argument was that reservations for deprived people like Jagjivan Ram was acceptable but not for his grandson. Look at the way the MPs are living in New Delhi. I went to see one MP. I would not name him, but he rode a swanky car, he was floating in money. He had come up from a village and was hardly literate, and he rose due to the reservation and vote bank politics. His next generations however did not qualify for the same benefits against those who remained backward irrespective of their caste.

First, by one stroke of pen the Government of India should completely abolish reservation for anybody. Let there be open competitions. Second, the age-restriction of 21 to 26 years for entry into the civil service, with three years relaxation to for the Scheduled Castes and Scheduled Tribes should be restored. The creamy layer, for example, sons of MPs, IAS officers, High Court Judges and Army Generals should stand in the queue. Why is there the 'Reserved Constituency'? We abolished the separate electorates of Hindus and Muslims and yet created the Reserved Constituency. What is the need? There is no end to this kind of practice. It is people like V P Singh and Arjun Singh who supported reservations. Is this the time to create this kind of divide? We are facing global competition, we are facing China, and we are facing terrorism. These are some of the major issues in which it is the fittest who survives.

Pseudo-secularism and minority-ism are the kind of issues that are coming up. The State should give basic education to every child. In every district, there should be a school where every poor child can study – and the rich shouldsupport the community-based or government schools. Our government has to put more money in education. By and large, the time for reservation is over now, but nobody seems to have the courage to say so. Reservation may be on the economic criteria. Where is the question of an IAS officer's or an MP's son getting reservation benefits? One can imagine as to what the income of an MP is. If he cannot educate his child even then, then he is not fit to be an MP. If an MP cannot manage his own home and family with all the facilities that he has got, how can he tackle problems of the nation? This is a very serious issue. In the next election, if anybody has the courage, he should take up this issue.

Some Notable Personalities

Jairamdas Doulatram was totally devoted to the tribal people. When he was the Governor of Assam, Raj Bhawan was full of tribal relics. He was a great man and was very fond of touring. At his age and in spite of all his family problems, he toured as much as any old British Collector would have toured. His daughter was very ill and his wife was dead. He was a refugee from Pakistan, a barrister-at-law and a Congressman. Once when he came on a visit for one day, we had put up a hut of aluminium sheets. Then, the aircraft which was to take him back could not land and so he stayed on for seven days. How does one host a Governor in a small town! But he kept himself busy with translation of all the *Abhangs*, the tales which the tribal priests sing. The Abhangs are something like the four Vedas which were composed by the rishis. These would have disappeared from the North-East but for the tribal priests. The priests sing about origin of man and origin of the adivasi or what we call the Adis of Siang. Doulatram took a lot of interest in these things. He mixed extremely well with the tribal leaders and they had great respect for him.

S H F J (Sam) Manekshaw, the Chief of the Army Staff (1969-72) always addressed Indira Gandhi as the 'Prime Minister'. He did not call her 'Madam'. The word 'Madam' is often used to express servility. Servility is the worst thing that can happen to anyone. When the government servants start having sycophants around them, they remain honest advisors no more. They become sycophants who hang around the politicians. Manekshaw was above all that.

Govind Ballabh Pant was extremely good as the Chief Minister of Uttar Pradesh. Although he held an open durbar, he also had the members of the ICS to help him. His ministers were known for their honesty.

Babu Raghubir Sahai was a lawyer and was one of the few educated people in the Badaun District. The Congress had some intellectuals who joined the movement and he was one of them. He was an out and out Congressman. One result was that he suffered in his law practice. A Congressman, he served Badaun as a Member of the Lok Sabha from 1952 to 1962 and was in some of its committees. Not servile by any chance, represented a unique type of a political leader in contrast to politicians like Bhajji Maharaj, who were totally servile. Raghubir Sahai was one of the few persons of independent stature. He never went to a District Magistrate to request for gun licences for his party MLAs and MPs. Badaun was on one bank of the Ganga. First comes the Ganga, then Ram Ganga, Bareli and Badaun. On one side is Rampur. So, the district was large and consisted of a very large population of Rohilla Pathans and some old traditional *Lalas* and *Brahmins*. Badaun had a mixed population. Abul Fazal and Fani Badayuni were among its residents. Khwaza Nizamuddin Aulia and some Sufis were also from there. Being readily approachable, Raghubir Sahai very popular. During the first General Elections he got a Congress ticket because he was the only educated person around. I think, in the second General Elections, he did not get a Congress Party ticket. He had the makings of a Central minister, but everybody cannot become a minister.

Fani Badayuni, whose real name was Muhammad Shaukat Ali Khan, was an eminent Urdu poet from Badaun where Khwaja Nizamuddin Aulia was born and whose dargah is there. Badaun had a tradition of cultural unity and communal amity but later on, with the coming of separate electorate, the situation changed. As a lawyer, Fani Badayuni did not succeed very much in his law practice, neither did he join any political movement. Having been reduced to penury, he moved out of Badaun and migrated to Hyderabad in the hope of getting some help from the Nizam. There he wrote poetry till his death. He would not be well known had his works not been discovered. Fani Badayuni was a person who can be ranked with Raghupati Sahai Firaq Gorakhpuri. Not much of his poetry is available but his legacy was taken up by Shakeel Badauni who started writing ghazals and became very famous with the coming of the film era in Bombay.

Harivansh Rai Bachchan taught me English Literature. In fact, he was not only a lecturer at that time, he was also my tutor. Each student was allotted a tutor and three or four students sat and discussed one subject once a week, once with one tutor and then with another tutor. The system was like that of Oxford and Cambridge Universities, and Allahabad University continued that tradition. Bachchan was with the Department of English, even though he wrote in Hindi. He was a complete teetotaller, extremely polite, very well-meaning and quite unobtrusive. There was no show and no airs about him, unlike Dr Amarnath Jha who was a cigar smoker and had western manners and style of talking English. Dr Jha acquired the British accent and was very well dressed all the time. Bachchan was a very good teacher and we were hugely impressed by him. He spoke very well and specialised in two poets, John Keats and Perey Bysshe Shelly.

Outside the university, he was mostly busy with his Hindi poems. He was not to be seen in the games and sports events. He did not socialise. He would be available to us during the tutorials; otherwise he was aloof and kept to himself; hee was just a quiet person. At that time, he was about to get married. I think he was courting Teji Suri, a Sikh girl from Punjab. Then he married her in 1941. That was the first inter-caste marriage in Allahabad; and one may say inter-province and inter-lingual. Bachchan was from a very ordinary family, not very rich but in Allahabad University, he had a certain stature.

Teachers were very popular among the students. In fact, one had to seek time to meet them outside the class room if one so wished. They were all nationalists. They had a small circle of their own and were totally dedicated to their own profession. They were not active in games and sports and were not even social.

Their views on politics were there but I do not think they took an active part in the national movement. But they never dissuaded their students from participating in the 1942 movement. If a student did not attend a class it did not matter. They overlooked absence of students if it was for participation in political agitations. In private meetings they expressed sympathies with the movement. Dr Moolchand, Dr Tara Chand and Dr Ishwari Prasad, none of them were politically active. They were good teachers who had their views and very popular among the youth. They were sympathetic to the freedom movement. But they did not take part in political agitations the way Congressmen did. Allahabad University was a place of learning and teaching and the teachers did not mind students going into political activities. But they themselves did not give up their teaching and court arrest. Active politics meant that one has to attend meetings of the Pradesh Congress Committees. They would never go there. They would never go to Jawaharlal Nehru's home in Anand Bhawan to seek his guidance, the way active Congressmen would do. Dr Tara Chand was picked up by Jawaharlal Nehru and sent as an Ambassador to Iran.

Josh Malihabadi whose real name was Shabbir Hasan Khan was, of course, a very great Urdu poet. He used to come to our hostel. I heard his mushairas. He belonged to the old world and there was nothing modern about him. He was very fond of his drinks and was a thorough nationalist and a Leftist. He belonged to a galaxy of people of that time like Dr Amarnath Jha, H R Bachchan and Firaq Gorakhpuri.

Firaq Gorakhpuri was a class by himself. He was the most brilliant teacher I have ever had. He had a very thorough command over the English language and spoke with great confidence, although I do not think he had ever been to England or outside Allahabad. His Urdu poetry was, of course, perfect. He was also in the Department of English and not in the Department of Urdu.

I remember *Jigar Moradabadi* alias Ali Sikandar came to some mushairas. He was among the permanent invitees. Jigar was also a very fond of his drinks. Most of the *shayars* (poets) were addicted to alcoholic drinks. They did not drink in public. They came on stage in the *mushairas* which were always held in venues outside the University and in the evening.

Mushairas did not interfere with the University's schedule. Students and women used to attend these. Of course, there were very few women in Allahabad University, but there was no purdah system. I never saw any 'burkawali' women in Allahabad University, not one. I also did not see any burkawali women in the public meetings of the Congress Party which I attended and which were addressed by eminent leaders like M A Jinnah and C Rajagopalachari. The communal divide was not there; but only in the sense that the meetings of Jinnah were attended mostly by Muslims. Meetings of the Congress Party were mass meetings with processions.

P D Tandon, the journalist, was virtually my guru in writing. There were two Tandons. One was Purshottam Das Tandon, the Congressman who was a rightist and very orthodox. He even resisted taking the anti-cholera injections. He was anti-Nehru, but Jawaharlal Nehru thought well of him. The other person was P D Tandon, the journalist. He was a great admirer of Jawaharlal Nehru and wrote for the 'National Harald' and the 'Leader'. He used to wear a khadi shirt and tie. He was always very upright and there was none of this yellow journalism in him. M Chalapathi Rau and Acharya J B Kriplani were also there.

P D Tandon was my brother's contemporary. So, my brother gave me a reference when I first went to Allahabad, and I went to meet him. He was also a Congressman. I do not think he ever courted arrest but he used to write for the Congress Party. I used to go very often to P D Tandon, the journalist. He would occasionally give me a book to review.

I met *Asoka Mehta,* the famous Socialist, when I came back from Afghanistan. Mehta had his own views on planning and other things. Mehta, Achyut Patwardhan, Aruna Asaf Ali, Jayaprakash Narayan and Acharya Narendra Deva were all intellectuals. Somehow or the other, they were known to be Leftist. Jawaharlal Nehru himself was a Leftist but these leaders became identified as anti-Nehru. They were all of the same age and maybe there was some kind of internal jealousy.

Chaudhary Badan Singh was elected a Member of Lok Sabha in 1952 and in 1957. He had a very humble beginning and was from what is now called the Kurmi caste which is a Scheduled Caste. He was the first Matriculate in his village and rose to become Chairman of the Badaun District Board. A man of the masses, he was arrested several times. He always used to wear khadi and was a committed Congressman. He and Raghubir Sahai were the two top leaders of Badaun.

So, these are some prominent people I had the privilege of knowing throughout my years of service.

ANNEXURE 1

List of First Batch of Civil Servants Posted as Political Officers Post-Independence

1. Renalte Khating
2. Surendra Mohan Krishnatri
3. Sunil Dutt Lakhar
4. Nausher Ferdonji Suntook
5. Krishna Chandra Johorey
6. Harmander Singh
7. Rashid Yusuf Ali
8. Raj Kumar Bharat Singh

EPILOGUE

Major Krishna Chandra Johorey, IAS, a Padma Shree awardee of the 1963 era and known amongst his peers as 'KC', retired as Secretary to Government of India in 1985. Post retirement, KC worked for World Wildlife Foundation (WWF) as its Secretary General. Subsequently, he took over as the Secretary General of the Organisation for Industrial, Spiritual and Cultural Advancement (OISCA), India.

Having completed his stint in these organisations, Mr Johorey devoted his energies to the establishment of the 'Bhartiya Academy' in Roorkee as a venture of the Soni Foundation – in collaboration with its prominent co-trustee, Major General S N Dubey (Retd). This school has, over the years, developed to be a key primary as well as secondary educational institution for the boys and girls of the villages around. Mr Johorey remains active in administration of this academy to this day.

KC went on to create a Non-Governmental Organisation (NGO) called the Eco Development Foundation, in which prominent members of the society joined in to the purpose of serving the cause of ecology and education for the marginalised children. In that endeavour, Mr Johorey – by the sheer dint of his indomitable will power – veneration in society and deference among his peers, started the Diksha School and Shiksha Bharti Primary School in Palam Vihar, Gurugram. Children of migrant labours and daily workers are given free education and mid-day meal in these schools. Consequent to the passing of the Right to Education Act, Mr Johorey with assistance from the education department and district administration, has devoted to the proper implementation of the Act on the ground. Presently, over 500 children are being supported by his NGO, the Eco Development Foundation.

Active in preventing child labour and preservation of the environment, Mr. Johorey is currently focused on a rural project on empowering women and children in Moradabad, Uttar Pradesh.

Truly, Major Krishna Chandra Johorey, IAS, a soldier-civil servant and social activist, has dedicated his long and eventful life to the betterment of the society. It has been a remarkable life indeed, and it finds its expression through the grace of publisher Rajan Arya, CEO of the Pentagon Press, New Delhi.

Lieutenant General Gautam Banerjee, PVSM, AVSM, YSM (Retd)
Former Colonel Commandant, The Bengal Sappers and Trustee,
The Soni Foundation, Roorkee
New Delhi
9th June, 2017

INDEX

1. Kamet Expedition in 1952, Capt Johorey standing on the left

2. Yatung Snow Games, India House, Yatung, Tibet, 1957-58.
(R to L) Singh, JE, Major KC Johorey

3. Maharani of Sikkim (Centre) visiting Mr. KC Johorey in Yatung with her entourage, 1957

4. Pundit Jawaharlal Nehru visiting Tibet, September 1958

5. Flag Hoisting Ceremony in Yatung. KC Johorey with Mr Tempo Namgyal Barphungpa, Vice-Chief of Mission, Yatung, Tibet

6. KC Johorey with Gylwa Karamppa in Yatung, Tibet

7. On Re-entering Bomdi-La after the Chinese withdrawal

8. Nehru on his visit to Tibet, along with Ambassador Apa Pant

9. KC Johorey with his daughter Geeta, Ms. Indira Gandhi and Omem Mayong (virtually brought up by Johorey family; went on to become an MP - representing Arunachal Pradesh)

10. Vice President DB Jathi presenting an 'Achievement Award' to Mr. KC Johorey

11. His Holiness the Dalai Lama, receiving the Organization for Industrial Spiritual & Cultural Advancement (OISCA) Award from Venezuelan Ambassador Zulm Guelman; World President of OISCA (HQ in Tokyo), Dr. Yoshiko Y Nakano; India Presisent of OISCA, Mr DN Sinha and Secretary General of OISCA, Mr KC Johorey - in Dharamsala

12. Mr. K C Johorey at his desk, at his last posting as Chief Secretary to the Govt. of Goa, Daman & Diu